MONEY

A HISTORY

MONEY
A HISTORY

**Catherine Eagleton
and Jonathan Williams**

with Joe Cribb and Elizabeth Errington

FIREFLY BOOKS

In memory of our colleagues

Martin Price (1939–1995)

and Nicholas Lowick (1940–1986)

A FIREFLY BOOK

Published by Firefly Books Ltd. 2007

First printing

Publisher Cataloging-in-Publication Data (U.S.)
Eagleton, Catherine
  Money: a history/Catherine Eagleton and Jonathan Williams;
with Joe Cribb and Elizabeth Errington. – 2nd ed.
Originally published: NY: St. Martin's Press, 1997.
[272] p.: photos. (chiefly col.); cm.
Includes bibliographical references and index.
Summary: A highly illustrated, cross-cultural introduction
to the history of money, from the earliest civilizations to
the modern period.
ISBN-13: 978-1-55407-282-8 (pbk.)
ISBN-10: 1-55407-282-4 (pbk.)
1. Money. 2. Money – History. I. Williams, Jonathan.
II. Cribb, Joe. III. Errington, Elizabeth. IV. Title.
332.49 dc22   HG231.E245   2007

Library and Archives Canada Cataloguing in Publication
Eagleton, Catherine
  Money: a history/Catherine Eagleton and Jonathan Williams;
with Joe Cribb and Elizabeth Errington. – 2nd ed.
Includes bibliographical references and index.
ISBN-13: 978-1-55407-282-8 (pbk.)
ISBN-10: 1-55407-282-4 (pbk.)
  1. Money – History. I. Williams, Jonathan, Dr. II. Cribb, Joe.
III. Errington, Elizabeth. IV. Title.
HG231.E25 2007   332.4'9   C2006-906467-9

Published in the United States by Firefly Books (U.S.) Inc.
P.O. Box 1338, Ellicott Station
Buffalo, New York 14205

Published in Canada by Firefly Books Ltd.
66 Leek Crescent
Richmond Hill, Ontario L4B 1H1

The first edition of this book was published to accompany
the British Museum's HSBC Money Gallery, opened on
30 January, 1997.

AUTHORS: Jennifer Adam, Marion Archibald,
Andrew Burnett, Barrie Cook, Joe Cribb,
Catherine Eagleton, Virginia Hewitt, Richard Kelleher,
Venetia Porter, Helen Wang and Jonathan Williams,
with contributions by Roger Bland and Clive Cheesman
Illustration coordination and maps: Elizabeth Errington
Coin and banknote photography: Stephen Dodd,
Jeff Hopson and Jerome Perkins
Index: Vesta Curtis

Designed by Harry Green
Cover illustration: Detail from a gold twenty-dollar coin
of the United States, 1908

Printed and bound in China

Contents

The Trustees of the British Museum

acknowledge with gratitude generous assistance

towards the HSBC Money Gallery

and the production of this book

from

HSBC Holdings plc

Preface

The first edition of this book was published to accompany the opening of the HSBC Money Gallery at the British Museum on 30 January 1997. This revised edition marks its tenth anniversary. The HSBC Money Gallery has already been visited by almost ten million people and continues to engage and fascinate visitors to the British Museum.

The gallery provides a unique insight into human history, tracing the phenomenon of money throughout the world from its earliest appearance in written sources down to the present day. The gallery's structure allows the history of money in different parts of the world to be presented as a whole, juxtaposing parallel and divergent trends within the same time frame, comparing, for example, the early development of coinage systems in Greece, India and China in the same display case. This book serves to complement the gallery displays by tracing the evolution and cultural context of money within its separate traditions, showing for example the continuity of money in China from its earliest evidence in the second millennium BC down to its current forms in the twenty-first century.

Money continues to change in both form and function, at the same time as cultural attitudes towards it evolve. This new edition enables us to bring the history of money up to date and to add some elements in the story of money which it now seems important not to omit.

The aim of both the gallery and this book has been to enable non-specialist visitors and readers to engage with the history of one of the most important aspects of their everyday lives. Money's place in our lives has become more and more essential. It enables us to manage in an increasingly complex world. The most basic transactions require access to money. From a social perspective the amount of money we have access to is no indicator of happiness or success, but it is increasingly difficult to survive in the modern world without some level of access to it. This book is intended to use our familiarity with money in our own lives to open up a route to the past. The history of money embraces the whole of human history since the earliest written records and enables us to observe the ways in which people in the past have dealt with the everyday issues that fill our own lives.

It is usual in the modern world to see money as a purely economic phenomenon which also affects other aspects of our lives, but the history of money presents it in a different light. The earliest evidence from Mesopotamia, China, India and the Mediterranean world shows money's early development firmly located in the social sphere. Pre-modern money in Africa and Oceania shows a similar focus for money as a social device.

The dynamics of this history encourage us to reassess the meaning of money's place in our own society. Both the gallery and this book highlight the interactions between political, social, economic, cultural and religious structures in the sphere of money. Money even reaches beyond life and creates an understanding for many people of their relationship with the spiritual world, an aspect best illustrated by the long tradition in China of providing the dead with money for use in their afterlives.

The history of money has much to inform us about the state of the world we live in today and how it came to be as it is. Perhaps the most dramatic element of that history, which we are increasingly conscious of today, is the role of money and monetary institutions in globalisation. From the silver tetradrachms of the Athenian Empire to the universal acceptability of the US dollar, money has been a crucial element in this process.

The global history of money presented here is also echoed in the development of HSBC Holdings plc. HSBC Holdings is one of the largest banking and financial services companies in the world. Its generosity has allowed the British Museum to create the HSBC Money Gallery and to publish this book. Further backing will also be given for the continuing development of the gallery. For this continuing support the British Museum is extremely grateful.

JOE CRIBB
Keeper of Coins and Medals
British Museum

Acknowledgements

The editors and authors wish to thank the following who have helped in the preparation of both editions of this volume:

BRITISH MUSEUM
Coins and Medals: Richard Abdy, Philip Attwood, Annette Calton, Beverley Fryer, Ray Gardner, Alison Harry, John Hore, Molly Hunter, Shah Nazar Khan, Janet Larkin, Andrew Meadows, Caroline Meadows, Brendan Moore, John Orna-Ornstein, David Owen, Cathy Sheffield, Emma Smith, Luke Syson and Gareth Williams

Conservation Department: Celestine Enderly

Ancient Egypt and Sudan: Richard Parkinson

Africa, Oceania and the Americas: Ben Burt, John Mack, Shelagh Weir and Michael O'Hanlon

Greek and Roman Antiquities: Lucilla Burn

Asia: Robert Knox and Michael Willis

Prehistory and Europe: Catherine Johns and Val Rigby

Ancient Near East: Christopher Walker and John Curtis

British Museum Development Trust: Julian Marland and Frances Dunkels

British Museum Press: Teresa Francis, Emma Way, Catherine Wood, Julie Young, Beatriz Waters and Axelle Russo

BANK OF ENGLAND MUSEUM: John Keyworth
ROYAL MINT MUSEUM: Graham Dyer, Kevin Clancy
MIDLAND BANK ARCHIVES: Edwin Green and Sarah Kinsey
ASHMOLEAN MUSEUM, OXFORD: Luke Treadwell
AMERICAN NUMISMATIC SOCIETY, NEW YORK: Michael Bates
OTHER: Maggie Claringbull, Howard Simmons, Michael O'Grady, Bernhard Rieger, John Kent

THE HSBC MONEY GALLERY
Project manager: Andrew Burnett

Curator: Joe Cribb

Assistant curator: Alison Harry

Section co-ordinators: Barrie Cook, Virginia Hewitt and Andrew Meadows

Designers: Jonathan Ould and Ann Lumley

Gallery editor: Gill Hughes

Building project manager: Sat Jandu

Clerks of works: Graham Allen and John Foster

Introduction

It is easier to write about money than to acquire it; and those who gain it make great sport of those who only know how to write about it.

VOLTAIRE, *Philosophical Dictionary (1764)*

Writing about money can be a hazardous enterprise, and involves treading on sensitive ground. Few phenomena in human history have been the focus of so much constant and fevered attention, occasioned so many moral and religious strictures and been the cause of so much violent strife and competition between individuals and states. This book attempts to describe how this happened, and to give some idea of the reasons why.

How are we to approach this difficult subject? We might begin by generalising about human nature, examining the role of money in different cultures and societies from an anthropological perspective. Or we might treat the problem as one of economics, looking at the statistics and general theories which are the basic tools of the economist and the economic historian. The approach taken in this book, however, is neither anthropological nor economic, but historical.

| Fifty-dollar note of The Hongkong & Shanghai Banking Corporation, 1934. From its founding in 1865 the Bank has been the principal note-issuer in Hong Kong. It has also played a pioneering role in the introduction of modern Western banking practice in several countries in East Asia. Today it is a subsidiary of HSBC Holdings plc. (× ⅞)

2 Scene from the Hollywood musical *Gold Diggers of 1933*, featuring Ginger Rogers. The chorus line, dressed to sing the famous hit number 'We're in the money', is suitably wearing costumes decorated with US silver dollars. The dreams of millions during the 1930s world economic slump found expression in the mass medium of film.

Yet this is not simply a traditional history of money from its 'origins' to the present day. Rather it is several histories, broadly chronologically arranged, each investigating money in one of a number of cultures as diverse as ancient India and modern Europe.

The diversity of the forms of money described in the following chapters necessarily raises the question of general definitions. In the abstract, money is often defined primarily as a means of exchange, while on a concrete level the word refers to those classes of object commonly used to perform this function. As this book, and Chapter 8 in particular will show, definitions such as these are mostly unhelpful, being a reflection of an inherently modern and Western point of view. There is more to the history of money than just buying and selling.

All the chapters in this book have been written by curators in the Department of Coins and Medals in the British Museum, specialists in particular areas and periods of the history of coinage and paper money. Their responsibilities include the care and presentation of the Museum's collections and the acquisition of new and important pieces. But behind the care of objects – relics of the past and apparently of interest only to antiquarians and collectors – lie the particular historical contexts which underpin and explain the bewildering variety of functions and material forms that money has adopted. In the chapters that

follow we shall be concerned not only with the objects themselves, but with what people in history have done with money, what they have thought about it and what effects it has had on them. The real history of money lies not in statistics, nor even in numismatics, though both can be found in this book, but in human attitudes and behaviour.

Take, for example, the painting in fig. 3. It was produced around 1514 by the Flemish artist Quentin Matsys. The two main characters are husband and wife. He is a money-lender, sitting at a table and carefully weighing a pile of coins. His wife sits on his left and also concentrates on the transaction taking place, while absent-mindedly fingering the book of devotional reading that lies half-open in front of her. There is a third participant in the scene, artfully concealed as a reflection in the mirror standing on the table. We assume that he is the customer of the money-lender, come to conclude a deal.

On one level, the painting is simply a well-observed scene of daily life in the Netherlands of the early sixteenth century, when trade was booming and the merchants of the Low Countries were among the richest in Europe. But if we look again, we may see it also as a story, a scene from the dramatic narrative of the history of money. Where is the focus of action and attention in the work as a whole? There is no obvious interaction between the couple in the picture, nor between them and us, the viewers. The picture is not primarily about relationships between people. All eyes, ours included, are fixed on the coins being counted out on the table. Money seems to be the focal point of the human world depicted here. As such, it appears to be competing with two other central features of the European society of that period: religion (witness the wife's neglect of her prayer-book) and the sacred bond of matrimony (the money lying on the table draws the married couple's attention away from one another and inexorably towards itself).

We might possibly conclude from this interpretation that Matsys meant us to understand the work as a fairly straightforward, moralising attack on money, a tirade against its destructive effects on human values. But perhaps this picture is not just a sermon in line and colour. It may in fact be considerably more subtle in its implications. After all, the woman may be momentarily looking away from her prayer-book, but she has not abandoned it completely; nor has she entirely left her husband's side for other distractions. A more complex interpretation of the painting might suggest that the artist is attempting to represent the ways in which money, religion and family actually co-exist in the real world, the world of history, rather than depicting a simplistic or moralising opposition between the material world of wealth and the higher realms of spiritual and emotional life.

3 Quentin Matsys (1464/5–1530), *A Money-lender and his Wife, c.* 1514 (Paris, Louvre).

The central characters in the painting are looking at a heap of physical objects – objects which for them meant money. Money, for early fifteenth-century Europeans, was for the most part gold and silver coins, and this fact is important. Other histories of money have perhaps tended not to look very hard at the objects involved, because of an unfortunate divergence in approach between historians and numismatists. In this book, however, coins and other objects will often take centre stage. Without them, an account of the history of money would be incomplete.

A book such as this cannot claim to be comprehensive, but neither is the choice of subjects arbitrary. The emphasis of the chapters will vary according to the nature of the period and culture under discussion, and each will attempt to characterise what is specific to that period or culture, in order to

4 One-dollar banknote, USA, 2003. George Washington first appeared on US $1 bills in 1869. The first Federal Reserve Bank $1 notes were issued in 1963, and the design has not changed since. Used every day across the world, the average life of a $1 bill is just twenty-two months. (× ¾)

illustrate the immense geographical and chronological variety within the history of money. The first half traces the development of money in the 'Western' tradition, beginning with the civilisations of Egypt and Mesopotamia, where the first written records of monetary and commercial activity have been found, and moving on to the Aegean civilisation of the Greeks and to the Mediterranean and continental world of the Roman Empire and medieval Europe. In the subsequent chapters the 'Eurocentric' balance is redressed with a triple focus on the perhaps less familiar histories of the Islamic world, India and China, and a chapter considering the indigenous monies of Africa and Oceania. In the final chapter, however, which looks at the modern world, it has been difficult to avoid considering the subject from an almost exclusively Western point of view. This can largely be justified by the increasing influence of European and, later, American culture on world history as a whole, and on the history of money in particular. The processes of colonialism, the two world wars and the developments in communications and technology which have led to the increasing 'globalisation' of the world economy perhaps make this bias inevitable, as the ori-

5 Cartoon by Hector Breeze (*The Guardian*, 9 January 1996), referring to a new United Kingdom £2 coin with a design celebrating the *Euro '96* football championships. In the past coin designs, often reflecting important historical themes and events, were frequently a focus of lively public controversy. The coin designs of the present day commemorate many different types of events, but, as the irony of the cartoon suggests, are rarely noticed.

gins of these various factors seem to lie mostly in the West. Modern monetary practices are so firmly rooted in the 'Western' tradition that even in the eastern countries of the Pacific Rim, with their own diverse traditions, Western-style money has been adopted as an integral tool in their ever growing economic power. If money is among the most influential factors shaping humanity in the modern world, then this, perhaps, is a particularly appropriate time to take another look at its history.

Mesopotamia, Egypt and Greece

Then there passed by Midianites, merchant-men, and they drew and lifted up Joseph out of the pit, and sold Joseph to the Ishmaelites for twenty pieces of silver, and they brought Joseph into Egypt.

GENESIS 37:28 (Authorised Version, 1611)

The earliest-known records of one very important strand in the history of money, broadly characterised by the monetary use of precious metals, can be traced back to the third millennium BC in Mesopotamia and Egypt. Over succeeding millennia this practice has continued, firstly in Europe, the Middle East and South Asia with the spread of coinage, and then throughout the world via the channels of Western colonialism and the rise of modern industrial societies in all parts of the globe. We should not, however, confuse the earliest records of what might appear to be the pre-eminent tradition in the history of money with the origins of money itself.

6 Ancient Egyptian wall-painting from a tomb at Thebes, *c.* fourteenth century BC, showing gold rings being weighed on a balance. It is unclear whether the Egyptians did in fact use gold rings as money or whether their form on such paintings is simply an artistic convention.

Mesopotamia and Egypt

We begin, then, with ancient Mesopotamia and Egypt, and by the end of this chapter we shall have arrived at a point in history, about 250 BC, when coinage in gold, silver and bronze was the most widespread form of money throughout most of the Mediterranean world, the Near East and India. While coinage only makes its earliest appearance in the late seventh century BC, the tradition of using precious metals, and especially silver, as money takes us back as far as the twenty-fourth century BC in Mesopotamia.

The transaction envisaged in the passage of Genesis quoted above, an amount of silver in exchange for a slave, is quite plausible for the historical period in which the biblical story of Joseph is supposed to have been set (early second millennium BC), but with one vital qualification. The seventeenth-century English translators of the text wrongly thought that this passage referred to coins ('pieces of silver'). The most important point to remember about the monetary use of metals in Mesopotamia and Egypt is that they passed as bullion by weight and not as coins, and that consequently the value of the metal to be used in a payment would have been assessed on a pair of scales on each separate occasion. 6 It is also important to place the occurrence of monetary phenomena within the overall context of ancient Near Eastern and Egyptian economic life, which is generally thought to have been typified by a system called 'centralised redistri-

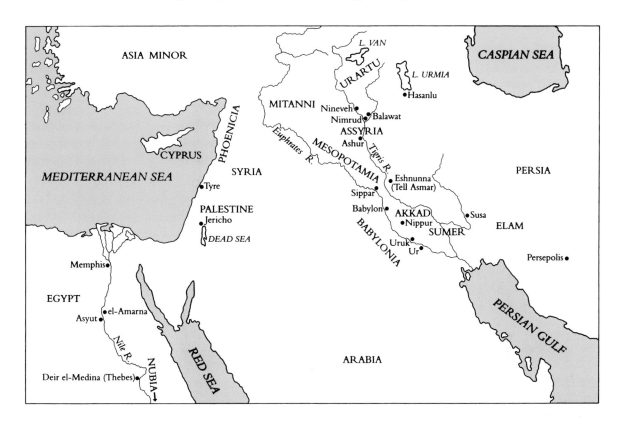

7 The Ancient Near East and Egypt.

bution', a technical term describing the primary process whereby goods were distributed among the population. This was not done through the action of the market; rather, manufactured goods and agricultural produce seem to have been collected from the people by the authorities, kings and temples, and then redistributed among them according to status and occupation.

Despite the dominance of central power in articulating much of what we would describe as economic life in these ancient societies, silver was recognisably used as money in a number of ways. Several early texts documenting the principles of law and justice in Mesopotamia are preserved on clay tablets and stone inscriptions from the royal and temple archives and monuments of the cities in the region. They provide us with some evidence of the social framework within which precious metal was used as money. In the 'law codes' (which were proclamations of the role of the king in establishing justice rather than legal codes of practice) a wide range of payments is documented in terms of fixed amounts of weighed silver. Some codes also identify the king as the authority for establishing the standard weights, and some surviving weights also bear the name of the king as testimony to this. Fines for harming another's person or property were usually reckoned in silver. For instance, according to the law code of the king of Eshnunna in northern Mesopotamia (beginning of the second millennium BC), the fine for biting a man's nose was 1 *mina* of silver (about half a kilo), a significant amount, while a slap in the face was reckoned at 10 *shekels*, a sixth as much. The same law code also sets out an ideal price list of common goods, as an expression of the benefits of prosperity brought about by royal justice, listing nine different commodities by weight and volume that should be worth one shekel of silver. Interest rates, too, figure in these quasi-legal texts. Both the Eshnunna code and the more famous Code of Hammurabi of about 8 two centuries later mention an interest rate on loans in silver at 20 per cent. They also show that debts could be paid off in grain with interest according to a silver–grain rate, if the debtor had no silver. Grain by volume seems in appropriate circumstances to have performed monetary functions – for payments to agricultural workers, for instance. The Eshnunna law code quantifies the ideal daily wage of a harvester in both grain and silver (12 *se*, about half a gram). Grain is also used in these texts to express the value of foodstuffs, whereas silver is used to express the value of a wider range of goods, from metals to oil and from lard to wool. From the same period, documents from the city of Ur in southern Mesopotamia containing the balanced accounts of merchants demonstrate that the representation of the monetary use of silver and grain in the law codes largely reflects everyday practice. Many such texts show that silver by weight was used as a standard means of accounting for the value of different goods, and that silver itself was often used as a means of payment in commercial transactions, together with barley.

How did this silver standard work? When the metal itself was paid from one party to another for whatever purpose, silver was weighed out on a balance according to the amount determined by law in the payment of a fine, say, or the sum agreed by the

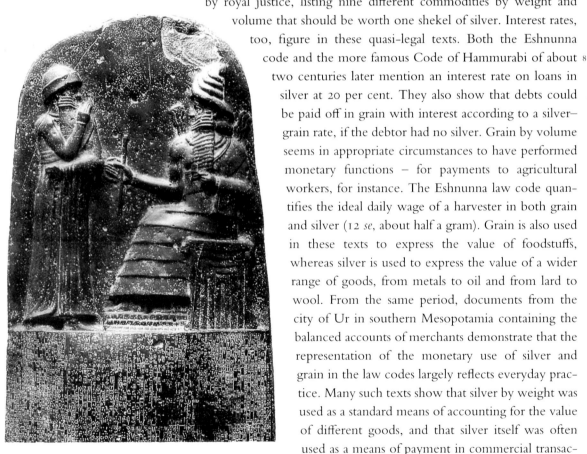

8 Stele of the Babylonian king Hammurabi (1792–1750 BC) found at Susa (southern Iran), where it was taken as booty in 1157 BC. This detail of the upper section shows the king, who stands facing the seated sun god with horned headdress. A 'law code' in cuneiform writing, describing many payments in weighed amounts of silver, is inscribed on both sides of the stone and runs to about 3,500 lines. The code continued to be used and copied for over 1,000 years (Paris, Louvre).

parties to a transaction. Hoards of silver found by archaeologists in Mesopotamia and Iran suggest that the metal was made into large ingots, cut into small scraps or drawn out into thin wire in order to facilitate the correct weighing out of the silver in bullion form. The silver wire was also made into rings which, documentary evidence suggests, were sometimes made to a certain weight.

In Mesopotamian cities, temples played a central role in what we might call the monetary sphere. They were probably the guardians of the official weights, and were generally important in the regulation of the silver system. As prestigious and literate institutions and wealthy repositories of silver and gold, temples were also the centres where records of payments and loans were made and kept. A document dated to 1823 BC (British Museum, WA 82279) records a loan from the temple of the god Shamash in the city of Sippar:

> Puzurum son of Ili-kadari has received from the god Shamash 38 ⅙ shekels of silver. He will pay interest at the rate set by Shamash. At the time of harvest he will repay the silver and the interest on it.

Silver itself, then, was commonly used as a monetary medium in ancient Mesopotamia. The king and the temples established the weight standards and published in inscriptions the values of certain commodities in silver (though it is uncertain how far this should be understood as representing official price-fixing) as well as the amounts of silver to be paid according to law in a range of circumstances – fines, interest, wages, and so on. But these authorities did not concern themselves further with the public supply of silver. It seems that the monetary 'circulation' of silver bullion was a social custom regulated to some extent by king and temple, but not directly administered by them. The metal had to be imported into the region from surrounding areas, and much of it would have been consumed – in effect hoarded – by kings, aristocrats and temples through taxes, tributes and plunder. As such, silver was a highly valued substance with strong symbolic associations with royalty, wealth and power, and the substantial surplus that was not immobilised in treasuries was potentially available for monetary use.

Similarly deprived of local sources of silver, ancient Egypt was, however, rich in gold from Nubia and in the agricultural wealth resulting from the yearly flooding of the Nile. In a letter to King Amenhotep III (now in the British Museum), Tushatta, King of Mitanni (c. 1390–1352 BC), says that in Egypt 'gold was more common than dust'. There is frequent mention in texts from the later New Kingdom (c. 1295–1069 BC) of standard weights (the *deben* of 91 grams, and its tenth, the *kite*), according to which metals were used as money in much the same ways as in Mesopotamia – both as a direct means of payment and in accounting for value across a range of goods in transactions by barter. A document preserved from the New Kingdom period records how a policeman, Amunmes,

bought an ox valued at 50 deben of copper (about 4.55 kg) from a workman, Penamun, but only 5 deben were actually paid in copper. The balance was made up by a variety of other commodities whose values were also expressed in deben of copper – fat (30 deben), oil (5 deben) and clothing (10 deben). This text comes from the village of Deir el-Medina near the city of Thebes, inhabited by the skilled craftsmen who worked on the royal tombs in the Valley of the Kings. A large number of such documents have survived from this highly literate community, which show that buying and selling on this system were frequent and that silver was a commonly used metal to express units of value in payments. Indeed, the Egyptian word for silver (*hedj*) seems to have taken on a broader meaning approaching that of money. This can be seen in a document from Deir el-Medina

9 Wall painting from the tomb of Rekhmira, chief minister to the Pharaoh Thutmose III, fifteenth century BC, showing a man carrying tribute in the form of a copper ingot.

10 Ancient Egyptian tomb-painting, *c.* fourteenth century BC, showing Nubians from the south of the kingdom carrying tribute in gold rings and other forms.

20

11 Part of a hoard of precious-metal objects found at el-Amarna, Egypt. The hoard of gold and silver ingots, wire and fragments was buried in a pot in the fourteenth century BC. (× ¼)

which records the repayment of a loan of 'silver' (in other words, money) to the sum of 76 deben of copper by one Shedydemduat to a workman named Pennuit. Fifty-four deben had already been repaid, and the remainder still to be returned was therefore 22 deben, 'in order to complete the amount of "silver"'.

Though the amounts are expressed in terms of copper deben, the payments could in fact have been made in a variety of goods. But silver, when available, was clearly highly acceptable as a means of payment, and hoards of gold and silver bullion have been found in Egypt. One such hoard, found during excavations in el-Amarna, the city of King Akhenaten (c. 1352–1336 BC), part of which is in the British Museum, contained both gold and silver ingots and pieces of cut silver, much of which is in rings, and a small silver figurine. The weights of some of the individual ingots of gold and silver seem to approximate to multiples and fractions of the deben. The hoard as a whole illustrates the forms in which assorted fragments of precious metal were weighed out and passed from hand to hand in Egypt within a system which commonly used the value of precious metal in payments.

As in Mesopotamia, the evidence for monetary practices from Egypt is of course restricted to the literate elite of the population and those who had access to the services of a scribe. We should perhaps not take their practices as necessarily representative of the life of the people of ancient Egypt as a whole. The artisans of Deir el-Medina were familiar with complex accounting systems, but whether this was also true for the mass of illiterate peasants in their daily lives is doubtful. How far the precious-metal standard extended down the social scale in either Egypt or Mesopotamia may be uncertain in economies which were orientated more towards the redistributive mode than to private enterprise. But as an aspect of the dominant royal, priestly and aristocratic culture, its existence is important for our appreciation of these ancient societies.

Coinage and bullion

One can observe basic similarities between the otherwise quite different societies of Mesopotamia and Egypt. Common to both is the adoption of a standard of value, expressed either in terms of grain by volume or precious metal by weight. In particular, the weights used in

12 Detail of an obelisk from Nimrud (ancient Calah of the Bible; now in northern Iraq), c. 865 BC. The panel shows tribute being paid to the Assyrian king Shalmaneser III in the form of copper ingots, which are being weighed on a pair of scales.

Mesopotamia, the shekel and the mina, became widespread in the Mediterranean world and were adopted by the Greeks in the early first millennium BC. Long-distance trade presumably played a significant role in the use of precious metal as money, because it must have been crucial for merchants to sell their goods in all regions of the Mediterranean. Though most of these would have been exchanged by barter, metals such as gold and silver would also have changed hands. They were valuable possessions in themselves and hence easily valued and exchanged against other goods. The fact that metals

13 Detail of a bronze strip from the monumental wooden gates of a royal building at Balawat, near Nimrud (northern Iraq), c. 845 BC. The scene depicts tribute (perhaps ingots) being brought by the Phoenicians to the Assyrian king.

were not subject to short-term decay or to yearly fluctuation of supply (like grain) must have increased their usefulness for traders. Thus gold or silver, even in small amounts, could constitute an effective means of making actual payments, whether of a commercial, legal or social kind, because of their general acceptability.

The main restriction on their usefulness was the problem of limited supply,

though this was of course one of the reasons why these metals were valuable in the first place. Regions .that found themselves in possession of a source of gold or silver were thus likely to have a privileged access to riches and, often, political power. Such indeed was the case for the kingdom of Lydia in western Asia Minor. The might and wealth of its last king, Croesus (whose reign ended about 547 BC after the conquest of his kingdom by the Persians), was legendary in antiquity. Apart from collecting large sums of money from their subjects, the Lydians were said to derive their wealth from the local river Pactolus and from mines, both of which provided them with electrum, a naturally occurring alloy of gold and silver. From this metal were made the objects that are usually understood as the first coins in the Western tradition, though bronze arrow-shaped objects made from around 600 BC in the area of the Black Sea also 16 seem to represent some form of proto-coinage (coincidentally, the Chinese were also developing 'coinage' in bronze at about the same period). The

14 Detail of the black obelisk of Shalmaneser III, King of Assyria, found at Nimrud, c. 825 BC. The scene shows part of a tribute paid by Jehu, the biblical king of Israel. Among the tribute paid to the king of Assyria and mentioned in the cuneiform inscription above the scene are gold, silver, golden goblets, golden buckets and tin. The figure on the right seems to be carrying ingots above his head.

15 Bronze or copper bar ingots of the eighth to seventh century BC, found at Tepe Hasanlu in north-western Iran. They range in length from about 20 to 28 cm and in width from 1.5 to 2.5 cm. (× ¼)

16 Bronze 'dolphin', made at Olbia on the northern shore of the Black Sea in the fifth century BC. In this area cast bronze objects in the shape of arrow-heads or dolphins seem to have been used as a form of currency.

17 Electrum coin from Lydia, seventh century BC. The earliest coins were made of electrum, a mixture of gold and silver, and so have a pale yellow colour. Early coins have the imprint of one or more rough punches on one side and a figural design on the other. This coin has the head and neck of a lion, to the left of which can be seen some Lydian letters which represent part of the inscription *Valvel*, a personal name, presumably referring to the person who was responsible for making the coin. (× 2)

Lydian pieces have a rough oval shape, thus resembling nuggets of gold, but they correspond to systems of regular weights, ranging from a group of larger coins (17.2 grams, 16.1 grams, 14.1 grams in weight) down to tiny pieces that weigh one ninety-sixth of the larger pieces. A large proportion of the surviving pieces are of these lesser weights, a fact which points towards a society that was accustomed to precision when it came to dealing with small weights.

The 'coins' are marked with one or more punches on one side, and, although some are blank or have simple parallel lines on the other side, most of them have a figurative design, often an animal (a lion, stag or ram, for example). This large repertoire of types is not fully understood, which makes attribution to specific minting authorities difficult. The lion's head and paws are generally associated with Lydia, as they strongly resemble designs on its later coins. Some designs are associated with cities in Asia Minor (Miletus and Phocaea), though no names are inscribed. There are, however, some rare inscriptions on the electrum which seem to mention individuals rather than states or cities. Two of them, apparently Lydian personal names, read VALVEL and KALIL in Lydian lettering. 17 Another, in Greek, is more explicit and reads 'I am the sign of Phanes' or, on smaller pieces, simply 'of Phanes'. These inscriptions refer to an individual with the Greek name of Phanes, and the grazing stag on the pieces may be his personal badge. Some of the designs on electrum can also be found on seals or rings of the same period, where they definitely represent personal devices, and one may wonder whether individuals were not also responsible for some of the early electrum coins. But who were they? Were they private, wealthy individuals, local rulers or state officials of the kingdom of Lydia? This is an important question for our understanding of the development of coinage, but the question of who made these early electrum pieces must remain open in the present state of our knowledge.

Can we glean any evidence from the places where the electrum coins have been found? The most famous discovery was made during the excavations at the temple of Artemis at Ephesus, where ninety-three electrum pieces and seven unstamped 18 silver nuggets were found underneath the temple itself, suggesting that they were buried there as a religious dedication. Similar coins were probably made on the island of Samos, but in general one can say that the production of these pieces was restricted to western Asia Minor, though some pieces were also found in neighbouring areas (Hellespont, Black Sea). Thus their production and use appear locally rather restricted, a fact that is already suggested by their often minute size: they were not intended to be handled frequently or to circulate

18 Electrotype copies of electrum coins from the hoard found at Ephesus during the excavations of the Temple of Artemis conducted by the British Museum at the beginning of the twentieth century.

widely in long-distance trade. So why were they made? There is a whole spectrum of non-commercial possibilities: perhaps they were used as a new way of making personalised dedications to the gods, or as prestigious gifts to dependants.

Herodotus mentions that Croesus sent a gift of two *staters* of gold to each of the citizens of the Greek city of Delphi, the site of the famous oracle of the god Apollo, in gratitude for what he took to be a favourable response from the god (*Histories*, 1.54). Though this episode would have happened some time after the first electrum coins appeared, it seems plausible that objects with such attractive designs would have been presented to individuals. No doubt these pieces, being intrinsically valuable, might also change hands in the course of trade, like jewellery or ivory, but that need not mean that they were produced to facilitate such trade in the first instance.

Furthermore, if we look at these early electrum objects from the perspective of the older uses of metal that we met in Mesopotamia, the introduction of a range of stamped designs and fixed weight standards need not appear so very momentous. It is hard to imagine how they could have been used without being weighed on scales, just like pieces of silver bullion, as, from the evidence of the pieces themselves, it is not clear that their value would have been readily intelligible from their size and diameter. This is an important point if the metal in question was to be recognised and accepted at 'face value', that is like later Greek coins, rather than by weight as bullion, as had always been the practice with regard to precious metal previously. But if we look at the pieces from the perspective of the later coinages, to which we will now turn our attention, their appearance in western Asia Minor in the late seventh century BC points towards a crucial change in monetary history.

The age of silver

Electrum coinage ceased to be minted after the middle of the sixth century, and in its place we find in many regions coinages made of silver and occasionally of gold. A few cities (Cyzicus, Lampsacus, Phocaea and Lesbos) continued to mint electrum coins, but they are very much the exception to the otherwise predominant silver coinage in the late sixth and fifth centuries BC. Why was electrum abandoned? As we have seen, silver had for a long time been the principal metal currency in the ancient Near East, and the succeeding dominance of silver coinage should occasion no surprise. Moreover, being a mixed alloy of two principal metals (but with some other additions such as lead), electrum was not easy to value, as the amount of gold in the alloy could potentially have made a significant difference to the value of a coin.

The earliest silver and gold coins were made in the kingdom of Lydia, perhaps in the reign of Croesus (*c.* 560–547 BC). These coins, which are usually

19 Electrum stater, perhaps minted during the revolt of the cities of Ionia, Asia Minor, *c.* 495 BC. The Ionian cities, led by Miletus, rebelled against Persian rule from 500 BC. Some electrum coins have been attributed to the period of the revolt, even though silver had by this time become the standard metal for coinage. (× 2)

19

20–21

20 Silver stater from Lydia, Asia Minor, mid-sixth century BC. Some of the earliest silver coins were made in Lydia, with a design showing a lion and a bull. The back of the coin continues to have the crude imprint of two punches.

found in western Asia Minor, depict a forepart of a lion and a bull. Other silver coinages were minted in Caria and other parts of Asia Minor at about the same time as the appearance of the first coins in Greece proper. Aegina (an island off 33 the coast of Attica), Athens and Corinth were the first Greek city-states to mint 34 their own coinages. Although in the earliest stages of silver coinage there are close similarities with the electrum issues in technique of manufacture and design, there are significant differences between the two groups. First, silver coinage was made in a larger geographical area than electrum: it was produced in many places in mainland Greece and particularly Macedonia, as well as in 25 Italy, Sicily, Cyprus, the Aegean islands, Cyrenaica (North Africa), southern 26 France and Asia Minor. Second, it was produced on a much larger scale, and it seems also to have moved into many other regions around the Mediterranean (including those where no coinage was produced, as we shall see below). Third,

21 Gold stater from Lydia, mid-sixth century BC. Lydian gold and silver coins had the same designs, a lion and a bull. The design was thought to have been introduced by Croesus, the last king of Lydia (c. 560-547 BC). The Greeks called the coins 'Croesean staters', although many were minted after the conquest of the Lydian kingdom by the Persians. (× 2)

22 Scene from the 'Darius vase', made in southern Italy, fourth century BC. The vase is named after the principal figure, who is identified by the inscription as Darius, King of Persia (522-486 BC). It has a scene showing the royal treasurer seated at a table and recording tribute brought to him in sacks. The Greek letters shown on the table represent values from 10,000 shekels to ¼ shekel.

23, 24 Silver siglos and gold daric of the kingdom of Persia, late sixth to fifth century BC. The 'lion and bull' coins minted by the Persians in western Asia Minor were replaced by coins with new designs, showing the kneeling figure of an archer drawing a

bow (and sometimes holding a spear), although the other side retained the rough punch-marks used on the earlier coins. The silver coins were called *sigloi* (the same word as the Hebrew *shekel*), and the gold ones *darics*, named after the Persian king Darius I (522-486 BC), under whom they were first made. (× 1½)

the custom developed of stamping a design or an inscription on the coinage to identify the community that had made it.

The reasons why coinage was adopted are more difficult to understand. Why should some states at certain periods wish to put out silver in this form? Already in antiquity people were discussing this question: in a famous passage of his constitutional treatise, the *Politics*, the fourth-century philosopher Aristotle suggested that the adoption of stamped coins in place of measured pieces of silver was

25 Silver didrachm of Athens, mid-sixth century BC. Like the earlier electrum coins of Asia Minor and unlike other early silver coinages, the earliest silver coins of Athens were without inscriptions and had varying designs, such as the facing head of a bull. The exact significance of the designs is not clear, though they may have been badges of prominent families or references to the cult of the goddess Athena. (× 1½)

27, 28 Silver tetradrachms of Athens, fifth century BC and second century BC. From the late sixth century, the various designs of Athenian coins were replaced by the standard design of the head of Athena and her sacred bird, the owl. The design of the earliest pieces was modified in about 480 BC by the addition of olive leaves on Athena's helmet and a small crescent moon behind the owl. The coins were produced in very large numbers from the silver mined at Laurium, and were so important economically that the archaising style was retained throughout the fifth and fourth centuries, although it would by then have come to look very dated. In the second century BC a new design was produced, still showing the owl, but standing on an amphora within a wreath. (× 1½)

simply one of convenience, to save the bother of weighing them out for every transaction. The addition of a design was simply a mark of value (*Politics*, 1257a). Though this explanation sounds plausible enough, it does not answer the question why nobody came up with this solution at an earlier date, if the change from bullion to coinage was so inevitable.

One of the most obvious explanations, one might say, is the minting of silver coins for economic reasons. This was already suggested in the fifth century BC by Herodotus (*Histories*, 1.94), who suggests a link between coins and trade within communities. External trade must also be considered as a possibility. Many early Greek coins have been found in Egypt, the Near East or in the region of the Black Sea, which suggests that the coins were used for long-distance commerce. The silver coins of Athens and northern Greece are frequently found in these areas, and it may well be possible that silver bullion was exported in the form of coinage. In the fourth century merchants coming to Athens could export silver in this form if they did not have any other return cargo of goods. As the writer Xenophon explains in one of his treatises, 'it is sound business to export silver; for wherever they [i.e. the merchants] sell it,

26 Silver stater of the Aegean island of Naxos, *c.* 500 BC, showing a cup for drinking wine; bunches of grapes are shown on either side and a vine-leaf above. The reverse still has only a punch-mark. (× 1½)

they are sure to make a profit on the capital invested' (*Ways and Means*, 3.2). But the numerous cut coins, ingots or pieces of scrap silver found mixed with 29–31 coins in hoards indicates that the coins were seen as silver bullion rather than as coins of a fixed value. It is hard to see how long-distance trade alone would have led to the development of coinage, and we need to look at other possible explanations.

Smaller-scale transactions in communities, involving buying and selling goods for everyday consumption, required small coins. Though low-value coins were used within cities from an early date, as we shall see below, it remains uncertain whether this constituted a vital factor in the production of coinage. The smallest coins, such as half *obols*, would still have been of considerable value and too

29 Silver stater of the Aegean island of Melos, *c.* 500 BC. The design shows a pomegranate (in Greek, *melon*), a punning reference to the issuing state. This piece was found in a hoard from Asyut in Egypt, where it had been imported from the Aegean along with many hundreds of Greek coins. Like this one, a number of them had been partially chopped up, indicating that they were treated as bullion when they were used in Egypt, an area that did not produce coinage at the time. (× 1½)

30 Silver stater of Terone, northern Greece, *c.* 500 BC. The design is a wine amphora or storage jar, a reference to the importance of the area for the wine trade. This coin, found at Asyut, had been cut by a chisel, presumably to check that it was made out of solid silver. (× 1½)

31 Silver stater of Acanthus, northern Greece, *c.* 500 BC. The design on coins of Acanthus is a lion attacking a bull, and the composition has been skilfully adjusted to fit the circular shape. This piece, found with a hoard of Greek coins in the Nile Delta in Egypt, had been tested for quality by a chisel cut. (× 1½)

32 Scene showing men bargaining with prostitutes, from a Greek painted cup made in Athens, early fifth century BC. The man on the left offers a purse to the woman in front of him. The man in the centre is perhaps trying to fix a price with another woman: he holds up three fingers but she counters with four.

high for everyday retail trade. A member of an Athenian jury, for example, was paid an allowance of three obols a day at the end of the fifth century BC, which probably represented roughly the cost of a whole day's subsistence.

Many coins were issued by Greek cities or rulers, who would have struck coins to meet various payments. As we have seen, Athenian citizens were paid by the state for jury service and for other activities such as attending the Assembly. Military expenditure, such as pay for oarsmen in the fleet or mercenaries, also required coins. It is therefore not surprising to find that states took an interest in minting activities, and that coinage is therefore linked with the increasing role of the state and law in Greek political life. Indeed, states may have made a profit by minting coins: there is some evidence from the Hellenistic period to suggest that a coin had a higher value within its area of issue than the bullion from which it was made. If this were also true in earlier centuries, it could provide a plausible explanation as to why so many Greek cities struck coins and why silver coinage spread so quickly in the late sixth and fifth centuries BC. Considerable savings and revenue would accrue to the states by taking over the production of silver and imposing an overvalued and state-regulated coinage. To work effectively, the system would have needed to fulfil two conditions. First, it would have to be regulated by a legal authority in order to enforce the overvaluation of silver when paid in the form of acceptable coin. The importance of the state's involvement in this regard would explain the choice of designs symbolising its role in maintaining the value of the coin. Second, the state imposing a coinage system would have to have a strong commercial attraction for traders, whether trading in silver itself or in some other commodity, for otherwise they would be put off by the loss involved in accepting overvalued silver coins. This might explain why coinage was produced by those states with a strong 'trade balance' in their favour, such as Athens or 27–8 Aegina. The silver coins of both states became international coinages and are 33 found in many parts of the Mediterranean world.

We might also look to certain currents in Greek thought for a means of interpreting the rapid and wide spread of coinage as money in the ancient world. Greek philosophers in the sixth and fifth centuries BC were concerned with the concept of law and how it could be applied. Thus the Athenian statesman Solon, who reformed the Athenian laws in the beginning of the sixth century, combines the issues of the city-state, wealth, administration and laws in his writings. The introduction of coinage in Athens took place somewhat later than his reforms, which transformed the Athenian state and society, but the spread of coinage can nevertheless be seen within the general context of the development of the Greek city. One of the Greek words for coinage (*nomisma*) derives from the same etymological root as the word for law (*nomos*), suggesting that the coins were recognised as a product of social conventions. Though ambiguous, our

33 Silver stater of the island of Aegina, fifth century BC. Aegina was one of the first Greek states to make silver coins. Its early coin design, a turtle, was replaced during the fifth century by a tortoise, as seen here. (× 1½)

29

Coinage and the city-state

The widespread adoption of silver coinage in the Greek world during the sixth century BC saw the introduction of designs and inscriptions which referred to the authority of the city-states which made the coins. The state's authority guaranteed the quality and value of the coins and protected them against abuses such as forgery.

The designs were chosen to symbolise the authority of the state by referring to its religious cults and mythological past, or by using puns to refer to its name, and were accompanied by inscriptions giving the cities' names. This pattern remained characteristic from the earliest Greek coins to the latest, made five hundred years later in the Hellenistic world, although the shape of the coins and the artistic style changed greatly.

34b Silver didrachm of Corinth, *c*. 450 BC. The standard design on coins of Corinth, an important commercial city in southern Greece, was the winged horse Pegasus. According to legend, Pegasus had been tamed by the hero Bellerophon near Corinth. (× 2)

34c Silver stater of Tyre in Phoenicia, fourth century BC, showing a bearded figure of the god Melqart riding on a winged sea-horse; beneath the waves is a dolphin. The design reflects the importance of the city as a maritime trading centre. (× 3)

34a Silver tetradrachm of Athens, *c*. 510 BC. Athens used the designs of a helmeted head of Athena, the patron deity of the city, and the owl, the bird sacred to Athena; as a result the coins came to be known as 'owls'. Next to the owl are the three Greek letters A, TH and E, the beginning of the Greek word for 'of the Athenians'. The design was introduced in the late sixth century and remained standard until the end of Athenian silver coinage in the first century BC. (× 2)

34d Silver tetradrachm of Myrina, Asia Minor, mid-second century BC, depicting the head of Apollo, the city's principal deity, wearing a laurel wreath. The much thinner and wider shape of the coin, characteristic of the second century, allowed the engraver greater scope for his treatment of the design. (× 2)

34e Silver tetradrachm of Eretria, a city on the Greek island of Euboea, showing the goddess Artemis. Mid-second century BC. (× 2)

34f Gold stater of Smyrna, Asia Minor, first century BC. This very rare coin depicts the head of the Tyche or personification of the fortune of the city. The Tyche wears a crown of miniature walls, which are supposed to symbolise those of the city. The reverse represents the cult statue of Aphrodite Stratonikis. The inscriptions refer to the city (*Zmyrnaion* = 'of Smyrna') and its Executive Board (*prytaneis*), which was responsible for the minting of these emergency gold coins during the war fought in Asia Minor between the Romans and King Mithradates VI of Pontus. (× 4)

34g Greek cities.

35 Silver tetradrachm of the Greek city of Messana (modern Messina), Sicily, fifth century BC. The coin depicts a hare above a cicada. The design was mentioned by Aristotle, who states that Anaxilas, the tyrant of Messana, was responsible for introducing hares into Sicily; this may perhaps suggest that the coins were called 'hares', just as those of Athens were called 'owls'. (× 2)

literary evidence for laws on weights and measures in Athens is particularly rich for the sixth century, and it comes as no surprise that the increased use of silver coinage falls into the same period.

It is clear from the preceding discussion that the origins and spread of silver coinage may have had different sorts of explanations. But once coinage had spread to cities across the Greek world it seems that it rapidly became the predominant form of precious metal money there. There is much evidence for the widespread use of coins from fifth-century Athens in the literature of the period. A number of inventories and accounts of state expenditure (like those of the building works of the Parthenon on the Acropolis) have survived inscribed on stone. It is clear from these inscriptions that coinage was the normal form of money, although uncoined bullion or precious metal in other forms was also mentioned, in particular in the lists of assets belonging to temples. According to the historian Thucydides, the great Athenian statesman Pericles made a speech on the eve of the Peloponnesian War against Sparta (431–404 BC) in which he reminded the Athenians of their financial strength (Thucydides, 2.13). He mentions that their annual income from the allies was 600 talents, while their reserves consisted of

> 6000 talents of coined silver . . . as well as uncoined gold and silver in the form of private and public dedications, the sacred items used in festivals and games, plunder from the Persians and other things, worth no less than 500 talents. There were also substantial sums in other temples, which they could use, and if all else failed they could use the gold which adorned the goddess herself [i.e. the colossal gold and ivory statue of Athena on the Acropolis]. . . . But he said that if they used it for their own preservation then they must restore at least as much.

36 Silver stater of the Greek city of Terina, southern Italy, fifth century BC. The winged figure on the coins of Terina is probably a personification of the city, but the iconography is complex. Like Victory, she is winged and holds a wreath; she sits on an amphora, perhaps symbolising the source of a local spring or river, and holds a *caduceus*, a symbol of peace. (× 2)

37 Gold stater of
Panticapaeum, a Greek city in
the Crimea on the northern
coast of the Black Sea, late
fourth century BC. The coin
has a head of the god Pan, a
punning allusion to the city's
name. The minting of gold
coins, otherwise unusual,
reflects the availability of gold
in the region, a wealth
exemplified by the rich burials
of Scythian rulers in this area,
which often included gold
objects. Pan is shown with
characteristically pointed ears
and a snub nose, and wearing a
wreath of vine-leaves. (× 5)

38 Silver tetradrachm of
Rhodes, early fourth century
BC. The island of Rhodes was
one of the most prosperous
states in the fourth and third
centuries BC and issued many
coins. The head of Apollo is
shown almost full-face, a mark
of the skill of the engraver who
made the die. The rose on the
back refers to Rhodes, since
the Greek for rose was *rhodos*.
(× 3)

39 Bronze 'coin' made at the Greek city of Acragas (modern Agrigento) in Sicily, *c.* mid-fifth century BC. Before the introduction of bronze coins, pyramid-shaped pieces of bronze currency were cast in Sicily. This example is decorated with two eagles' heads and three dots on top to indicate its value. (× 1½)

40 Bronze coin of Acragas, late fifth century BC. After making objects like **39**, the city produced coin-shaped bronzes by the normal coin-striking process. This piece depicts a crab and other sea creatures, reflecting the city's maritime situation. The six dots which surround the design represent its value. (× 1½)

This passage shows the primacy of silver coinage over other forms of wealth, both in quantity and in function: temple treasures and the like could be used *in extremis*, but would have to be replaced later. Coins in silver formed the bulk of the city's wealth. But while silver *tetradrachms* were suitable for state transactions or large payments, the lowest silver denominations in the fifth century were still too valuable to cater for small-scale individual purchases. Nevertheless, people seem to have adapted to using coins, and eventually the smallest of the silver coins were replaced by bronze coinage. The idea of making low-value coins out of bronze, a cheap metal, seems to have originated in the cities of southern Italy in the late fifth century BC, but spread throughout most of the Greek world during the fourth and third centuries BC. From then onwards any transaction in the market-places of Athens or other cities could have been carried out in coinage: the new medium of bronze provided small enough coins, such as the *chalkous* (an eighth of a silver obol).

Coinage is only one part of the story of money in the Greek world, albeit the most significant. Though most ancient cities may have used coins, the majority did not actually produce coinage themselves in the Archaic and Classical periods (*c.* 600-320 BC) for a variety of reasons – some perhaps because they had no access to silver and some for political reasons. The most famous of these cities was Sparta, where no coins were made until the third century BC, and the Spartans may have used iron spits instead. The ownership of gold and silver was regarded as contrary to the Spartan warrior ethos and characteristic of a base, mercantile mentality which the manly Spartans affected to despise. Nevertheless, to defeat the wealthy Athenians in the Peloponnesian War, they had to accept huge subsidies in coin from the Persian king in order to finance a fleet with which to challenge the Athenians' maritime power.

Money and credit

International warfare faced Sparta with new demands which its primitive monetary system could not meet unaided. By contrast, other states in Greece, in particular Athens, used coins and money in a more developed way, such as through banks. Athenian banks are first attested towards the end of the fifth century BC, but most of our evidence comes from the fourth. We should not think of these as sophisticated financial institutions like modern banks, but as a cross between a *bureau de change* and a pawnbroker. Bankers operated in a private capacity and were not subject to any state regulation. Their most visible activity was money-changing, primarily for foreigners who arrived at Athens with non-Athenian currency. We hear of moneychangers doing business from behind tables set up in the Agora (market-place); even now the modern Greek word *trapeza* means both 'table' and 'bank'. Bankers also accepted money on deposit, but appear to have paid no interest. What they offered was effectively a safe-deposit box – a

41 Bronze coin of Athens, late fourth century BC. This, one of the earliest bronze coins made by the city, shows an owl with two bodies, perhaps suggesting a double denomination (2 chalkoi or 2 kollyboi). This type of coin was minted in huge numbers, and almost a thousand specimens have been recovered so far in the excavations in the Agora or central square of Athens. (× 2)

service of particular use to foreign merchants who had nowhere else to store their valuables while at Athens. But we also hear of Athenians who kept money with a banker, possibly for security but perhaps in order to conceal the extent of their wealth from the prying eyes of the taxman. Finally, bankers lent money – both their own and that of depositors – to private individuals, typically at an interest rate of 12 per cent a year. People naturally preferred to borrow from friends or relatives, and most credit transactions were of this kind. Bankers therefore tended to be used only as lenders of last resort.

The banker of whom we know most, Pasion, rose from being the slave of a banker to acquire not only control of the bank but also Athenian citizenship. By the time of his death in 370 BC he was worth over 60 talents (360,000 *drachmae*). The scale of his private wealth is graphically illustrated when we recall that in the fifth century the rich city of Byzantium paid 16 talents a year to Athens. But banking was a high-risk business: Pasion was nearly ruined early in his career when he was sued by a disgruntled client, and we hear of many other banks going broke.

In the Greek world there was no equivalent of a state bank. The surplus wealth of Athens was stored under the protection of Athena on the Acropolis and was regarded in some sense as belonging to the goddess, so that thieves would be deterred by fear of committing an act of sacrilege. Hence, when the Athenians needed extra money to finance military operations, they 'borrowed' it from Athena with a promise to repay it when they could. When their finances were in crisis, they even melted down the gold cult-statues of the goddess. We also know that some temples lent their money to individuals. Inscribed accounts of the fifth century from a temple in the Athenian countryside show loans being made in units of 200 and 300 drachmae.

In the Greek world financial transactions were conducted solely in coined money; there were no cheques or exchangeable bills. Therefore the smooth running of the economy required there to be sufficient coins in circulation. In Athens we find that coins were minted on an increasingly regular basis and in

42 Bronze coin of Ptolemy II, King of Egypt, 286–246 BC. The coinage system set up in the Ptolemaic kingdom of Egypt was designed for the purpose of reserving silver for dealing with foreign merchants. Consequently, large bronze coins were made in substantial quantities to meet the internal needs of the kingdom. The coin depicts a head of the god Zeus Ammon, with a ram's horn. (× 2)

43 Bronze coin of Agathocles, King of Bactria (modern Afghanistan), early second century BC. Like the Hellenistic kingdoms further west, the kingdom of Bactria produced bronze coins, although these were sometimes square, like Indian coins. On one side the legend was in Greek, but the other, which depicts a figure of an Indian goddess holding a lotus, has an Indian (Brahmi script) inscription.

Hellenistic portraiture

The vast conquests of Alexander the Great (336-323 BC) transformed the ancient world. New areas, from Greece to India, fell under the domination of Greek rulers, and the Greek world was transformed from a collection of city-states into a series of monarchies, known today as the Hellenistic kingdoms. These changes had profound effects on the coinage. Royal portraiture was introduced shortly after Alexander's death, while the spread of Greek culture to the east meant that similar designs were also adopted there, in the kingdoms which succeeded the empire of Alexander.

Since most rulers wished to emulate Alexander or claimed to be his legitimate successors, their portraits usually show them in his pose, with the head turned upwards and eyes raised, and with the *diadem*, a white ribbon which was the symbol of kingship. The portraits died out in the first century BC, when the independent kingdoms succumbed to the Romans, but although the Romans had a very different tradition of portraiture, the earliest emperors used portraits influenced by those of the Hellenistic kings.

44c Silver tetradrachm of Eumenes II, King of Pergamum, Asia Minor, 197–158 BC. The kingdom of Pergamum achieved its most brilliant period in the reign of Eumenes II, whose coins depicted a posthumous portrait of Philetaerus, the founder of the royal dynasty in the third century BC.

44d Silver tetradrachm of Antiochus VI, King of Syria, mid-second century BC. The young king is shown wearing the royal diadem and a crown of rays. Antiochus regarded himself as a god on earth and this crown was a symbol of divinity. The use of divine symbols was a feature of the portraits of Hellenistic kings of the late fourth and early third century BC, but is unusual on coins of later kings such as Antiochus VI.

44e Silver tetradrachm of Mithridates II, King of Pontus (modern northern Turkey), mid-third century BC. The coin portrait itself and the use of the diadem show how Greek ideas were adopted in other areas by non-Greek dynasties in the wake of Alexander's conquests. (× 3)

44a Silver tetradrachm of Lysimachus, king in Thrace (northern Greece) and Asia Minor, 305-281 BC. The coin depicts Alexander the Great, since Lysimachus wanted to legitimise his position by emphasising that he was Alexander's successor. The portrait has the characteristic hairstyle of Alexander, and, as well as the diadem, his head is decorated with a ram's horn, a symbol of the god Zeus-Ammon, whom Alexander had claimed to be his father.

44b Gold octodrachm of Ptolemy II, King of Egypt (286–246 BC), and his second wife Arsinoe. The Greek legend *adelphon* refers to the fact that Ptolemy (shown nearer the viewer, wearing the royal diadem) and his queen were also brother and sister, in continuation of earlier Egyptian royal practice. (× 3)

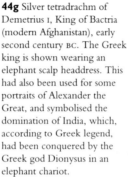

44f Silver tetradrachm of Bagadat (Baydad), priest-king of Persis (modern south-west Iran), late third or early second century BC. The idea of placing the ruler's portrait on the coin and its style are derived from Greek practices introduced after Alexander the Great, although the appearance of the subject is Iranian, with a moustache and earring. (× 3)

44g Silver tetradrachm of Demetrius I, King of Bactria (modern Afghanistan), early second century BC. The Greek king is shown wearing an elephant scalp headdress. This had also been used for some portraits of Alexander the Great, and symbolised the domination of India, which, according to Greek legend, had been conquered by the Greek god Dionysus in an elephant chariot.

44h Gold aureus of Augustus, Roman emperor 31 BC– AD 14. The portrayal of individuals on Roman coinage during their lifetime was introduced by Julius Caesar in 44 BC and became a feature of Roman imperial coins. The Roman emperors copied this idea from Hellenistic practice, although they avoided the symbols of kingship such as the diadem and instead portrayed themselves wearing a laurel wreath, a symbol of victory.

44i The Hellenistic kingdoms *c.* 275 BC.

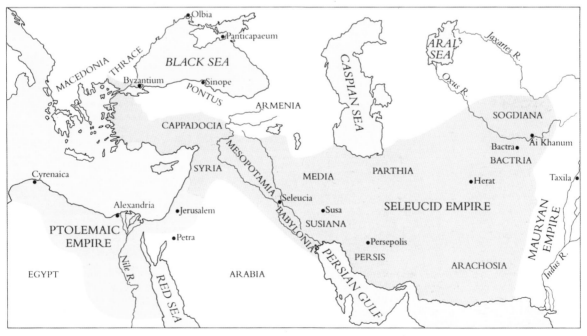

45 Silver tetradrachm of Philip II, King of Macedon, 359–336 BC. Under Philip, the Macedonian kingdom began to expand, and he conquered all the independent cities in northern Greece and took possession of the gold and silver mines there. This access to wealth was an important factor in Philip's rise to power, and he minted large numbers of coins. The silver coins depict a young rider on a huge racehorse and commemorate Philip's own victory at the Olympic Games of 356 BC. The Greek inscription gives the king's name (*Philippou*). The rider is shown holding a laurel branch and wearing a wreath, both symbols of victory. (× 3)

46 Silver tetradrachm in the name of Alexander the Great (336–323 BC), struck in 280 BC at Cyzicus in Turkey. Alexander made large numbers of gold and silver coins to finance his conquests. The coins, struck at many mints throughout his empire, were of standard types; the silver depicted Heracles and the seated figure of Zeus. The same designs continued long after Alexander's death.

large quantities. Evidence for the widespread use of coinage in day-to-day transactions in the late fifth century is found in the plays of Aristophanes, where characters talk of buying fish and sickles in the market-place, and of storing small coins in their mouths! And the vignettes of the fourth-century satirist Theophrastus contain numerous references to coins – buying, selling or lending money. By this stage the Athenians had started to mint low-denomination bronze coins for everyday use: excavations in the Athenian Agora have brought to light over 16,000 coins, mostly of bronze, which had presumably been dropped. The sheer number of these finds vividly illustrates the extent to which coined money had become the norm by this time. Similarly, most hoards dating from the end of the Classical period consist of coins rather than, as had earlier been the case, of bullion. Monetised societies depended upon coinage for most financial transactions, and as a consequence states were required to maintain the reputation and value of their coins in various ways. At Athens the passing of fake coins was strictly forbidden, and a law of 375 BC instituted the checking of coins by public slaves.

Conclusion

Access to gold and silver was one of the secrets behind the extraordinary success of the Macedonians under Philip II (359–336 BC) and his son Alexander the Great (336–323 BC) in conquering Greece and defeating the might of the wealthy Persian Empire. Philip's seizure of the mines of Thrace enabled him to produce a massive coinage in gold, silver and bronze to pay his army, while Alexander's conquest of Asia gave him control of the accumulated wealth of the Persian king – estimated at 180,000 talents in total – all of which was subsequently distributed, either as coin or booty. These are sums of a completely different order from those we have met thus far, and foreshadow the imperial wealth of the Roman Empire after its conquest of the Mediterranean world. Coinage was produced in greater quantities and over a much wider area in the Hellenistic period, but the basic monetary culture did not change.

2

The Roman World

Around [the Mediterranean] lie the continents far and wide, pouring an endless flow of goods to you [Rome]. There is brought from every land and sea whatever is brought forth by the seasons and is produced by all countries, rivers, lakes, and the skills of Greeks and foreigners. . . . So many merchantmen arrive here with cargoes from all over, at every season, and with each return of the harvest, that the city seems like a common warehouse of the world.

These words, taken from the speech *To Rome* written by Aelius Aristides, a second-century AD Greek rhetorician from Asia Minor, convey something of the enormous scale of the city of Rome as the metropolis of a great empire. Rome had grown to a city of perhaps over a million inhabitants, the largest European city known to history until the eighteenth century. With this growth of city and empire came an economy and use of money on a vast scale, altogether unprecedented in the ancient world of the Mediterranean and the Near East.

Early Rome

Rome itself had already had a long history before Aelius Aristides' time, having been founded, according to Roman tradition, in 753 BC. Rome's origins lay in a small city, at first governed by kings and then by a republican constitution under an aristocratic ruling class, and for the first 400 or so years of the city's history it developed within a strictly regional and Italian context. One aspect of Rome's geographical and cultural limits was the lack of coined money, a situation that endured until about 300 BC, some 200 years after it had become a normal feature of life in the Greek world of the Aegean and indeed of the Greek colonies in Sicily and southern Italy.

Later writers thought that the earliest form of money in Rome had been sheep and cattle, as they derived the Latin word for 'money', *pecunia*, from the word for 'cattle', *pecus*. But, while it is possible that certain values had been expressed in terms of head of cattle in Rome as elsewhere in the ancient world, it is less likely that they ever served as a form of payment. There is better evidence for the monetary use of bronze bullion measured by weight among the early Romans, as well as among the other indigenous peoples of Italy, including the Etruscans. Since bronze is a relatively cheap metal, considerable quantities were needed: the historian Livy (first century BC) mentions a tradition that Roman senators from the time of the early Republic had to carry their wealth in carts (Livy, 4.60.6). From this period date the early roughcast lumps of

bronze known today as *aes rude* ('unworked bronze') 48–9 and the cast bronze/iron *ramo secco* ('dry branch') bars with a crude design resembling a branch. Neither form of currency was specifically Roman, indeed the ramo secco bars were generally in use further to the north of Italy, but they were used by the Romans as a form of valuable bullion. They were not, however, made to a consistent weight standard and were often chopped up into smaller pieces.

How was this bronze bullion actually used? From the surviving fragments of Rome's earliest law code, the Twelve Tables, dating from 450 BC, we know that fines for various crimes were assessed in terms of units of bronze by weight. Perhaps at about the same period Roman society was organised into different classes, based on a wealth qualification assessed in terms of the same units. Army pay (*stipendium*, literally 'an amount weighed out') was introduced at some point between about 400 and 340 BC; it too seems to have been assessed in units of bronze and perhaps paid in bronze as well. If the state paid out bronze, it must also have collected it in some manner, so taxes (*tributum*) were also probably assessed in terms of weighed bronze units.

Against this background, it is perhaps understandable why the earliest Roman coinage, dating to about 300 BC, should have consisted of two quite separate and apparently unrelated elements: on the

47 Cast bronze currency bar of the Roman Republic, third century BC. The image represents a tripod (a ritual vessel with three legs), a design also found on the coins of Greek cities of southern Italy. This example was found at Castel Gandolfo near Rome (near the ancient Latin city of Alba Longa) in 1819. The idea of making large currency bars was derived from earlier Italian bars.

48 Broken piece of bronze used for currency in central Italy in the fourth to third centuries BC, now known as *aes rude*, meaning unworked bronze.

one hand, large bronze bars and heavy discs cast in bronze made in the native 47
Italian tradition and, on the other, struck silver and bronze coins. The struck 50
coins were modelled directly on Greek coins made in southern Italy; indeed,
some may even have been manufactured for the Romans in a Greek city, perhaps Neapolis (modern Naples). They can be distinguished as Roman only 50a
by their inscriptions. The designs, weight standard, level of silver purity and
even technique of manufacture are all borrowed straight from those of the
contemporary Greek cities in southern Italy. And even in the case of the heavy
bronze bars and discs, the form of their decoration was derived from the
iconographic world of the Greeks, with designs such as tripods or dolphins
adapted directly from Greek coins.

The adoption of the Greek idea of coinage, the copying of Greek models 50b
and the Hellenisation of an Italian form of currency took place in the very
period that Rome began to emerge as a significant power in the Mediterranean
world. The Romans' success in repelling the invasion of the Greek king Pyrrhus
(280–275 BC) left them as rulers of the whole peninsula, and with their victory
over Carthage in two long wars (264–241 and 218–201 BC, the latter being the
famous war against Hannibal) they became the dominant power in the western
Mediterranean. It is no accident that the Romans adopted coinage at this time,
when many aspects of their culture – art, architecture and religion – were
transformed by an influx of foreign, particularly Greek, influences. The entry
of the Romans into the 'civilised' world dominated by Greek culture was thus
marked by an intense Hellenisation, including the adoption of coined money.

After about a century of development from these origins, the Roman monetary system was reformed about 212 BC in response to the unprecedented
financial demands on the state caused by the long war
against the Carthaginians under Hannibal. This
brought about the establishment of a coinage consisting solely of struck silver and bronze pieces on
the Greek model. The principal coins in the new
system were the bronze *as* and the silver *denarius* 50f, j

49 Part of a bronze currency
bar of north and central Italy,
fifth to third centuries BC.
Analysis of the metal of such
bars has shown that the bronze
contains a large proportion of
iron. Such an alloy is typical of
the product of the first smelting
of iron-rich copper ores.

The early development of the Roman monetary system

Weighed amounts of bronze seem to have been used as money in early Rome. Finds of bronze bar ingots and scrap bronze fragments in Italy suggest that this form of money was in use among Rome's neighbours by the fourth century BC. Rome introduced its own bronze ingots during the early third century BC. Some of these were bar-shaped, while others took the round shape of Greek-style coins, but were considerably larger and cast like the bars. Contact with the Greek cities of south Italy and Sicily also led Rome to copy their forms of money and make struck silver and bronze coins. These new coins betray in their designs the Greek influences responsible for their existence. Gold coins were struck only occasionally. During the early years of Rome's Second Punic War (218–201 BC) against the Carthaginian general Hannibal, the costs of the war forced the Romans to reorganise their coinage. A new monetary system was introduced in about 210 BC, based on the denarius, a silver coin valued in terms of the bronze unit called an as. The denarius was one of Rome's longest-lasting denominations.

50d Silver quadrigatus, *c.* 225 BC, so called from its four-horse chariot (*quadriga*) design. This was the principal silver coin of the Romans from *c.* 225 BC until the introduction of the denarius in *c.* 210 BC. (× 4)

50a Bronze coin, *c.* 300 BC, with the Greek inscription *Romaion*, meaning 'of the Romans', above the foreparts of a bull. The design was copied from coins of the Greek city of Neapolis (modern Naples). (× 2)

50b Silver 2-drachma coin, *c.* 300 BC, showing the head of Mars, the Roman god of war. (× 2)

50c Cast bronze as of the Roman Republic, late third century BC, showing the head of Janus, the Roman god who guarded doors and the start of the calendar. Janus's head, which faces in both directions, is commonly found on early Roman coinage. The coin-shaped copper ingots of this kind are now known as *aes grave*, meaning heavy bronze.

50i Bronze uncia, one twelfth of the as, *c.* 210 BC. This struck coin depicts the Roman goddess of war, Bellona, with a single dot representing its value below. (× 2)

50e Gold stater, *c.* 215 BC. Gold issues were very infrequent under the Republic, and were usually made in response to financial emergencies. This coin was issued during the crisis caused by Hannibal's invasion of Italy in 218 BC. The design represents two warriors taking an oath in the traditional manner: each touches with the point of his sword a pig held by the figure kneeling between them. (× 4)

50j Bronze as, *c.* 200 BC. Smaller and lighter versions of the as, like this example, were struck to replace the large cast *aes grave* because the relative values of bronze and silver coins had changed during the Second Punic War.

50g Silver quinarius, worth half a denarius, with the Roman numeral v, signifying its value of five asses. (× 2)

50k Silver victoriatus, about 200 BC. Of baser silver than the denarius, the victoriatus circulated in large numbers during the early decades after the introduction of the denarius, but its relationship to the other coins of this period is uncertain. The coin is named after its design of a winged Victory crowning a trophy of arms. (× 2)

50f Silver denarius, *c.* 210 BC. The x, the Roman numeral 10, behind the head of Roma is the value mark of the coin in terms of bronze asses. The reverse shows the Dioscuri, the heroes Castor and Pollux. (× 2)

50h Silver sestertius, a quarter denarius with the Roman numerals IIS, standing for two and a half asses (S = *semis*, half an as). (× 2)

(so-called because it was originally worth 10 asses). There was a fixed relationship between them which changed only once in the next 400 years, when the tariff of the denarius was increased to 16 asses in about 140 BC.

Metal	Denomination	Value (from 210 BC)	Value (from c. 140 BC)
Silver	denarius	10 asses	16 asses
Silver	quinarius	5 asses	8 asses
Silver	sestertius	2½ asses	4 asses
Bronze	as	1 as	
Bronze	semis	½ as	
Bronze	triens	⅓ as	
Bronze	quadrans	¼ as	
Bronze	sextans	⅙ as	
Bronze	uncia	¹⁄₁₂ as	

The Romans had started the third century with a relatively undeveloped system of coinage and state finance in which coined money had played an insignificant role. This had been sufficient for the conquest of Italy, but the establishment of the overseas empire required more complex and stable arrangements. Coinage was now indispensable to the efficient running of the Roman state, and it seems quite likely that from about this time Roman society had become as monetised as any other major city of the contemporary Mediterranean world. The output of low-value bronze coinage was greatly expanded, partly in consequence of the need to pay the army, and finds of coins in modern excavations suggest a transformation in the amount of coined money in circulation in the second and first centuries BC.

Coins in the Roman world

In order to understand how people in the Roman world actually used coins we need to turn to written sources, such as the extant texts on papyrus from Roman Egypt or literary texts. Most ancient writings pay scant attention to everyday realities, but notable exceptions are the three synoptic gospels of Matthew, Mark and Luke from the New Testament. They are full of parables and other stories told by Jesus, drawing on experiences from the lives of people from the lower strata of society in Palestine and often involving coins. Many stories from the gospels mention the payment of sums of money: for example, in the story of the Good Samaritan, the innkeeper who

51 Coinage in the third century BC.

takes in the wounded man is paid 2 denarii as part payment for board and lodging for a few days (Luke 10: 35). Elsewhere Jesus implies that a denarius is a fair day's wage for a worker in a vineyard (Matthew 20: 1) and in another story he asks, 'what woman, having ten silver drachmae [a drachma was the Greek equivalent of a denarius], if she loses one coin, does not light a lamp and sweep the house and search diligently until she finds it? And when she has found it, she calls together her friends and her neighbours, saying "Rejoice with me, for I have the coin which I had lost"' (Luke 15: 9). Clearly a denarius was a very valuable object for most ordinary people: in another story (Mark 12: 42) Jesus commends the poor widow who puts into the alms box all that she has, two *lepta* – the equivalent of a quadrans (there were 64 quad- 52 rantes to a denarius). Small copper coins which are clearly the same as the lepta (or 'widow's mites') referred to in the story are found in considerable quantities in present-day Israel. Larger sums of money are also mentioned: Jesus's disciples assume that it would cost 200 denarii to buy enough bread to feed the five thousand (Mark 7: 37), while the ointment that Mary Magdalene breaks over Jesus's feet (Mark 14: 5) is said to have been worth 300 denarii – clearly a very substantial sum.

These references suggest that the relatively poor people who came to listen to Jesus regarded coins as a familiar feature of ordinary life. Much the same picture is evident from the everyday receipts and letters that have survived from Roman Egypt. These, too, indicate a widespread use of coins for even small transactions and, indeed, for more developed systems of credit transfer, so that payment might not even require the exchange of actual coins.

If the use of coinage seems to have become customary in much of the Roman world (at any rate the Mediterranean provinces), it would, however, be misleading to think of a unitary monetary system in place throughout the territories conquered by or subject to Rome. The denarius was only one of the silver coinages produced in the lands controlled by the Romans. As they expanded their control across those areas of the Mediterranean which already had a tradition of coinage, the Romans usually took a pragmatic view and permitted the existing coinages to continue. It was generally characteristic of the Roman attitude to the administration of their multi-cultural empire that existing systems would be left alone or simply incorporated wholesale into the Roman system, rather than being subjected to the imposition of centralised uniformity. So it was with administrative and financial organisation: existing tax regimes continued after Roman conquest, while functioning monetary sys- 53–5 tems and coins were allowed to continue and to co-exist with Roman coins. In two particular provinces, for example, the Romans preserved the profitable closed currency systems that had been operated by their previous rulers. Both the kingdom of Pergamum, acquired by the Romans in 133 BC as the province

52 Bronze lepton (known as *prutah* in Hebrew) from Roman Judaea: an example of the 'widow's mite' referred to in Mark 12: 42. The coin, showing three ears of corn, was issued in AD 29 by the Roman procurator of Judaea, Pontius Pilate, in the name of the Roman emperor Tiberius. (× 1½)

53 Silver denarius produced by an Iberian community in Spain, under Roman rule, second century BC. Its inscription in Iberian script, *Ikalesken*, names the local community. The design is based on the Dioscuri of the Roman denarius (**50f**), but omits one of the riders. (× 1½)

54 Bronze coin of Gozo, near Malta. Gozo and Malta were captured by Rome in 218 BC and formed part of the Roman province of Sicily. Gozo (called Gaulos at this period) made a few bronze coins of its own throughout the second and first centuries BC. The coin shows the Phoenician moon-goddess Astarte, reflecting the Phoenician origin of the island's population.

56 Base-silver 4-drachma coin of the emperor Nerva (AD 96-8) minted at Alexandria for circulation in Roman Egypt, which had its own separate coinage based on the system of the Ptolemies. The base-silver 4-drachma coin was maintained as the standard denomination until the reforms of Diocletian in AD 294-6.

of Asia, and the kingdom of Egypt, conquered by Octavian (Augustus) in 30 BC, had struck coins containing less silver than those notionally of the same value which were circulating in the surrounding areas. The kings of Pergamum and Egypt had stipulated that their coins were the only legal silver currency within their realms and, since their coins were not accepted outside their kingdoms because they were too light, the governments were able to make a profit when traders had to change their coins on entering and leaving the kingdom. The Romans were not about to abolish such a comfortable arrangement just for the sake of ostensible imperial uniformity.

56–7

If the preservation of the status quo was the normal Roman response to the monetary institutions of annexed territories, the Romans were quite capable of intervening forcefully in extreme circumstances. So in 146 BC, at the end of their third and final war against Carthage, urged on by Cato's catchy slogan '*delenda est Carthago*' (Destroy Carthage!), the Romans utterly demolished the city and obliterated its coinage by removing it from circulation and melting it down, as a symbol of the Carthaginians' power and wealth which had been the cause of such trouble to the Roman state for over a century.

Wealth and corruption

The wide plurality of monetary systems in the empire was, however, inevitably eroded. This was a result not of official action, but of the draining of huge amounts of precious metal out of the provinces towards the city of Rome through the exaction of booty upon conquest and, later, through taxes. In the second and first centuries BC the brilliant successes of the Roman legions began to extract immense quantities of loot from newly conquered areas in the Greek east on a scale never before seen in Rome. The spoils won in a major war in Italy in 293 BC against the people of the Samnites amounted to 1,830 pounds (592 kg) of silver, a large sum in those days. One hundred and twenty years later, however, the booty accruing to the Romans in 167 BC from the defeat of the king-

55 Bronze coin of the Roman emperor Augustus (27 BC–AD 14), minted at Ilici in eastern Spain. Local copper alloy coinages in the name of Augustus and his successors were issued throughout the Roman Empire. By the second half of the first century, Roman coinage had replaced local coinage in the west, but in the eastern half of the empire local issues continued until the late third century.

57 Base-silver 4-drachma coin of the emperor Gordian III (AD 238–44) minted at Caesarea in Cappadocia, Asia Minor. Cappadocia became part of the Roman Empire in AD 17, and Caesarea remained a mint for silver coins until the reign of Gordian III. This coin was part of the large issue struck to pay for his war against the Parthian kings of Iran.

dom of Macedon alone was 75 million denarii, equivalent to about a million pounds (324,000 kg) of silver. And Macedon was by no means the richest of the Hellenistic kingdoms the Romans would conquer. The spoils of war, and hence the Romans' wealth, had by the second century BC increased exponentially. The flow of wealth from new territories to Rome led to the impoverishment of the provinces, at least in respect of precious metal, with the result that there was not enough silver left with which to make coins. This resulted in the gradual disappearance from the Roman provinces of silver coinages other than those made in Rome. The plentiful silver coinage of Athens survived the Roman conquest of Greece in 146 BC intact, but gradually petered out by the middle of the first century BC. Julius Caesar's conquest of Gaul in the 50s BC stripped the region of its reserves of gold and brought the previous gold coinages of the area to an end; silver managed to survive for only another generation. Even in wealthy Asia Minor the Greek cities also by and large stopped producing their own silver coins under the Roman Empire, but hundreds of communities continued to issue bronze coins down to the third century AD, with designs reflecting their local civic identities.

Later commentators saw the extraordinary wealth that flowed into Rome after her conquests in the second and first centuries BC as the cause of a catastrophic decline in public morality. The Greek historian Polybius commented on the higher standards that prevailed among the Romans at the time when he was writing, in the middle of the second century BC:

58 Gold aureus of the Roman Republic issued by the magistrate Aulus Manlius in 80 BC. The design represents the equestrian portrait statue set up in honour of Lucius Cornelius Sulla, *dictator* (temporary head of state) of Rome 82–79 BC. This was one of the earliest representations on Roman coins of a living statesman, a sign of the shift in power from the aristocratic senate to the successful generals of the first century BC. (× 4)

Among the Greeks, . . . members of the government, if they are entrusted with no more than a talent, though they have ten copyists and as many seals and twice as many witnesses, cannot keep their faith; whereas among the Romans those who as magistrates and legates are dealing with large sums of money maintain correct conduct just because they have pledged their faith by oath. Whereas elsewhere it is a rare thing to find a man who keeps his hands off public money, and whose record is clean in this respect, among the Romans one rarely comes across a man who has been detected in such conduct.

POLYBIUS, 6.56

A hundred and fifty years later, however, the historian Livy reflected on the decline in standards that came about as a result of the great increase in wealth in Rome during the intervening period:

> No state was ever greater, none more righteous or richer in good examples, none ever was where avarice and luxury came into the social order so late, or where humble means and thrift were so highly esteemed and so long held in honour. For it is true that the less men's wealth was, the less was their greed. Of late, riches have brought in avarice. . . .
>
> LIVY, Preface, 11

The Romans often blamed contact with corrupt Greeks and other Easterners for the perceived decline in standards. Livy again:

> It was through the army serving in Asia that the beginnings of foreign luxury were introduced into the city. These men brought into Rome for the first time bronze couches, costly coverlets, bed curtains and other fabrics and – what was at that time considered gorgeous furniture – one-legged tables and sideboards.
>
> LIVY, 39.6.7

If we believe the historian Sallust, the venality of Romans in the late Republic was even remarked upon by their foreign enemies. Jugurtha, king of Numidia in North Africa, is reported to have believed that he could bribe Roman senators in order to avoid war, 'for he was convinced that at Rome everything was for sale' (Sallust, *The War Against Jugurtha*, 28). Looking back on the causes of the catastrophic civil wars of the first century BC, the Romans commonly blamed the accumulated effects of excessive wealth and the corrupting extravagance it brought in its wake. The extravagant expenditure on the circus games organised in 58 BC was, for instance, thought to mark a turning point in the moral corruption of Rome (Pliny, *Natural History*, 36.113). The poet Lucan (first century AD) wrote:

> Fortune introduced excess of wealth and morals collapsed before prosperity; the spoils of war encouraged extravagance. . . . This was not a people to be satisfied by peace, growing fat on its liberty and forgetting the sword. . . . Public office was stolen through bribery, while the people, selling its own support, together with deadly corruption, returned each year with their venal struggles at the elections. Enter ravenous usury and interest, greedy for the passage of time. Trust was shattered, and war was a source of profit for many.
>
> LUCAN, 1.160–82

The Romans occasionally attempted to pass laws to limit the amounts of money that could be spent on luxurious living, but the regulations were never

59 Silver denarius minted for Julius Caesar in the early months of 44 BC. The Latin legend hails him as *Caesar dict perpetvo*, 'Caesar, perpetual Dictator'. Caesar was the first Roman ruler whose portrait bust appeared on Roman coins during his lifetime. The introduction of such a design acknowledged his absolute power, representing him as though he were a king, like Alexander the Great and his successors on Greek coins. (× 4)

60 Silver denarius minted by the Roman general Marcus Brutus in 43–42 BC. The Roman historian Dio relates that Brutus 'stamped his own portrait, and a cap of liberty with two daggers on the coins which he struck, indicating thereby and by means of the inscription that he and Cassius had freed their country'. The reverse inscription reads *Eid[ibus] Mar[tiis]*, 'the Ides of March', the date on which Brutus and Cassius and their fellow conspirators assassinated Julius Caesar.

observed. Pliny tells us that by the middle of the first century AD over 25 million denarii each year were spent on luxuries from China, India and Arabia. It is impossible to say how accurate this figure might be, but it is certainly the case that Roman coins are commonly found in India. And a recently discovered tax receipt from a ship plying the trade with India through the Red Sea suggests that it may have been even greater than Pliny suggests.

Pliny also records how 'Marcus Crassus [a contemporary and rival of Julius Caesar and Pompey] used to say that no man was rich who could not maintain a legion on his income' (*Natural History*, 33.134). Implicit in this statement is a close association between access to money and military power, a factor that had a dramatic effect on the history of the late Republic in the first century BC. The Romans might have been wrong in the extent of their moralising about an imagined past of frugal simplicity, but they were correct in perceiving the considerable impact of new wealth on the social and political life of their community. Politicians borrowed huge sums to buy their way into public office in the late Republic, against the prospect of making even more during their year as a magistrate. We are told that Caesar alone owed 25 million denarii in 61 BC, a debt he managed to recoup many times over in the course of his conquest of Gaul in the 50s. Money-lending and banking thus assumed considerable political importance in Rome. Money could buy political influence and it could also pay for an army to seize absolute power. It is no coincidence that the emperor Augustus, the eventual victor in the civil wars that put an end to the Roman Republic in the 40s and 30s BC, also became incomparably the richest individual in the empire, capable of dispensing financial patronage and largesse to the

58–60

61–3

61 Silver denarius showing Octavian (later called Augustus) and his adoptive father Julius Caesar. The inscription names Caesar as 'the God Julius' and Octavian as 'Son of the God'. Octavian used Caesar's image on his coins to help legitimise his own position as heir to Caesar's power. (× 1½)

62 Silver denarius of Octavian, showing Victory standing on a ship's prow. This symbolises Octavian's naval victory at Actium in 31 BC, where the forces of Antony and Cleopatra were defeated. (× 1½)

whole Roman world. In his inscriptional biography Augustus records that 'the total sum which he donated to the public treasury, to the Roman plebs and to discharged soldiers was six hundred million denarii', a colossal sum made possible only by his unique access to the wealth of the whole empire. From then on, there was nobody whose fortune could compete with that of the emperors, and this was one of the main instruments of their dominance. The sums of money available to the Roman elite increased in magnitude until one man managed to amass a sum of truly imperial proportions and transformed a free republic into a monarchy.

The empire

The coinage itself expressed the new imperial orientation of money. No longer produced in the name of elected monetary magistrates, every coin bore the emperor's portrait or that of a member of his immediate family. This fact alone would have sent a palpable message to all those who came into contact with the coins, that they were inhabitants of the Roman Empire. Some of the impact that the new coins must have had can be gathered from a story in St Mark's Gospel. Jesus is being asked by some Pharisees, who are trying to lay a trap for him, whether it is lawful for Jews (who had never accepted the legitimacy of Roman rule) to pay taxes. Jesus says to them:

'Bring me a coin and let me look at it.' And they brought one. And he said to them, 'Whose likeness and inscription is this?' They said to him, 'Caesar's.' Jesus said to them, 'Render to Caesar the things that are Caesar's, and to God the things that are God's.'

MARK 12: 15–17

Within one generation of Augustus's death Jesus could turn to a coin with a portrait of the emperor as a symbol of imperial authority.

However, despite the fundamental change that had taken place in the ideology of coin designs

63 Gold aureus of Octavian, 28 BC. The reverse of this rare coin shows Octavian seated on the curule chair of a consul, chief magistrate of the Roman Republic, with the Latin legend *Leges et ivra P[opvli] R[omani] restitvit,* 'he restored the laws and rights of the Roman people'. This resonant phrase refers to Octavian's 'first settlement' of 28–27 BC, when he claimed to restore the Republican constitution after the end of the devastating civil wars which followed the assassination of Julius Caesar. (× 4)

64 Copper as of Nero (AD 54–68). (× 2)

the monetary system remained largely unchanged from the period of the Republic. The principal denomination, the silver denarius, continued to be struck at much the same size and weight. The bronze coinage, whose production had been more or less 64–5 abandoned in the first century BC, was revived in a new form. Asses were now made of pure copper, while *sestertii*, which had formerly been made of silver, were now minted in brass. Gold coinage also became a regular part of the Roman monetary system, and the new gold coin, the *aureus*, was tariffed at 25 denarii. The regular production of these new high-value coins can perhaps be seen as a reflection of the dawn of Augustus's new golden age of peace, law and prosperity, and they certainly marked a significant increase in the amount of money in circulation. In fact one unique source of evidence, the coins found at the city of Pompeii destroyed by the eruption of Mount Vesuvius in AD 79, suggests that the gold coins in circulation were worth more than twice as much as the silver and base-metal coins put together. In terms of their value in sestertii, the coins from Pompeii were worth the following: base metal, 2,312 sestertii; silver, 22,302 sestertii; gold, 54,800 sestertii.

These figures indicate the importance of the new gold coinage and reflect the scale of the Roman Empire's monetary economy and resources, which were unprecedented in the context of the ancient Mediterranean world. It is the sheer scale of Roman coinage that distinguishes it from the many coinages of the earlier Greek and Hellenistic world. For example, hundreds of millions of coins were struck during the third and fourth centuries. This is a staggering output, and one that was not repeated until modern times.

It was, indeed, because of the vast size of the empire that coin production was required on an astronomical scale. It has been estimated that the imperial budget in the middle of the second century AD amounted to around 225 million denarii (or 9 million gold aurei) a year. Three-quarters of this probably went on paying the army, which consisted of over 400,000 men; the remainder would have been needed for the civil service, building projects, subsidies to enemies across the frontiers of the empire and other expenses. This enormous yearly expenditure was supported by the taxes and revenues gathered from the empire – an extremely complex system of land taxes, rents and sundry dues which funded the central operations of the empire and the emperor.

65 Brass sestertius of the emperor Titus (AD 79–81), showing the Flavian amphitheatre, the Colosseum in Rome, which was completed under Titus and dedicated in AD 80. (× 2)

66 Silver coin of Tincomarus, king of southern Britain *c.* AD 10. Though the Romans had yet to subdue Britain, the coinage of some British kings already displayed considerable Roman influence: the head wearing a wreath on this coin seems to have been copied from the portrait of Augustus on a coin made at Lugdunum (Lyons, France). (× 1½)

Just as the scale of the Roman economy and coinage production grew, so did its geographical diffusion. Coins were already well known in the Mediterranean world prior to the advent of the Romans, from the influence of the Greeks and Carthaginians. The peoples of northern Europe, including Britain, also began to issue coins before their conquest by the Romans. But under the Romans coin use expanded greatly throughout the continental regions of the empire, mostly through the agency of the army. A letter dating from the early second century AD, preserved on a wooden tablet (now in the British Museum) and excavated from the fort of Vindolanda near Hadrian's Wall, on the very edge of the Roman Empire, provides vivid evidence for the entrepreneurial activities being carried out there in coin by members of the army. These business dealings clearly involved the transfer of considerable amounts of coins:

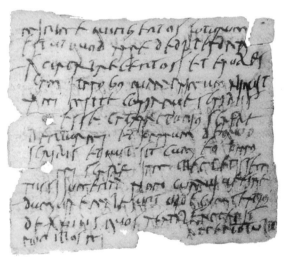

> Octavius to his brother Candidus: greetings. The hundred pounds of sinew from Marinus I will settle up. From the time when you wrote to me about this matter, he has not even mentioned it to me. I have several times written to you that I have bought about 5,000 modii of grain, on account of which I need cash. Unless you send me some cash, at least 500 denarii, the result will be that I shall lose what I have laid out as a deposit, about 300 denarii, and I shall be embarrassed. . . . See with Tertius about the 8½ denarii which he received from Fatalis. He has not credited them to my account.

67 Letter recording monetary transactions, written on a wooden tablet found at the fort of Vindolanda on Hadrian's Wall in northern England. Second century AD.

68 Plated forgery of a silver denarius of the Roman Republic, 85 BC. The silver plating has partly come away, revealing the bronze core beneath. Forgery was a common phenomenon in the Republic, as later, and surviving coins often show cut-marks indicating that they have been tested for authenticity. (× 2)

69, 70 Bronze as of Claudius (*left*) and a privately made imitation of the same. The Roman provinces of Gaul and Britain also experienced a shortage of bronze coinage, met as in Italy by unofficial copies.

Coins became so necessary to the workings of the provincial economy in Britain and Gaul that epidemics of forgery broke out in the reign of Claudius (AD 41–54) 69–70 and again in the 270s, the 340s and the 350s, at periods when there was a shortage of official coin. The forgeries, mostly of low-value coins, can hardly have fooled many people. They supplemented the insufficient output of official mints which was restricting the money supply and met the growing demand for coins in the provincial economy.

Archaeology can tell us a great deal about coins and money in the Roman economy. In Britain, for instance, although Roman coins regularly entered the province after the invasion of AD 43, they are only found on archaeological sites identifiable as large towns or military outposts for the

71 Relief from a Roman tomb of the second century AD at Neumagen (the Roman town of Noviomagus) on the Moselle near Trier, showing the payment of rent by tenants.

next two centuries. In this period the indigenous rural population of Roman Britain, that is, the majority of the island's inhabitants, seems not to have used coins at all. This is a useful reminder of the gaps in our evidence concerning money in the Roman world. But in the middle of the third century AD large numbers of low-value coins entered Britain and seem to have been very widely used, as they are found on all sorts of sites, including rural sites and settlements where previously coins appear not to have been used at all. The increase in coin use that occurred after AD 260 appears to have been sustained throughout the fourth century until the Roman withdrawal from Britain shortly after AD 400.

Money and inflation

The increased use of coinage in Britain from the middle of the third century AD may have been facilitated, at least partly, by the enormous increase in coin production that took place during that century and which was accompanied

72 Base silver antoninianus of the emperor Caracalla (212–17). The emperor is shown wearing a radiate crown, identifying him with the sun-god Apollo, in order to distinguish this denomination from the denarius, on which the emperor wore a wreath. This coin is now called a radiate from its design, or an antoninianus from the name of the emperor, Marcus Aurelius Antoninus Pius (Caracalla was his nickname). (× 1½)

73 Base silver antoninianus of Tetricus I (272–4), ruler of the so-called Gallic Empire, a break-away state consisting of Roman Gaul, Britain and Spain. By the 260s the antoninianus had replaced the denarius as the main Roman denomination, but progressive debasement had reduced its silver content to below 10 per cent. (× 1½)

and made possible by a fall in the silver standard of the coinage itself. For more than four centuries the coinage system based on the denarius had remained unchanged, but the amount of silver in the coinage had fallen gradually yet constantly from the reign of Nero (AD 54–68) onwards, until, by the mid-260s, the *radiate*, the coin that had replaced the denarius at double its face value, contained no more than 2–3 per cent of silver. Under the 72 emperor Tetricus (who ruled in France and Britain between AD 271 and 274) 73 the radiate reached its lowest point, with a silver content of no more than 0.5 per cent; as a consequence these coins were produced in great quantities.

The crisis in confidence in the coinage being issued at this time is illustrated by the following official decree that has survived on a papyrus from Egypt dating from the middle of the third century:

> From Aurelius Ptolemaeus also called Nemesianus, chief official of the Oxyrhynchite nome [district]. Since the public officials have assembled and accused the bankers of the banks of exchange of having closed them on account of their unwillingness to accept the divine coins of the Emperors, it has become necessary that an injunction should be issued to all the owners of the banks to open them, to accept and exchange all coin except the absolutely spurious and counterfeit, and not only to them, but to all who engage in business transactions of any kind whatever, knowing that if they disobey this injunction they will experience the penalties ordained for them previously by his Highness the Prefect [of Egypt].
>
> *Oxyrhynchus Papyri*, XII.1411

The dramatic debasement of the silver coinage in the third century AD appears to have been caused largely by the exhaustion of supplies of silver, and it seems that some of the silver mines in Spain declined after the second century. However, an exacerbating factor must have been the increasing strain on the imperial resources caused by the incessant frontier wars, as successive waves of barbarian peoples attempted to force their way into the prosperous territories of the empire. A declining stock of silver was therefore forced to go further and further, as coin output increased. The consequences were debasement of the coinage and a rise in prices: in short, inflation. One illustration of this can be provided by the increase in the pay of a Roman legionary soldier, which greatly accelerated after AD 200:

Reign	*Amount per annum*
Julius Caesar (*c.* 46 BC)	225 denarii
Domitian (AD 81–96)	300 denarii
Septimius Severus (AD 193–211)	600 denarii
Caracalla (AD 211–17)	900 denarii
Maximinus (AD 235–8)	1,800 denarii

74 Gold coin of the emperor Gallienus (253–68), showing him in the guise of Hercules, carrying the god's club and wearing his lion-skin cloak. (× 1½)

75 Base-silver coin of the emperor Aurelian (270–75) from the mint of Antioch, showing on the reverse the head of Vabalathus, King of Palmyra in Syria, who had reached an accord with Aurelian in 270 which gave him the rank of Roman consul. The placing of his portrait on the coins tacitly acknowledges his unofficial position as Aurelian's co-emperor. (× 1½)

Inflation also meant that low-denomination bronze coins became increasingly uneconomic to produce, and they ceased to be made during the reign of Gallienus (AD 253–68), much in the same way as the farthing and the half- 74 penny were removed from the British denominational system in the latter half of the twentieth century. The same process also put an end to the local bronze coinages of the cities of the eastern part of the empire. Even the gold coinage was destabilised, being struck on a variable weight standard and in debased metal. It seems that by this time the old fixed relationship between the silver and the gold coinages must have broken down.

The problems of inadequate resources and constant warfare affected much more than the monetary system. Indeed, the whole fabric of the Roman Empire was almost destroyed. Huge parts of the empire seceded: in the west, Spain, Gaul and Britain fell under the rule of the separatist 'Romano-Gallic' emperors for fifteen years, from AD 260 to 274; in the east, all of Syria and Egypt was taken over by the Palmyrene rulers Odenathus, Vabalathus and Zenobia from AD 261 to 271. The empire was eventually saved by the vigorous emperor Aurelian (AD 270–75), but the inherent problems were greater 75–6 than one man could manage effectively. The idea of having a board of co-emperors was formalised by Diocletian (AD 284–305), who split the empire into eastern and western halves and established a collegiate system comprising two senior rulers in each part of the empire and two deputies who would succeed them. This 'tetrarchic' system did not formally survive Diocletian's

76 Gold aureus of Aurelian. Despite his relative lack of renown in the modern world, Aurelian was one of the most successful and dynamic emperors of the third century. He recovered the territories lost to the Gallic and Palmyrene empires and he reformed the coinage. (× 4)

abdication, and even though Constantine the Great (AD 306–37) established 77–8 himself as the principal ruler of the Roman world after a long series of civil wars, the principle of having more than one co-ruler was firmly established and led in AD 395 to the eventual division of the empire into two halves.

It is no coincidence that the two emperors who tried hardest to sort out

78 Gold solidus of Constantine the Great. According to the Church historian and bishop Eusebius (260–340), Constantine, the first Christian emperor, 'directed his likeness to be stamped on a gold coin with his eyes uplifted in the posture of prayer to God'. This type of portrait is derived from those of Alexander the Great and his successors. (× 3)

77 Bronze nummus of Constantine the Great (307–37) showing a *labarum* (a banner topped with the Christian *chi-rho* symbol) piercing a serpent, one of the earliest references to Christianity to appear on a coin. (× 2)

79 Gold bar cast in the city of Hermopolis in Egypt, third century AD. The bar was made for control purposes, and bears two stamps: the smaller one gives the name of the city in abbreviated form in Greek and Latin, while the larger and more ornate one names the official Accueppus who checked the quality of the metal.

the military problems of the empire, Aurelian and Diocletian, also tried to deal with its money and its administration. Diocletian continued the process 80 of the reorganisation of the provinces which had already begun in the third century, and both attempted reforms of the coinage. The details are not fully clear to us, but the decisive change was to free the value of the gold coin from that of the debased silver coins. At some point in the third century, possibly under Gallienus or Aurelian, gold coins had ceased to have a fixed relationship with other denominations and instead came literally to be worth their weight in gold. We know that this was the case under Diocletian, since his Price Edict specifically states that the price for gold should be the same 80g whether in coins or bullion. The 'floating' of the gold coinage was to have far-reaching consequences for the use of money in the Roman world in that 79 gold coins came to be treated as bullion. Surviving papyri from fourth-century Egypt show that the value of gold coins, and hence their relationship with the base metal coinage, could change from month to month.

Coinage reforms in the late third to early fourth century

The third century AD saw Rome's traditional monetary system gradually succumb to the combined weight of inflation and political crisis. Genuine attempts at resolving matters were eventually made by two strong personalities at the end of the century, the emperors Aurelian (270–75) and Diocletian (284–305). Aurelian reformed the very debased antoninianus by publicly guaranteeing its silver content at 5 per cent. He also restored the high quality of the gold coinage, and reintroduced the denarius and perhaps the as. But his reforms were not fully effective, and twenty years later, in 294, Diocletian introduced a new coinage with a new silver coin, the argenteus, and new bronze denominations. He also set up across the empire a network of fifteen existing and new mints to strike his new coinage. Diocletian's reforms were far-reaching in economic, administrative and military spheres, but his monetary changes were no more effective than Aurelian's, and further reforms followed in the fourth century. Chief among these was the introduction of the lighter gold coin, the solidus, by Constantine the Great (307–37) in about 309. In contrast to earlier Roman gold coins, it soon became the principal element of the precious metal coinage, and survived to become the main denomination of the Byzantine Empire. Alongside the solidus, new small silver and copper denominations were also introduced.

80e Bronze nummus of Diocletian, a new standard bronze denomination introduced by Diocletian.

80h Silver miliarensis of Constantius II (337–61).

80i Silver siliqua of Constantine the Great.

80f Bronze radiate of Diocletian.

80j Bronze nummus of Constantius II, showing the reverse type probably introduced to mark the thousandth anniversary of Rome's foundation in 348, reading *Fel[icium] temp[orum] reparatio* ('the restoration of fortunate times').

80g Fragment of Diocletian's decree revaluing the coinage in 301, found at Aphrodisias in Asia Minor.

80a Base silver antoninianus of Aurelian. The Roman numerals XXI on its reverse signify the reformed standard of the coin: 20 parts copper to 1 part silver.

80c Bronze as (?) of Aurelian.

80b Base-silver denarius of Aurelian.

80d Silver argenteus of Diocletian. The figure XCVI on the reverse of this new denomination indicates that 96 of these coins were struck to each pound of silver.

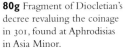

80k Silver siliqua of Theodosius I (379–95).

81 Gold medallion of the emperor Constantius II (337–61), struck at Antioch, showing him distributing largesse from a chariot. Objects for distribution are shown below the chariot. The medallion itself was doubtless made for donation on just such an occasion (Berlin, Münzkabinett der Staatlichen Museen).

The later Roman Empire

The fact that gold coins had come to be literally worth their own weight in gold explains why we also find that, from the middle of the third century AD onwards, precious-metal plate and jewellery increasingly came to have a monetary function. Now that the value of gold coins was determined solely by their weight and the current price of gold, they were in effect no different from any other form of precious-metal object in their monetary potential. We know that fourth-century government officials received payment not just in coins but also in other precious-metal objects. Some of these objects survive today: one such is a silver dish in the British Museum, bearing an inscription celebrating the tenth anniversary of the reign of the emperor Licinius (AD 308–24), which was presumably presented to a senior official on that occasion. In the same way, hoards of precious-metal coins of this period quite commonly include jewellery and plate, suggesting that they were used as money in addition to coins. Another feature of the coinage of the 81–4 fourth and fifth centuries is the large and impressive gold and silver medallions which were probably presentation pieces given out by emperors on occasions such as their anniversaries.

Now that the circulating value of gold coins was dependent on the price of

82 The insignia of the post of *Comes Sacrarum Largitionum*, Count of the Holy (i.e. Imperial) Largesse, as depicted in the *Notitia Dignitatum*, a register of the official administration of the empire dating from about 400. This official was in charge of minting in the later empire. In addition to coins, the picture shows buckles and other precious-metal ornaments that could be used for payment (Oxford, Bodleian Library).

83 Gold medallion of Diocletian (AD 284–305). The head is a good example of the portrayal of depersonalised imperial authority of the period. This giant coin is the equivalent in weight to ten gold aurei.

bullion, it was free to rise, and the coinage as a whole was rendered even more vulnerable to inflation, which seems to have accelerated towards the end of the third century AD and continued into the fourth. Such rampant inflation understandably caused considerable economic and social distress, as we can learn from the impassioned preamble to Diocletian's Price Edict of AD 301: 80

> Who does not know that wherever the common safety requires our armies to be sent, the profiteers insolently and covertly attack the public welfare, not only in towns and villages, but on every road? They charge extortionate prices for merchandise, not just fourfold or eightfold, but on such a scale that human speech cannot find words to characterise their profit and their practices? Indeed, sometimes in a single retail sale a soldier is stripped of his donative and pay.... Aroused justly and rightfully by all the facts set forth above ... we have decided that maximum prices of articles for sale must be established.

Diocletian's edict was a misguided attempt to stop inflation simply by making it illegal. It tried to establish maximum legal prices for all sorts of commodities and services across the Roman Empire. For example:

1 army modius (about a bushel) of wheat: 100 denarii
1 Italian sextarius (about half a litre) of ordinary wine: 8 denarii
1 Italian sextarius of Falernian wine: 30 denarii
1 Italian pound (about 325 grams) of beef: 8 denarii
1 Italian pound of pork: 12 denarii
1 Roman pound (about 325 grams) of gold: 72,000 denarii
1 Roman pound of silver: 6,000 denarii
1 Roman pound of copper (second cheapest type): 60 denarii
1 day's wages for a farm labourer (with maintenance): 25 denarii
1 day's wages for a baker: 50 denarii
Barber, per man: 2 denarii
Scribe, for writing 100 lines: 20 denarii

84 Silver coin of Priscus Attalus, who was installed as emperor at Rome by Alaric the Goth in 409 and reigned for little over six months. He was again proclaimed emperor by the Goths in Gaul in 414, but lasted only until 416. His giant silver coins, apparently struck at four to the Roman pound, were the equivalent of gold solidi.

Price control has also been favoured by some modern politicians, and the attempt was as futile in 301 as it was in the 1970s: people simply withdrew their goods from sale, and no amount of official threats were able to avert the inflationary pressure.

If the inflation was at least partly caused by changes in the nature of the coinage system, it also had serious effects on the coinage. The gold coinage was exempt, of course, because of its floating value. Gold coins continued to be made much as before, but their value in terms of denarii and in terms of numbers of base-metal coins increased enormously (the denarius had become a unit of account by this period, and was no longer the name of an actual coin).

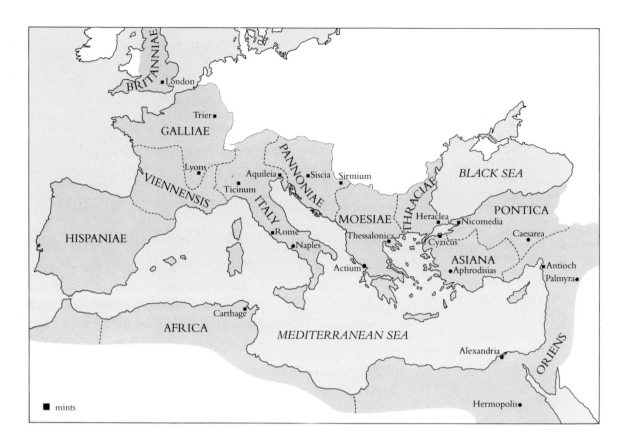

85 Mints and dioceses under Diocletian (AD 284–305).

86 Bronze follis of Constantine the Great, with the inscription *Providentiae Avgg* ('To Imperial Providence') and showing a fortress, a reference to the emperor's role in protecting the empire. (× 1½)

Various remedies, all more or less in vain, were tried to save the base-metal coinage. Its weight was reduced and its value increased, as we know from a fragmentary inscription dating from AD 301. Neither strategy worked for more than a few years. The Roman monetary system of the fourth century was punctuated every few years by a fundamental reform, whereby all earlier base-metal coinage was taken out of circulation and replaced by an entirely new system, which then proceeded to succumb to inflation.

The inherent instability of the late Roman monetary system stands in stark contrast to the permanence of the Republican and early Imperial system. But, paradoxically, the diversity characteristic of the earlier period was replaced in the third and fourth centuries by a visual and physical uniformity across the empire. From the reign of Diocletian onwards, Roman coins were produced at 85 about a dozen mints across the empire. They were all made to the same dimensions and metallic quality and, for the first time in the history of the Roman world, with the same designs. Similarly, the images of the emperors on the coins also became more uniform and less individualised. The imperial portrait had become an icon of imperial authority rather than a portrait. The same applies to the other designs on the coins. One type, for example, depicts a fort, but it does 86 not represent an actual structure. It is rather an allusive symbol of the emperor himself and his role in defending the security of the empire.

The late Roman Empire was also the period of most widespread and intense coin use in the whole of Roman history. In western Europe coins would not play such an important role again until perhaps the nineteenth century. But the Roman monetary system had become deeply polarised internally, and the government was unable to maintain a relationship between the high-value gold coinage, whose circulation must have been restricted to the wealthier classes, and the token base-metal coins. There was thus no internal cohesion in this crucial area of imperial administration.

Conclusion: change and continuity

It was perhaps a similar lack of cohesion between the rich and poor sections of the population in the western empire that led to the collapse of imperial control and the end of the Roman Empire in the west. The Greek east, on the other hand, was both financially and socially more stable, and managed to survive under Roman control to become what is known as the Byzantine Empire. Significantly, one important turning point was the reform of the base-metal coinage after the chaos of the fourth and fifth centuries by the emperor Anastasius (491–518). His rigorous financial control enabled him to die with a surplus of 320,000 Roman pounds of gold (104,000 kg) in the treasury, laying the foundations for a secure imperial future.

The structure of society in the western empire had changed radically in the third and fourth centuries AD. Towns had gone into decline, and the rich retreated to their villas and estates in the countryside, seemingly turning their backs on public life and the defence of the empire. Wealth and property became increasingly concentrated in fewer hands, while the Christian Church also took a large slice of the available wealth away from the community, as rich Christians preferred to endow churches and monasteries than to provide public buildings or monetary largesse for their fellow-citizens. The abandonment of Roman civic culture in the post-imperial kingdoms of the west, which we shall look at in the next chapter, was anticipated before the actual fall of the western empire itself.

87 Gold solidus of the emperor Arcadius (383–408), ruler of the eastern portion of the empire. This frontal military portrait is characteristic of the later Roman coinage for the eastern empire. Similar imperial portraits continued to be used on the coins of the east, later known as the Byzantine Empire, after the fall of the western part of the empire in 480. (× 4)

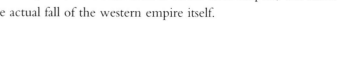

Medieval Europe

It gives me no pleasure to recount all of the different civil wars which afflicted the Frankish people. . . . What are you trying to do? You have everything you want! . . . In your treasuries the gold and silver are piled high. Only one thing is lacking: you cannot keep peace, and therefore you do not know the grace of God.

GREGORY OF TOURS (AD 539–94), *History of the Franks*, 5.1

The medieval world lived in the long shadow of the imperial Roman past, particularly so in western Europe where so much had changed. The end of the western Roman empire resulted in the disappearance of most public institutions that the Roman world had known, including the system of coinage and state finance which had kept money in production and in circulation. The Germanic kings who conquered the western half of the Roman Empire had little use for the complex taxation system on which the Roman state had depended for the support of its expensive infrastructure and standing army, neither of which existed in Germanic society. Precious metal continued to be of prime importance for the kings and nobles of the post-Roman world. But instead of circulating throughout the body politic as it had done in the Roman period, gold and silver began to pile up in the private treasure-houses of kings and bishops. It would be many centuries before something approaching the centralised complexity of the Roman monetary system was re-established in Europe.

Money in the wake of Rome: c. AD 450–c. 750

The barbarian peoples neighbouring the Roman Empire in the first centuries of our era seem to have regarded coins principally as bullion, but they were already familiar with money both in concept and in practice. Imperial coins are found in all the lands bordering the Rhine and Danube frontiers, and even in the far north. Among the barbarians, Roman gold and silver coins were often mounted as prestige jewellery or were melted down to make other luxury objects, but they also retained some measure of their monetary function. In times of peace there was a lively trade across the imperial frontier, and while barter served for many transactions, both gold and silver coins were used to settle imbalances and in the purchase of high-value merchandise such as furs and slaves. The leaders of the more coherent barbarian groups received imperial gifts in coin and plate, distributed with a nice regard both to the barbarians' value as erstwhile allies and to their potential threat as future enemies. The spectacular dish of 500 pounds (162 kg) of gold given in AD 451 by Aetius the

88 Silver half siliqua of Odovacar (476–93), struck in his own name at Ravenna early in his reign. Odovacar presents here the imperially correct view of his position: although proclaimed king by the barbarian troops of the 'Roman' army in Italy, he adds no royal title, wears no diadem and is shown as *magister militum* (commander of the army). (× 2)

89 Gold solidus of the Frankish king Theodebert I of Metz (534–48). Theodebert was the first barbarian ruler to place his own name on the solidus. Such self-aggrandising usurpation of the emperor's prerogative was noted with disapproval by the contemporary Byzantine historian Procopius. (× 4)

Roman general to the king of the Visigoths may be contrasted with the modest silver bowls that ended up at second hand in the grave of a seventh-century English king at Sutton Hoo.

Large sums were also handed over to barbarian neighbours in tribute payments and in subsidies for defending the empire from more ferocious tribes further to the north and east. The scale of this drain on the imperial treasury is recorded in literary sources and attested by the many coin hoards that have been found beyond the Roman frontier. Between the years 422 and 437 the annual subsidy paid to the Huns, for instance, rose from 350 to 2,100 pounds (113 to 680 kg) of gold. But even this was not enough to prevent them from invading Italy under Attila in 452. In contrast to the earlier Celtic tribes of northern Europe who had struck coinage of their own when in a similar position, none of the Germanic barbarian kingdoms produced any official coins until after they had settled, by invitation or conquest, in the heartlands of Roman Europe in the fifth century.

In Italy the pattern was set by Odovacar, a Roman general of Gothic parentage who brought the sequence of western emperors to an end in 476. He produced a series of imperial-style denominations in gold, silver and bronze which served the needs of the monetary economy that he had inherited and successfully maintained. A multi-denominational system in all three metals was followed by his Ostrogothic successors into the sixth century. After Justinian restored Byzantine control in Italy in 552, imperial gold coins and some silver and bronze were struck again at Rome and Ravenna. Other barbarian successor states which initiated coinage in a quasi-Roman context were the Vandals in their final home in North Africa; the Lombards of Italy in their kingdom in the north and their duchy of Benevento in the south; the Visigoths first in south Gaul and then in Spain; the Franks under the Merovingian dynasty in France; and the Burgundians, another Germanic people, along their eastern borders. Coinage thus continued to be produced in all the former territories of the Roman west, except for Britain. Roman coinage had already ceased to circulate there in the early fifth century, and no more coins were struck in Britain until the beginning of Anglo-Saxon minting in about 600.

Nevertheless, despite the geographical continuity, the monetary systems of western Europe changed radically after the end of Roman rule. Outside Italy the coins of the barbarian kingdoms

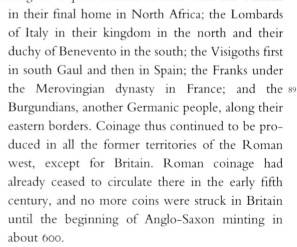

were almost exclusively gold. The reason for this concentration on high-value coins was essentially that the uses of money had altered from those in the later Roman Empire. The urban-centred economy was gradually replaced by a rural one based on the large country estate. The old Roman taxation system was less effective or had broken down, international trade continued but at a reduced level and the circulation of coin became more sluggish. In these circumstances there was less need for smaller denominations, but a continuing requirement for gold coin suitable for settling legal compensation payments characteristic of Germanic society, giving largesse, paying armies and supplying the needs of the larger-scale operator.

At first, the barbarian rulers regarded their territories as still technically within the empire and struck their gold coins in the names of the successive contemporary emperors at Constantinople. 90–91 Usually referred to as 'pseudo-imperial', these coins are often distinguished from their imperial prototypes only by their style, which is not always inferior to that of the official issues, just individually and consistently different. Lower denominations, if any, in silver and bronze increasingly bore the monograms or names of the barbarian rulers themselves. The imperial connection gradually weakened until all coins were struck in the names of the local issuing authorities.

The later sixth and seventh centuries brought change. In the less centralised Frankish kingdoms, there was a proliferation of mints and early signs of

90, 91 Gold tremissis of the Byzantine emperor Justinian I (527–65), struck at Constantinople, and a contemporary gold Visigothic tremissis in his name struck in Spain and distinguished by the cross on the chest. (× 4)

a relaxation in the Roman tradition of the ruler's monopoly of coinage in the assumption by others, particularly ecclesiastical authorities, of the right to coin. At this time, too, the wastage of gold coins was increased by the consistently unfavourable balance of trade in luxuries with the East and by the tendency of the wealthy and the Church to hoard what they had. Dwindling stocks of gold could not be augmented with new supplies as there were no significant sources of raw metal in the West, and the former regular infusions of imperial *solidi* in the form of subsidies from the Byzantine Empire ceased. There was a serious shortage of bullion and, throughout the barbarian kingdoms, gold was increas-

92 Gold tremissis struck in Merovingian France by the moneyer Lobosindus, *c.* 605–15, with the formula *Racio Dom[in]i* (treasury of the king). (× 2)

93 Silver penny of Archbishop Ecgberht of York (732/4–66) with King Eadberht of Northumbria (737–58), showing a full-length figure of the archbishop. The Church was involved in coin production from its beginning in England. (× 2)

ingly confined to the smaller denomination, the *tremissis* (worth one third of a solidus). The tendency, evident from the beginning, for the weight and fineness of their gold coins to fall away from the old imperial standard was considerably accelerated. The pace and extent of this process varied with the individual circumstances of each successor kingdom.

The problem became more acute as the demand for coin began to rise. Successful barbarian dynasties, despite internecine warfare, created more settled conditions and developed fiscal systems which promoted commercial life and the use of money. In addition, the newly granted markets and fairs called for a coin less valuable than the gold tremissis. At this point, the growing influence of the Christian Church was also important, on the one hand increasing the drain on bullion by converting gold coins into plate and ornaments, while on the other stimulating the circulation of money in its roles as collector and dispenser of alms, patron of craftsmen and as a participant in the revival of trade.

These developments are particularly clear in Merovingian France where, 92 during the first half of the seventh century, the tremisses and the rare regal solidi became rapidly paler as the gold was adulterated with silver. With a brief overlap, they were replaced in about 675 by silver coins, some of which carry the inscription DENARIVS. These were of approximately the same size and weight as the tremissis. Anglo-Saxon England, dependent on continental bullion, 93 could not sustain a gold coinage after the Merovingian standard had collapsed, and changed over to silver about the same time. The source of the metal is a problem, as silver was previously scarce. Long-held stocks in the form of plate no doubt contributed, but it seems likely that newly mined silver became available, most probably from the Melle region of western France, which was to be much more productive later. These west European silver pennies of small thick fabric are unhistorically, but usefully, known as *sceattas* (an Old English word with a derivative meaning of 'treasure'). Central to the rise in commercial activity and the use of coined money from about 700 were the Frisians, based in the Netherlands, who traded in slaves as well as exchanging northern commodities for southern luxuries. Their sceattas rapidly became a major element of northern European currency. Another series of early eighth-century sceattas is attributed, still with some reserve, to the southern Danish town of Ribe on the North Sea coast, an important outpost of this trading system.

During the second quarter of the eighth century the weight and particularly the fineness of the sceattas declined. Some of the latest issues in England have such a low silver content that they appear almost like bronze coins. The reasons for this collapse of the standard are complex. Problems of bullion supply and an adverse balance of trade again played their part, but perhaps most important was the suppression of the independent pagan Frisian kingdom by the Christian Carolingians.

The uses of money

The social institutions of the Germanic peoples who
settled in the former western Roman Empire, particularly
compensation payments for various crimes and aristocratic
gift-giving, were facilitated by the adoption of money and
stimulated its use. Payments to troops, purchases of
luxuries and property and donations to the Church all
employed coined money. While barter continued, money
was also used in commerce. As systems of taxation, tolls
and customs were developed in the established successor
states, money – while not a necessity – was increasingly
used. It was high denominations, essentially gold, that
were needed for these transactions. Even silver coins,
where they existed, were relatively high-value and it was
only in North Africa and Italy that lower-value copper
coins continued to be struck to facilitate small-scale
market purchases in an urban economy.

94a Gold and garnet Anglo-
Saxon pectoral cross set with a
gold solidus of Heraclius and
Heraclius Constantine of the
period 613–32, found at
Wilton, Norfolk. This
pendant adapts the pagan
tradition of using coins for
jewellery to the devotional
purposes of a recent Christian
convert. (× 1½)

94c Copper follis (40 nummi)
of Theodahad, king of the
Ostrogoths (534–6), struck in
Rome. The king is shown
wearing a jewelled
spangenhelm, the helmet-like
'crown' of Germanic kings.
(× 1½)

94b Leaf from the ivory
diptych of Orestes, Roman
consul, AD 530. The consul
sits between Rome and
Constantinople personified.
Above are medallions of the
Ostrogothic rulers Athalaric
(left) and his mother
Amalasuntha (right). Below,
servants pour money from
sacks, symbolising the consul's
customary largesse to the
populace and demonstrating
the continuity of Roman
tradition under the Germanic
kings (London, Victoria and
Albert Museum).

94d Silver quarter siliqua of
Pope Gregory III (731–41)
with the Byzantine emperor
Leo III, struck at Rome. The
pope's monogram appears on
the reverse. The coinage
reflects the passing of real
authority in Rome from the
Byzantine emperor, still in
nominal control, to the popes.

94e Bronze pan-balance and Roman coins used as weights, found in a pagan Anglo-Saxon warrior's grave at Dover, sixth century AD. Anglo-Saxon coins were not yet being produced and such equipment was used to weigh small amounts of gold and foreign gold coins. (× ⅓)

94g Hoard of 100 Frankish and Anglo-Saxon gold tremisses, buried (with a few ornaments) *c.* 645 at Crondall, Hampshire (from electrotypes of the originals now in the Ashmolean Museum, Oxford). The round sum of 100 gold shillings is thought to represent a *wergeld* (compensation payment for a killing). (× 1¼)

94f Detail of a drawing from the Eadwine Psalter, a mid-twelfth-century English copy of a Utrecht original of *c.* 820, illustrating Psalm 123: 'Behold as the eyes of servants look unto the hand of their masters . . . .' The king watches two servants tip money from sacks onto a table while another weighs the amount due to each waiting soldier (Cambridge, Trinity College).

94h Hoard of 118 Anglo-Saxon and continental silver pennies (sceattas), buried *c.* 730 and found at Woodham Walter, Essex. The hoard, found close to a road leading inland from the port of Maldon, contained many Frisian coins from the area of the Rhine estuary, suggesting that this was money used in trade.

95 Base-silver denier of Nemfidius, Patrician of Provence (*c.* 700–10), struck at Marseilles. The growing independence of the administrators of Provence at the expense of the weak Merovingian kings led them to replace the royal name with their own on the coinage. (× 1½)

96 Silver denier of Emperor Louis the Pious (814–40), struck at Melle, Aquitaine, 819–22. The mint name *Metallum* on the reverse means 'mine' in Latin, and refers to the rich local source of silver. (× 1½)

Meanwhile, the Visigoths in Spain were making do with ever baser gold tremisses and no silver until their issues were brought to an end early in the eighth century by the Arab conquest. In Italy the Lombard gold coins similarly declined in fineness, supplemented by only limited issues of silver. The duchy of Benevento in southern Italy, which apparently began striking in the late seventh century, sustained a coinage of solidi and tremisses of poor-quality gold into the ninth century, latterly alongside silver pennies of the reformed broad type inspired by those instituted by the Carolingian ruler Pepin about 755.

The monetary history of western Europe in these centuries parallels the transition from the essential unity of the empire to the plurality of the successor barbarian regimes, all with a shared Roman inheritance but with their own distinctive identities.

The age of the penny: c. 750–1150

At the dawn of the Carolingian age European currency was in transition: a vestigial Roman monetary system of coinage and taxation struggled on in the south, while in the north-west the framework of its medieval successor was already in place. The trend towards decentralisation characteristic of the new order was, however, about to be reversed, if only temporarily. The precursor of this development was the fall of Spain to the Arabs in 711–15. The whole of the peninsula became part of the Islamic world, adopting the monetary system used in the Umayyad caliph's other territories, which stretched from the Indus to the Atlantic (see fig. 134c). The eighty or so mints of the preceding Visigothic period were reduced to a single mint at Cordoba which served the entire country. There was a clear contrast between the monetary institutions of the post-Roman barbarian West and the Islamic world.

The signal for change in France was the overthrow of the last effete Merovingian rulers by the vigorous founders of the Carolingian dynasty. Its first king, Pepin the Short, carried out a radical reform of the coinage in about 755, by which the higher weight and silver content of the original penny were restored. The new money, also distinguished from the old by a broader, thinner fabric, was to remain the standard silver denomination in Europe for the rest of the Middle Ages. The reform also tightened royal control over minting operations, symbolised by the presence of the ruler's initial or name and title on all coins. The number of mints was reduced and coins of uniform design were soon struck throughout the king's or emperor's dominions, including northern Spain recovered from the Arabs and in the former Lombard kingdom in north Italy. The volume of Carolingian coinage was high, sustained by fiscal and commercial success and, in particular, by the effective exploitation of the Melle mines 96 in western France.

The political situation in southern England also favoured increased centralisation and an explicitly regal currency. The largely anonymous sceattas were superseded by broader pennies of Carolingian inspiration and of restored weight and fineness, struck in the name of Offa, king of Mercia (757–96), who had made himself master of all England south of the Humber. Fewer broad pennies were issued than sceattas in their heyday, and the total amount of silver in circulation was smaller, even after the greater intrinsic value of the new coins is taken into account. This decline, continuing a trend which had begun well before the reform, is probably to be explained by an unfavourable balance of trade and the absence of significant sources of raw silver to make up the deficit. A lack of bullion was even more evident in the local money of northern England, which consisted of coins with an ever decreasing silver content but which nonetheless met the needs of a lively internal economy. When fine-metal money was required, southern English and Carolingian coins were used, but the conquest of the Northumbrian kingdom by the Scandinavian invaders in 867 extinguished minting there for a generation.

The Viking menace was a factor of growing importance in ninth-century 97 Europe. It caused, at the same time, both the expansion and the weakening of west European money supply. Many new Carolingian mints were opened to meet the need for coin to pay the massive tributes demanded by the raiders. In southern England, once more politically divided, the volume of coin produced also rose steeply. More fundamentally, Viking activity disrupted agricultural and urban life and also the internal and external trade on which earlier prosperity had been based. Although severely strained, the Carolingian system, with its access to greater reserves and new bullion, coped better than the English one, which came near to collapse with pennies containing only 25 per cent silver or less.

During the same century the Vikings were developing their own trade routes across Russia to Constantinople and the Islamic caliphate further to the east. This commerce was heavily dependent upon the sale of slaves for silver in the form of Arabic *dirhams*, which were brought back to the north in large 97a numbers. The establishment of settled Viking communities in the British Isles in the later ninth century saw the extension of their trading network westwards across the North and Irish Seas, and their rulers soon produced money for the same range of purposes as their longer-established neighbours and former enemies.

Although there had been fundamental internal changes to the monetary system in large areas of western Europe, the geographical extent of regular coin use had scarcely changed since the days of the later Roman Empire. There had been an early extension of minting into Frisia, some advance into Germany following the Carolingian conquests and occasional issues in Scandinavia. But a rapid expansion eastwards occurred in the early tenth century when power in

The Vikings

The traditional view of the Vikings' role in monetary history from the eighth to the eleventh centuries is of plunderers and extortionists satisfying their thirst for silver by ruthlessly preying on the wealth of more financially advanced societies. Recent scholarship has been concerned to highlight their more positive activities in this area, particularly their contribution to the development of towns and trade. It is difficult to strike a just balance between these aspects: both represent part of the truth and are interrelated. In western Europe the raising of gelds (taxes) to pay off the Vikings stimulated the development of a money economy among their victims, and the exacting of tribute did not preclude commercial relations. The Vikings were responsible for developing trade routes through the eastern Baltic with Kiev, Russia and Central Asia, but a major source of their profit was the sale of slaves seized in raids.

Once established in settled communities in their conquered lands, the Vikings adopted existing monetary systems, or created them from scratch, as at Dublin, often using native or imported experts to operate them. The initial impetus may have been prestige or the need to make official gifts, but coinages for normal fiscal and commercial purposes usually followed. In their homelands the Vikings were mainly content to use foreign money and were slow to introduce exclusive national coinages because it took time to develop the institutions needed to run them successfully. But settled economies did not tame the Vikings' military energy or end the urge for expansion, and their heirs continued to fight for land and fortune under their more respectable name of Normans.

97a Silver dirham of Caliph Al-Mu'tamid (AH 256–79/AD 870–92), struck at Arminiyah, AH 277 (AD 890–91), from the Cuerdale (Lancashire) hoard buried c. 905 (see frontispiece). The Islamic coins found in England had travelled from the caliphate by way of Viking trade routes along the Russian river systems and through Scandinavia. (× 1½)

97c Silver penny of Anlaf Guthfrithsson (939–41), struck at York, showing the pagan motif of a raven. The Vikings, who intermittently controlled York during the tenth century, participated fully in the trading activities of the city and their coins were often struck by moneyers who had worked for their Anglo-Saxon predecessors. (× 3)

97b Srebrennik (silver coin) of Jaroslav the Wise, Prince of Kiev (1015–54). People of Scandinavian descent had settled at Kiev on the Dnieper, a focal point of Viking trade with Constantinople and the east, in the ninth century. Denominations and designs were Byzantine in inspiration (Stockholm, Kungl. Myntkabinettet, Statens Museum för Mynt Medali och Penninghistoria). (× 1½)

97d Silver penny of Sihtric III Silkbeard, Norse king of Dublin (993/4–1042), struck by the moneyer Fastolf c. 997. This issue, based on Aethelred II's crux-type penny, marked the start of minting in Ireland. Viking Dublin was an important centre for trade. (× 1½)

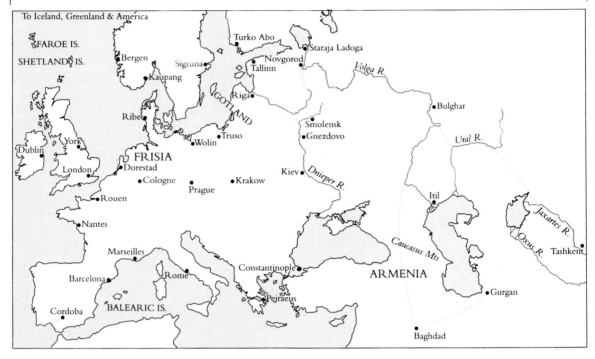

97e Main Viking trade routes.

97f Silver penny of Olaf Skötkonung of Sweden (c. 994–1022), struck at Sigtuna, c. 995. The earliest coins naming the kings of Sweden, Denmark and Norway were made about the same time. They all copy the crux-type penny of Aethelred II of England, used to pay large amounts of money to the Scandinavian invaders. (× 1½)

97g Silver penny of Cnut, Danish king of England (1016–35), struck at London. In 1018 Cnut exacted a geld to pay off his invasion fleet. In this way large numbers of English coins reached Scandinavia, where, like this example, they were often 'pecked', i.e. tested with a knife-point. (× 1½)

97h Silver pfennig of Otto III (as king in Germany, 983–96, with his grandmother Adelheid acting as regent), struck at Goslar after 991 in metal from the Rammelsberg mines. This coin is pecked and had circulated in Scandinavia. Many German coins travelled northwards in trade, but tribute and plunder were also involved. (× 1½)

97i This stone at Yttergärde in Uppland, Sweden, was dedicated in the 1020s to the memory of Ulv of Borresta. The runic inscription says that Ulv 'has in England taken three gelds. The first which Tosti paid. Then Thorkell paid. Then Cnut paid.'

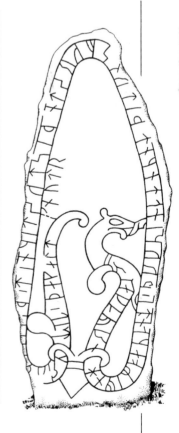

Germany passed to the Saxon dynasty with its centre in Bavaria. This political change was complemented by the discovery, around the middle of the century, of rich silver mines in the Harz mountains near Goslar in Saxony. The spread of money use and minting continued as peoples on the eastern and northern fringes of the German empire in Bohemia, Hungary, Poland and Scandinavia 98 developed settled states which first used foreign coin and then saw the advantages of converting this into money of their own. The adoption of Christianity

98 Silver penny of Boleslav II, Duke of Bohemia (967–99), struck at Prague. The obverse design, showing the Hand of God, was copied from a coin of Aethelred II of England of the early 980s. Anglo-Saxon coins reached Bohemia in trade, but the source for this type may also reflect political and religious affiliations, as Boleslav's wife, Emma, may have been English. (× 5)

in these lands also helped to promote the use and production of money. By the year 1000, coins were being struck from Dublin to Kiev, although Scotland did 97 not have its own coined money until more than a century later. Many of these early issues were small and intermittent, often produced for distribution rather than circulation; normal monetary needs were met by foreign coin which arrived in tribute or trade. National coinages developed more fully in eastern Europe from the eleventh century but often on a relatively limited scale compared with those of the more mature, and mine-owning, states in the West.

From the tenth to the early twelfth centuries the decentralising trend in France and Germany was intensified. First the French king and then the German emperor granted coining rights to ecclesiastical and lay magnates whose wealth and power had increased at the expense of central control. The strongest

99 Base-silver denier of Thibaut II, Count of Champagne (1125–52), struck at Provins. This coinage owed its success to the income generated by Champagne's international fairs. (× 1½)

100 Silver pfennig of Sigwin, Archbishop of Cologne (1079–89). The coins of Cologne were first regal, then struck in the joint names of the German emperor and the archbishop, and later, as here, in that of the archbishop alone, illustrating the extension of coinage rights. (× 1½)

101 Silver penny of William I 'the Conqueror' (1066–87), struck at Gloucester by the moneyer Ordric. The reverse illustrates the control measures, inherited from the Anglo-Saxons, used to maintain the high quality of the coinage. The inscription named the moneyer and the mint so that the issuer of coins deficient in weight or fineness could be traced and punished. (× 1½)

of these feudal coinages, such as those of the Abbey of Tours, the Counts of Anjou and Champagne, or the Archbishops of Cologne, dominated the money in regions far beyond the borders of their own territories. The need to maintain confidence and acceptability caused many coinages to become 'immobilised', that is, to continue to use the same basic designs and inscriptions for many years.

In the earlier part of this period the use of money, the volume of currency and the velocity of circulation all increased. Although revived Viking activity played a part, this expansion was principally based on renewable silver stocks and the growth in local and international trade exemplified by important fairs such as those in Champagne. By the mid-eleventh century, however, the Goslar mines in Saxony had been worked out and the resulting shortage of new silver brought a reduction in minting and money supply throughout Europe. There was also a related tendency for issues to decline in both weight and fineness. Although the volume of production had also decreased in England, the standard of the coinage was maintained, partly as a result of a favourable trade balance probably already involving the export of wool. Also contrary to the trend elsewhere in Europe, a steady reduction in the number of mints in England began in the later eleventh century. Neither did feudal currencies develop as they did in France, and the English royal monopoly established by the West Saxon dynasty survived both the Danish and Norman conquests. A few ecclesiastical authorities and lay magnates retained minting rights, but their coins conformed in all respects to regal issues. Only during the civil war in the 1140s were baronial coinages struck in England, but they did not survive the restoration of peace.

The sole currency coin throughout most of northern Europe during this period remained the silver penny. As market transactions became more common there was a growing demand for smaller denominations. Round halfpennies were struck from the mid-ninth century, but only intermittently, and needs were otherwise met by cutting the penny into halves and quarters – and even smaller parts in eastern Europe. Gold coins were struck almost exclusively for ceremonial use, although Byzantine and Arabic gold coins did occasionally reach north-west Europe to provide the bullion for these local issues.

In north and central Italy money developed largely along north European lines with the silver penny as the standard currency unit. Coinage remained the monopoly of the Carolingian rulers

102 Gold dinar of Offa of Mercia (757–96), copying a gold dinar of the Abbasid caliph Al-Mansur struck at Baghdad in AH 157 (AD 773/4). Offa's coin may have been struck to fulfil the promise he made in 786 to send an annual gift to the pope, but its condition shows that it was used in commerce. (× 2)

and then of their German imperial successors. Minting rights were not granted to other authorities until later in the twelfth century, beginning with the city of Genoa in 1138. The Papacy issued silver pennies in the joint names of current pope and Carolingian emperor from the eighth to the later tenth century, but never on a large scale. In south Italy and Sicily the currency remained outside the general European system. It reflected the region's position as a point of contact between the Islamic and Byzantine empires in including both gold and copper coins whose types were often derived from Arab or Byzantine models. The Normans who carved out principalities for themselves there in the eleventh century continued to issue gold and copper coins in the local tradition, but also incorporated a base-silver coinage into their system.

During the tenth and eleventh centuries the Arabs' power in Spain had declined as they first parted from the central caliphate and then broke up into many petty states, some of which issued coinage, generally on a very limited scale. In the late eleventh century they joined the empire of the Almoravid rulers of North Africa, which revived the issue of gold and silver coins. Northern Spain had been lost to Christian states, from which emerged the kingdoms of Leon, Aragon and Navarre, alongside the former Carolingian territory of Barcelona, now independent under a powerful dynasty of counts. These states produced silver pennies on the French model, but some also struck gold coins based on the issues of their Arab neighbours which they had obtained through normal trade and in tribute payments.

By the middle of the twelfth century the period of monetary recession in western Europe was about to be replaced by one of great expansion as a result of an infusion of new silver from the massive deposits discovered at Freiberg in Meissen. But before continuing with this story, we should take a brief look at the long and important history of the Roman Empire in the east, centred on the city of Constantinople, which has come to be known to historians as the Byzantine Empire.

Byzantium

[It] is accepted everywhere from the ends of the earth. It is admired by all men and in all kingdoms, because no kingdom has a currency that can be compared to it.

COSMAS INDICOPLEUSTES (6th century AD)

For centuries the Byzantine Empire lay between the worlds of medieval Europe and Islam, a crucial zone of influence and exchange as well as a great civilisation in its own right. Its coinage provided the model for the first independent currencies of its neighbours and successors, while for over half a millennium the gold solidus or *nomisma*, the bedrock of its monetary system, ruled supreme as the principal trade coin of the Mediterranean world, the 'dollar of the Middle Ages' as it has been called. It was also familiar as the *bezant* over a much wider area across Europe and Asia. When Western kings wished to make religious offerings in gold coin, they used bezants.

When 'Byzantium' begins is a matter of continuing debate. For the coinage a range of developments in the sixth century provides a useful marker. In about 498 the emperor Anastasius introduced a series of large copper coins to replace the tiny late Roman bronzes. Christian emblems such as angels and crosses replaced the pagan figure of Victory on the backs of the gold coins; a full-facing bust of the emperor became the normal imperial image on the front, while ornate robes replaced military costume as the usual imperial attire. In a long transition during the seventh century Greek took the place of Latin in coin legends, the most obvious consequence of which was the replacement of 'Augustus' by 'Basileus' as the imperial title.

A by-word for stability, the Byzantine gold coinage remained, from its origin as the solidus of Constantine the Great, unchanged in standards for centuries and seemingly always in plentiful supply. Its position was shaken by heavy debasement in the mid-eleventh century, but a revival of standards in 1092 under Alexius I Comnenus restored its reputation until the thirteenth century.

This coinage, like that of Rome before it, probably owed its form to the needs of the state rather than the interests of commerce. The constant availability of a stable gold coinage enabled the state to function, accumulating cash through taxation to pay for its standing army, civil servants, buildings, ceremonials and foreign subsidies – the armies alone may have regularly absorbed over half the state's income. The Byzantine state taxed and spent on an enormous scale in comparison to contemporary western Europe. A land tax was the basis of the system, and to pay it landowners sold their surplus produce – often to the state itself to supply the army, the administration and the imperial post.

Taxation in gold coin, rather than in kind, simplified collection and distribution, and also facilitated the building up of reserves of treasure. Treasure was important because the Byzantine state was not able to have much recourse to credit and loans – in a crisis the emperor had to look to his regalia, the Church or great magnates to tide him over.

While the gold coinage existed to fulfil the purposes of the state, it inevitably played a role beyond that in daily life. Furthermore, supporting it were lesser denominations, mostly in copper, which permitted smaller-scale monetary transactions to occur. In any case, provision of such a coinage helped maximise the state's holdings of treasure: taxes had to be paid in gold, but the state could make payments (including change out of gold offered for tax) in copper.

Initially there was a range of smaller gold and copper coins, though from the mid-eighth century the only lesser coin normally available was the copper *follis*.

103 Gold nomisma (solidus) of the Byzantine emperor Constantine VII and his son Romanus II (co-rulers 945–59), mint of Constantinople, showing the image of Christ. From the mid-ninth century religious images increasingly dominated the coinage. The figure of Christ became the normal obverse design, relegating the emperor to the reverse. (× 1½)

Intermediate silver coinages were only periodically provided, though the *milaresion* (1/12 nomisma) was in reasonable supply in the ninth and tenth centuries. In general the empire remained predominantly agricultural and rural, and, outside Constantinople and a few other centres, trade would have been confined to agricultural produce or low-level dealings and was probably highly seasonal. Merchants were of low status and subject to state regulation. The relative lack of low-level coinage between the seventh and twelfth centuries suggests a restricted urban economy.

PRINCIPAL DENOMINATIONS OF THE BYZANTINE EMPIRE

FIFTH TO EIGHTH CENTURIES

Gold	Silver	Copper	
solidus/nomisma	hexagram	follis (40 nummi)	
semissis (½ nomisma)		half-follis (20 nummi)	
tremissis (⅓ nomisma)		decanummium (10 nummi)	
		pentanummium (5 nummi)	

EIGHTH TO TWELFTH CENTURIES

Gold	Silver	Copper	
nomisma	milaresion	follis (1/288 nomisma)	
	(1/12 nomisma)		

TWELFTH TO THIRTEENTH CENTURIES

Gold	Electrum	Base silver	Copper
hyperperon	aspron trachy	trachy (1/48 hyperperon,	tetarteron
	(⅓ hyperperon)	later 1/20)	(uncertain value)
			half tetarteron
			(uncertain value)

104 Gold hyperperon of Emperor Alexius 1 Comnenus (1081–1118), struck after the reform of 1092. In the eleventh century the old nomisma denomination became broader and distinctly concave in shape. In the mid-century the coinage suffered serious debasement, until 1092 when Alexius 1 introduced a new gold coin, the hyperperon. This had the concave form of the debased nomisma, but its fineness was restored to a high level (20½ carats). (× 3)

In 1092 Alexius 1's reform supported the newly restored gold coinage (the *hyperperon*) with a wider range of pieces in electrum, base silver and copper, somewhat broadening the character of available money. In the last years of the diminished empire, from the recapture of Constantinople in 1261 to the final Ottoman capture of Constantinople in 1453, the once mighty bezant disappeared for good, replaced by a poor coinage in silver and copper.

The later Middle Ages in western Europe: c. 1150–1450

Men were subtle enough to devise the use of money to be the instrument of natural riches which of themselves administer to human need. . . . For money does not directly relieve the necessities of life, but is an instrument artificially invented for the easier exchange of natural riches. And it is clear without further proof that coin is very useful to the civil community, and convenient, or rather necessary, to the business of the state.

NICHOLAS ORESME (c. 1320–82), *A Treatise on the Origin, Nature, Law and Alterations of Money*

105 Avarice, from a medieval manuscript illumination. Images of money, particularly its hoarding and testing, have featured in Christian art with largely negative connotations. Above all, the miser is the classic symbol of avarice, one of the Seven Deadly Sins, as depicted in this manuscript: demons hover around him, both inspiring and reflecting the spiritually destructive allure of gold (British Library).

By the twelfth century the issue of coined money was an established factor throughout most of Europe, and minting was becoming more centralised. Lands coming late to coinage, such as the Scandinavian and eastern European kingdoms, retained a relatively centralised approach to the provision of money along with virtual royal monopolies; the same held good for the Christian kingdoms of Spain as they expanded at the expense of the Arabs. In England, where royal control of coinage had always been retained, the number of issuing mints was gradually reduced to a handful, dominated by London. In France the previously insignificant regal coinage expanded its role greatly in national currency at the expense of the coins of the feudal lords, which were restricted to the lands of their issuers. In the lands of the Holy Roman Empire (Italy, Germany and the Netherlands) the number of coin issuers continued to expand, but many of the most significant and influential were already established.

This interest in the control of minting in the twelfth century reflected the increased role that money was playing in European society. At a time of rising population, town and city growth and expanding commerce, both local and international, coinage had to be adapted to fulfil increasing monetary needs. New silver supplies both augmented the overall money supply and enabled a relatively high-value, fine silver coinage to be restored to areas such as north Italy and the Netherlands, where economic activity was making its greatest advances.

77

106 Silver denier tournois of Philip II Augustus, King of France (1180–1223), showing a stylised castle. The abbey of St Martin of Tours was an important coin issuer in western France. Philip Augustus took over the issue of its popular coin from 1204 and it joined the denier parisis as official royal coin. It also became the basis of the national money of account. (× 1½)

107 Silver grosso of Venice, issued by the Doge Giacomo Tiepolo (1229–49), who is represented receiving a banner from St Mark, patron of Venice. In the late twelfth century northern Italy was well placed to attract new silver supplies, and was also commercially advanced and urbanised. However, its coinage consisted solely of tiny base-silver denari. The pioneering Venetian grosso, probably introduced in 1202, was a fine silver coin, bigger than any seen in Europe since antiquity, and worth 24 of the local denari. (× 1½)

The spread of the new silver coin varied in the context of local coinage, but there was a strong tendency at first to make it worth twelve of the local pennies (or a suitable fraction or multiple thereof), thus fitting it into the widespread system of account of 12 denarii (pennies) to the solidus (*soldo, sou*, shilling), and 20 solidi to the *librum* (*livre* or pound). This system formed a money of account and played a vital part in late medieval money beyond its convenience in reckoning, acting as a common denominator for the changing values of coins as the monetary systems of Europe became more varied and complicated.

In the thirteenth and early fourteenth centuries larger silver coins, multiples of the old penny denomination, spread into most European coinage systems, usually under a name derived from the Italian term *grosso denaro*, or *grosso* ('big penny'), which in English became the groat. The pioneering Venetian grosso 107 was introduced in around 1202 and equalled 24 local denarii, though both it and the Florentine grosso of 12 denarii in fact weighed little more than a contemporary English penny. The French *gros tournois* (introduced in 1266) was worth 111 12 *deniers tournois* (one sou) but weighed twice as much as the grosso, while the 106 English groat, of similar size to the gros tournois, was worth four pence and only found its niche in English currency from 1351.

The silver that had allowed this new pattern of coinage to develop came from 108 a series of new mines discovered during the twelfth and thirteenth centuries. The first was at Freiberg in Saxony in the 1160s, to be followed by others in 109 Italy, Bohemia and the Alps. The last new mine, at Kutna Hora in Bohemia, discovered in 1294, would produce 20-25 tons (20,300–25,400 kg) of silver annually in the early fourteenth century.

The impact of new silver on Europe's money supplies was enormous. For instance, it has been estimated that the amount of coined money in circulation in England in 1300 was not equalled again until about 1600. Nevertheless, despite the new silver coins, high-value dealings were still often facilitated by the use of silver ingots. These may sometimes have been stamped to indicate their adherence to silver of the coinage standard of, say, the Venetian grosso or English sterling penny. Gold dust in sealed bags, weighed by the ounce, may also have been thus employed in the lands bordering the Mediterranean. Much of the dealing of money-changers would have involved exchanges between local coin and marks of silver or ounces of gold. Only gradually did the revival of gold coin displace this traffic.

108 Silver pfennig of Philipp I von Heinsberg, archbishop of Cologne (1167–91). Minting at Cologne expanded from the 1170s, from virtually nothing to over 2 million pfennigs a year, following the opening of the Freiberg silver mines. The Cologne pfennig came to be one of Germany's dominant coins, used widely in the Rhineland and beyond throughout the thirteenth century. (× 1½)

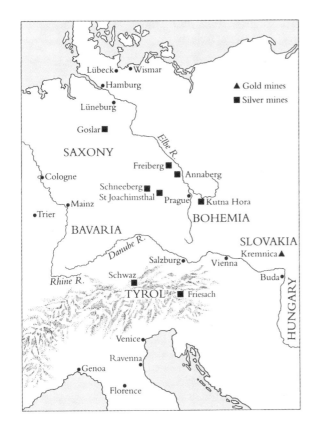

109 European mines in the tenth to sixteenth centuries.

The lowest level of transactions probably also occurred without much use of coinage. Barter and the offsetting of small-scale loans were presumably commonplace in local communities, and would long remain so. The provision of small change was, however, affected by the new types of coin. Increases in the money supply made the use of coin more familiar and regular. Complaints about the shortage of small denominations became common in the later Middle Ages, as demand conflicted with the reluctance of mints to give due attention to this part of the currency, which was more labour-intensive and less profitable to produce. These complaints may in part have been encouraged by increased expectations of the roles money was to fulfil. It is possible that people resorted to unofficial tokens in base metal to supplement the lack of low-value official coinage, though this has not been adequately demonstrated for the medieval period.

The old penny equivalents were, however, gradually debased in their silver content, and in many areas their value steadily declined against the fine silver money. As the proportion of copper to silver in their make-up increased, they earned the name 'black money'. This could have a knock-on effect on

110 Silver pfennig of the archbishops of Salzburg, Friesach mint, c.1216(?)–87, showing an angel under a canopy. Heavy production at Friesach began around 1195, reflecting the output of its silver mines. Until the 1230s Friesach and its neighbouring mints were immensely productive. In the thirteenth century Friesacher pfennigs dominated currency from the eastern Alps to the Carpathians. (× 1½)

111 Silver gros tournois of Louis IX, King of France (1226–70). This was the first large silver multiple north of the Alps, worth 12 deniers tournois. It was successful and became a familiar coin internationally, particularly in the Rhineland and the Netherlands. (× 1½)

112 Silver penny of Edward I, King of England (1272–1307). England's export trade ensured that the country had ready access to bullion, and its currency expanded to match the general growth in silver supplies from the late twelfth century. The type introduced by Edward I was to be long-lived and internationally popular. (× 1½)

113 Silver sterling of Jean d'Avesnes, Count of Hainaut (1280–1304), showing him wearing a garland of roses. English sterling pennies became plentiful in the Netherlands, and to defend or expand their mint profits local princes began to produce their own versions. In the 1290s perhaps 90 million continental sterlings were issued, in contrast to the 9 million English ones struck. (× 1½)

prices, as these coins were often the base coin of the money of account, but this process also encouraged the use of coin for ever smaller transactions. Where the base coin's value became too small to be functional it disappeared altogether and a multiple usually took its place in the system. Those lands, like England, which maintained fine silver for their smallest denominations (the halfpenny and farthing) saw these coins shrink to an impractical size while still retaining significant purchasing power.

The new silver multiples proved only a partial solution in the provision of high-value money. The next step was the revival of gold coinage and the creation of a multi-metallic system (gold, silver and often base silver) covering a range of denominations. A usable gold coinage of course required sufficient quantities of gold. Europe's own supplies were limited, with the most important sources being attached to the kingdom of Hungary, in particular Kremnica (modern Slovakia), which became productive in the 1330s. More importantly, in the thirteenth century, Italian trading cities, particularly Genoa, Florence and Pisa, increasingly captured the gold trade with North Africa, the gold coming ultimately from either the western Sudan or the west coast of Africa and being transferred across the Sahara to the Islamic lands of North Africa.

In 1251–2 both Genoa and Florence launched gold coins, the *genovino* and 114–15 the *florin*. The latter was to become enormously important in international trade for the next century, spreading the concept of gold coinage across Europe and inspiring a host of imitations. Florins of Aragon were important in the western Mediterranean, florins of Lübeck in the Hanseatic ports of the Baltic, and florin-based *gulden* provided a common currency for the varied principalities of the Rhineland. The florin's closest rival was to be the Venetian *ducat*, introduced in 1284, which gained the dominant role in eastern Mediterranean trade. As familiarity with gold coin spread, Western rulers in the fourteenth century adopted the new concept, though it often took much trial and error for them to produce coins that reflected the relative values of gold and silver sufficiently well to permit both to remain effectively in currency in a fixed relationship.

In the wake of Kutna Hora, the last great new bullion source of the central Middle Ages, the *praguergroschen* of Bohemia arose in the early

114 Gold augustale of the emperor Frederick II, as king of Sicily (1197–1250). Sicily had been part of the Islamic world, with a coinage of small gold tari which was continued by the Normans. In 1231 Frederick II added the augustale, a coin of 20½ carats gold, on the standard of the Byzantine hyperperon and of the African gold from which it was made. It became familiar in Italy, paving the way for the revival of gold coinages in the west. (× 3)

115 Gold florin of the city of Florence, 1252–1307, with a lily as its city badge. By 1252 enough African gold was passing through Florence for it to launch its own gold coinage. The florin was pure gold, initially valued at 1 lira in Florentine reckoning. Its international importance was immediate, both in the Near East and western Europe.

116 Gold ducat of Giovanni Dandolo, Doge of Venice (1279–89), showing him kneeling to receive a banner from St Mark. Venice had less immediate access to the North African gold trade, and also have continued its use of Byzantine coin. Only in 1284 did it produce its own, similar in standard to the florin and apparently primarily for international use. (× 2)

fourteenth century to act as eastern Europe's silver multiple. It was widely used in the region in combination with the gold ducats produced from the king of Hungary's mine at Kremnica. Bohemian and German silver flowed eastwards as well as westwards, with Venice dominating the export of bullion to the Islamic world, though Venetian coinage also spread widely in the Balkans and was copied there in the thirteenth century, as the new kingdoms of Serbia and Bulgaria began to produce coinage of their own. The Venetian ducat brought gold to the eastern Mediterranean, inspiring imitations in the Latin states there and competing with Islamic *dinars* in Egypt and Syria. In the north-east the production of coinage began to penetrate Russia in the late fourteenth century, in addition to the silver ingots known as *grivnas* or *rubles* which still acted as the principal form of precious-metal circulation there in the twelfth and thirteenth centuries.

The development of relatively stable international trading networks enabled systems to evolve which permitted the transfer of funds without the risk and inconvenience of moving huge amounts of coin. Money could be deposited, for instance, with the Order of the Temple or a Lombard merchant family, a credit note could be received and the equivalent sum in a specified form of currency (less charges) received at another place, where the same institution had an outlet. Large-scale trading systems could thus develop which minimised the transfer of physical sums of money. The fairs held in Champagne in northern France acted as a major international clearing house for the settlement of debts between Flanders and Italy. It must be stressed, however, that this network was relatively

117 Silver grivna of Russia, Novgorod type. Trading imbalances appear to have carried European silver in quantity to the Russian principalities via Novgorod, where it was recast into the ingots which functioned as the main means of exchange in Russia between the eleventh and fourteenth centuries. The local production and use of coin as money did not begin until the later fourteenth century.

118 Genoese bankers, from *De Septem Vitis*, a late fourteenth-century manuscript. Through the development of the bill of exchange the bankers of north Italy provided the international networks which permitted the transfer of funds across distances without requiring the movement of coin. Surviving Genoese registers record its origins in the late twelfth century and its full flowering in the thirteenth. Genoa was also a pioneer of advances in local banking, allowing transfers both between different accounts in the same bank and between different banks altogether. Genoese bankers also developed interest-bearing deposit accounts (British Library).

119 Gold florin of Humbert II, Dauphin of Vienne (1333–49). The minting of florin imitations began in Vienne in 1327, indicating the availability of Italian gold in the Rhone valley. This was encouraged by the arrival of the papal court in Avignon as the centre of a taxation system initiating bullion transfers across Christendom.

120 Silver praguergroschen of Wenceslas II, King of Bohemia (1278–1305). The praguergroschen became familiar across eastern Europe, and much Bohemian silver was exported east and south, instead of being coined. (× 2)

121 Gold ducat of Ladislaus V, King of Hungary (1453–7), showing St Ladislas with orb and battle-axe. By 1328 enough gold was coming from Kremnica for a gold coinage to be introduced. Production was high throughout the later Middle Ages, dominating supplies in Central Europe, where Hungarian ducats were long the preferred means of payment. (× 2)

restricted in extent, with no more than a dozen or so cities forming its core. Lübeck and the Hanseatic German trading cities of the north were not part of it until the fifteenth century.

The great merchant houses of Tuscany and Lombardy made important contributions to the nature of medieval money, though this involved circumventing the entrenched theological prohibitions of 'usury' – making money breed by charging interest on a loan – which was regarded as being against divine law. Nicholas Oresme (d. 1382) in his *Treatise on the Origin, Nature, Law and Alterations of Money* is severe and clear in outlining the ideological restrictions underpinning the official medieval view of money: 'There are three ways in which profit may be made from money, without laying it out for its natural purpose: one is the art of the moneychanger, banking or exchange; another is usury; a third is alteration of the coinage. The first way is contemptible, the second bad, and the third worse.' Yet the Italians were able to develop deposit-banking and the bill of exchange, enabling banking transactions to be carried out at a distance. They also began to extend credit and lend on a much larger scale than their Jewish predecessors who had dominated money-lending in the early medieval period. Exchange contracts used in long-distance trade, where an element of risk permitted charges, could be used to disguise loans, for instance. Thus a bill of exchange could represent a simple transfer of funds, or else an investment transaction.

Necessity overcame many scruples, and popes, kings and other rulers were able to borrow against future income, giving them more leeway in the ever more expensive fields of warfare and diplomacy. This period also saw the development of public debt among the states of Italy, a crucial innovation for the history of banking and public finance. Between 1303 and 1400 the public debt of the city of Florence rose from 50,000 gold florins to 3 million. By allowing credit and overdrafts beyond the totals of their deposits, Italian bankers were able qualitatively to increase the money supply, releasing it from the age-old restrictions imposed by the amount of coinage currently in circulation. However, most of the great Italian banking or financial houses eventually overextended themselves, usually in royal loans they could hardly refuse, and crashed when their royal debtors defaulted. The kings of England and France between them caused the failure of the Riccardi of Lucca in 1294; Edward III of England ruined the Florentine houses of the Peruzzi in 1343 and the Bardi in 1346. The Medici were the greatest bankers of the later Middle Ages, but

118

even they fell in 1494, when long-term trading imbalances tied up their funds away from Italy where they faced political pressures in Florence itself. Despite the refinements in banking and high finance, all imbalances ultimately still had to be settled in gold and silver.

Money was playing a much more important role in government and in society generally. Rulers increasingly paid their servants salaries rather than in grants of land. They ceased to rely on the old feudal levy to raise armies, which through tradition and precedent was too circumscribed and inflexible, and instead supplied and paid troops in cash. Larger-scale struggles, such as the Hundred Years' War between England and France (1337–1453), encouraged the subsidy of allies and payments of huge ransoms and dowries, while the Crusades and long-distance pilgrimages also necessitated the large-scale transmission of funds.

Feudal tenants increasingly commuted their labour services into cash rents, while their lords relied more on such cash payments or more directly and intensively exploited their estates to produce saleable surpluses. From the thirteenth century onwards networks of weekly markets made it possible for lesser monetary dealings to penetrate well outside the towns and cities. Prices in general rose occasionally, if nowhere near modern standards, but wages tended to keep pace, despite the interests of those benefiting from fixed rents and wedded to the concept of the just price and the just wage. The increased money supply was one

122 Silver gigliato of Charles II, King of Naples (1285–1309). Larger grossi, double the size of the first Italian grossi, came to dominate Italian silver coin in the later Middle Ages. The mines of Sardinia provided the silver for the Neapolitan gigliato, which became an important Mediterranean trade coin, rivalling, and in the 1330s supplanting, the Venetian grosso.

123 Gold pavillon of Philip VI, King of France (1328–50), showing the king beneath a canopy decorated with fleurs-de-lis. The introduction of gold coin to France was gradual. There were several issues, but only in the 1330s was there sufficient gold in the economy to ensure a satisfactory relationship between gold and silver. France's early gold issues had designs of high skill and set the style for other western rulers. (× 3)

124 Gold noble of Edward III, King of England (1327–77). The king is represented holding sword and shield and standing in a ship. By the 1340s foreign gold coins were familiar in England, and, with parliament's encouragement, the king introduced both local gold and silver multiple issues. The noble fitted into both of England's units of account, being half a mark and a third of a pound.

125 Gold saluto of Charles I, King of Sicily (1266–85), showing the Annunciation: the Archangel Gabriel approaches the Virgin Mary, a lily separating them. Religious imagery was common in medieval coin design. (× 2)

126 Gold gulden of Adolf II von Nassau, Archbishop of Mainz (1461–75), showing the arms of the Rhineland electors, the archbishops of Mainz, Cologne and Trier, and the Count Palatine. In 1385 these princes founded the Rhenish Monetary Union, co-ordinating their coinages and often their designs. This design represents the eighteenth Treaty of the Union, introduced in 1464 to last for twenty years.

reason for such rises, though other factors contributed. For instance, labour shortages following the population collapse of the Black Death (1346–7) helped raise wages.

Yet we should not overestimate the use of coined money at this time. It was much more familiar to most people than in the early Middle Ages, but nevertheless much of society still would not have employed coin on a daily basis. Most rural daily life would have been based on a large degree of self-sufficiency and small-scale barter, with coin acquired occasionally on the sale of surplus agricultural produce and disbursed equally occasionally to pay taxes, rents, dues, fines or rare payments for specialist goods or services. These certainly grew more frequent and substantial, as cash rents took over, but the use of money might easily be virtually seasonal, following harvest time. This was reflected in the usual dates fixed for the payments of dues and rents, All Saints' Day (1 November) and the feast of St John the Baptist (24 June). Richer folk would have had a greater store of wealth and more constant access to funds, but this was still subject to the sheer availability of coin.

Liquidity could therefore be a major problem. As the fourteenth century advanced with no new silver deposits being discovered and the older ones becoming increasingly less productive, bullion supplies diminished as the metal circulated through the continent and beyond. The flow of silver to the Near East as coin or bullion was one of Europe's major exports in exchange for the spices (which made winter food palatable) and the other Eastern goods Westerners craved, and the movement of precious metal brought great profit to middlemen like the Venetians as well as to the silver-producers themselves. Local shortages were always possible, if local mint prices were uncompetitive, or if local produce was in little demand. Bimetallism, the use of gold and silver coinage concurrently in an integrated currency system, could enhance such problems: some rulers tried to fix the gold/silver ratio at an unrealistic level, causing undervalued metal to be taken to a mint that offered a better price. But as the fifteenth century arrived, there were longer periods of severe money shortage, the so-called 'bullion famine', which curtailed trade and other economic activity, even for those rich in property and other goods. Thus, a system accustomed to, and often requiring, the availability of coin was faced with severe shortages of hard cash.

While mints of different rulers competed for available bullion, there were also pressures to link different currencies to facilitate ongoing commerce. In the fourteenth century the coinages of the Rhineland were linked by a series of 126

127 Silver witten of Lübeck, c.1366–80. Monetary conventions linked the towns of the Hanseatic League, beginning with Lübeck and Wismar, followed by Hamburg, Lüneburg and others. The first *Rezess* (convention) of the union was held in 1379, and successive such agreements regulated north German currency in the name of the Wendish Monetary Union until 1569. (× 2)

conventions between the region's princes, who agreed to strike their gold coinage, and sometimes part of their silver coinage, to a common standard. Similarly, from the mid-fourteenth century several of the cities of the Hanseatic League on the Baltic coast issued a silver coin (the *witten*) to common standards 127 in the Wendish Monetary Union. In fifteenth-century Italy many smaller coin issuers produced ducats to the Venetian standard. Political developments added to this trend. The House of Burgundy obtained control of most of the secular 128 principalities of the Netherlands (Holland, Flanders, Hainaut, Brabant and Luxemburg) and introduced a common coinage for the region; the various kingdoms of the Iberian peninsula (except Portugal) fell to a single ruling house, and Castilian coinage became the national coinage of Spain in the 1490s; and a network of royal mints across France reinforced the ubiquity of the national 130 currency, restored to stability after the tribulations of the Hundred Years' War.

By the mid-fifteenth century the tight monetary squeeze caused by the bullion famine was easing, a consequence of new discoveries of silver and developments in mining techniques. The impact of further new bullion supplies from the Americas was to transform money in Europe after the Middle Ages.

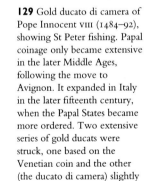

129 Gold ducato di camera of Pope Innocent VIII (1484–92), showing St Peter fishing. Papal coinage only became extensive in the later Middle Ages, following the move to Avignon. It expanded in Italy in the later fifteenth century, when the Papal States became more ordered. Two extensive series of gold ducats were struck, one based on the Venetian coin and the other (the ducato di camera) slightly lighter. (× 1½)

128 Gold lion of Philip the Good, Duke of Burgundy, as Count of Flanders (1419–67), named after its design of a lion beneath a canopy. The main principalities of the Netherlands fell into the hands of the dukes of Burgundy, and a unified coinage (covering Flanders, Brabant, Hainaut and Holland) was first issued in 1434; the lion became the main gold coin in 1454 under a revision of the system. (× 2)

130 Gold écu au soleil of Louis XI, King of France (1461–83). The name of the denomination was derived from its design: the crowned shield (*écu*) of France under the sun (*soleil*). The écu was the principal gold coin of France from 1385 well into the early modern period, subject to relatively minor alterations. Secret marks indicate which of the various French mints struck each coin (here an annulet under the *v* of *Ludovicus* indicates Toulouse). (× 2)

The Islamic Lands

There are two hungry wolves in our society, money and status.

IBN HANBAL, Book 3, p. 456

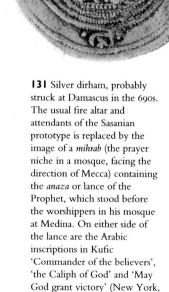

131 Silver dirham, probably struck at Damascus in the 690s. The usual fire altar and attendants of the Sasanian prototype is replaced by the image of a *mihrab* (the prayer niche in a mosque, facing the direction of Mecca) containing the *anaza* or lance of the Prophet, which stood before the worshippers in his mosque at Medina. On either side of the lance are the Arabic inscriptions in Kufic 'Commander of the believers', 'the Caliph of God' and 'May God grant victory' (New York, American Numismatic Society). (× 2)

The religion of Islam was revealed to the Prophet Muhammad in the early seventh century AD in Mecca, an ancient place of sanctuary and one of the principal trading cities of Arabia. The first year by which the Islamic or Hijra calendar is calculated, equivalent to AD 622, is the year of the flight (*Hijra*) of the Prophet Muhammad when, in conflict with the ruling elite of Mecca, he fled to Medina with his followers and founded the first Muslim community. It was at Medina that the first mosque was constructed, and from here began the conquests that would found the Muslim Empire.

At the beginning of the seventh century the lands that were to become part of the future Muslim Empire were under the domination of two main spheres of influence: the Byzantine emperors controlled the Mediterranean countries, while Sasanian emperors ruled Iran and Iraq. The border between them ran through what was known as the Jazira, 'the island', the lands lying between the rivers Tigris and Euphrates. Such was the speed of the Arab conquests that by the middle of the seventh century the Muslims had defeated the Byzantines in Syria and Egypt, overthrown the Sasanians, and then in the next fifty years proceeded to conquer a vast and disparate area that stretched from Spain to India.

Religion and the power of money

Islam was both a religious and a political system. Over the succeeding centuries, while empires were built up and fell apart, and different Islamic sects and schools of thought were established, the essence of the Islamic message – the belief in one God and his messenger Muhammad as the 'seal of the Prophets' – provided a thread of unity across time and space. At the outset, the Islamic caliphate had to reconcile the competing demands of God and of more temporal concerns, a tension that is reflected both in Islamic attitudes towards money and in the coins themselves. For the system of ethics established under Islam had to be reconciled with the needs of an earthly community and the monetary requirements of the state, such as the efficient collection of taxes, the successful organisation of commercial life, and so on.

From earliest Islamic times it was clear that a certain unease existed over the power of money. There are repeated warnings in the Qur'an about its transient nature: 'Woe to every kind of scandal monger and backbiter who piles up wealth and lays it by thinking that his wealth can make him last forever' (Sura

132 Gold dinar struck in Syria in 695–6, showing the Umayyad caliph Abd al-Malik dressed in traditional Arab robes and holding a sword. Around the margin is the *shahada*: 'There is no God but God; Muhammad is his prophet'. On the reverse, on either side of the modified Byzantine cross design, is the Arabic legend 'In the name of God struck in the year 76'. This coin type, also found on bronze coins, was struck shortly before Abd al-Malik's coinage reform. It reflects the arabisation of the Byzantine prototype. (× 3)

133 Gold dinar minted by the Arabs in North Africa in AH 97 (AD 715–16). Byzantine coins of Carthage were imitated in North Africa from the early 690s. The Arab imitations had legends that included Latin translations of the *shahada*. This example contains on the obverse the first half of the *shahada* in Arabic: 'There is no God but God', with place of striking and date in Latin, and on the reverse the second half of the *shahada*: 'Muhammad is his prophet', with the Latin testifying to the oneness of God. (× 1½)

104, v. 1–3). Added to this was an anxiety about the insidious tendency of money to distract the believer from the 'true path': 'Wealth and sons are allurements of the life of this world, but of the things that endure, good deeds are best in the sight of the Lord' (Sura 18, v. 46). The Prophet himself is supposed to have said 'Money puts my community to the test' (Ibn Hanbal, Book 4, p. 160).

As a consequence of this deep-seated unease about the power of money, the religion itself attempted to regulate its influence and prescribe certain conditions according to which the Muslim could possess money and remain ethically just. One of the principal conditions was to give *zakat*, the alms tax, calculated as a certain proportion of a person's wealth. This was laid down as one of the five main obligations of Islam. Furthermore, usury (*riba*) was explicitly banned in the Qur'an: 'Those who devour *riba* shall only rise again as one whom Satan strikes with his touch. . . . God has permitted selling and forbidden *riba*' (Qur'an, Sura 2, v. 275).

Despite these regulations, the Muslims developed a number of financial instruments, and the prohibition on interest proved an obstacle neither to trade nor to banking. Concern about the ethics of financial transactions led to the development of the post of the *muhtasib* in the major Islamic cities. The *muhtasib* was a functionary of the state and, at least in theory, was appointed by virtue of his high moral integrity and knowledge of Islamic law (*sharia*). His role was to make sure that in all areas of commerce the *sharia* was upheld. Thus he would check weights and measures, and even test for counterfeit coins. He made sure that merchants did not charge interest and dealt severely with hoarding. This was a practice that was frowned upon, although it evidently took place for a variety of reasons. A story from Aden in the thirteenth century is an apt demonstration of the kind of unease that an observing Muslim might feel about the moral provenance of the coins that came his way. In this story a jurist refuses to do business with someone, believing that the man's money is morally tainted because of lax observance of the *sharia*. Indeed he makes a point of separating his own coins from those of the other man's, fearing moral contamination.

Islamic coins, containing both religious and secular messages in their inscriptions, are reflections of these two components of Islamic society and monetary culture. How did the distinctive Islamic coinage tradition come about?

Coins and early Islam

The conquering Arabs inherited two principal monetary systems. In the west there was the gold-based currency of the Byzantine Empire, the principal coin 134a–b being the solidus. In Sasanian Iran, however, silver was the dominant metal, 134f–i with the *drachm* (a term based on the Greek drachma) the main currency. Solidi, Sasanian drachms and coins from Ethiopia are known to have been available to

The origins of Islamic coinage

The earliest Islamic coins were copies of the gold and bronze coins of the Byzantine Empire and the silver coins of the Sasanian Empire circulating in the lands conquered by the Arabs in the decades after the Prophet Muhammad's death. The Arab gold dinar and bronze fals were named after Byzantine coins, respectively the denarius aureus (solidus) and the follis, and the silver dirham from the Sasanian drachm. Reflecting their origins, these early coins are described as Arab-Byzantine or Arab-Sasanian. The coins illustrated show the modifications that took place, such as the removal of Christian imagery and the addition of Arabic inscriptions.

134a Gold solidus of the Byzantine emperor Heraclius (610–41), showing the emperor and his two sons on the obverse and the cross on three steps on the reverse. This is one of the Byzantine coin types imitated by the Muslims. (× 2)

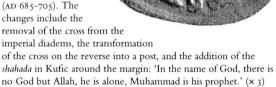

134b Gold dinar imitating the solidus of Heraclius, probably struck at Damascus in about 691-2, during the reign of the Umayyad caliph Abd al-Malik (AD 685-705). The changes include the removal of the cross from the imperial diadems, the transformation of the cross on the reverse into a post, and the addition of the shahada in Kufic around the margin: 'In the name of God, there is no God but Allah, he is alone, Muhammad is his prophet.' (× 3)

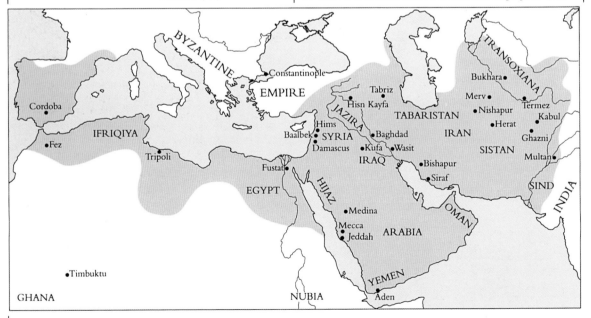

134c The Umayyad Empire.

134d Bronze follis of the Byzantine emperor Constans II (641–68), showing the emperor holding a cross and globe on the obverse and on the reverse the Greek numeral M indicating the denomination 40 nummi – features imitated in the Arab-Byzantine coinage.

134h Silver dirham of Khursid, the local ruler of Tabaristan (northern Iran), dating from AH 123 (AD 740). The province of Tabaristan retained its independence under the Dabuyid Ispahbad dynasty, long after the rest of the Sasanian Empire succumbed to the Muslims. The Ispahbads struck coins in the Sasanian style, but half the size. After the Muslim conquest of Tabaristan in AD 761, this local coinage was continued by the governors who represented the Abbasid caliphate in this area until the end of the eighth century.

134e Bronze fals imitating the follis of Constans II, struck at Hims (Syria). Mints for bronze coins in Byzantine Syria had been closed in the early seventh century, but were reopened by the Arabs to strike a wide variety of copper fulus (plural of fals). The dating probably ranges from the 680s to the reform of 696. The Arab-Byzantine imitations include ones closely following the prototype as shown here, as well as a host of irregular issues and countermarked coins.

134f Silver drachm of the Sasanian emperor Khusrau II (590–628), struck at Bishapur in Iran in 626, showing the ruler's portrait on the obverse and the Zoroastrian fire altar with attendants on the reverse. Khusrau II's coins were the main prototype for the Arab-Sasanian imitations.

134g Silver dirham struck at Bishapur in the name of al-Hajaj bin Yusuf, the powerful Umayyad governor of the eastern Islamic lands. Characteristic of coins struck before the reform, it shows the Sasanian bust of Khusrau II on the obverse with the addition of the governor's name and the *shahada* in Arabic Kufic script. On the reverse, the inscriptions around the fire altar and attendants are in Pahlavi (Middle Persian) and consist of the mint signature BYSH (Bishapur) and the year AH 76 (AD 695–6).

134i Base-silver dirham of the Abbasid governors of Bukhara in the province of Sogdiana (now in Uzbekistan) conquered by the Muslims in 674. Unlike the majority of Arab-Sasanian coins, this has the portrait of the emperor Bahram V (420–38) and not Khusrau II on the obverse. Bahram's coins had circulated in the province following his conquest of it from the Epthalite Huns. The inscriptions name the Abbasid caliph al-Mahdi (775–85) in Arabic Kufic and Bahram V in Bukharan script.

135 Gold dinar, probably minted at Damascus in 696–7. This coin without a pictorial design, dated AH 77, is the first issue struck by the caliph Abd al-Malik as part of his reform of the coinage. The inscriptions state the essence of the Islamic message: on the obverse, 'There is no God but God alone; he has no associate', 'Muhammad is the Prophet of God. He sent him with guidance and the religion of truth to make it prevail over every other religion'; on the reverse, 'God is one, God is eternal, he begets not nor is he begotten'; in the margin, 'in the name of God this dinar was struck in the year 77'. This new dinar was struck to a standard of 4.25 g, known as the *mithqal*.

136 Silver dirham struck at Damascus in AH 79 (AD 698–9). This is the first year for which there exist examples of reformed silver coins struck with Kufic legends, including the mint name.

the merchants of Mecca at the advent of Islam. In the west Byzantine coins were 134a–e first used and then imitated by the Muslims, but in a suitably Islamicised form, with specifically Christian symbols such as the cross removed, while in the east the Sasanian silver model was followed by the Muslims in the production of their *dirhams*. The portrait of a Sasanian ruler and the Zoroastrian fire-altar 134f–g design was maintained, but supplemented by the addition of the Islamic inscription *bismillah* ('In the name of God') in Arabic and of the Islamic governor's name, either in Pahlavi (Middle Persian) or bilingually.

The Sasanian style largely came to an end with the coinage reform of AH 77 (AD 696), although it was to reappear in provinces of the eastern Islamic 134h–i lands a generation or so later. The reform introduced a new and unequivocally Islamic coinage. The new gold *dinars*, followed two years later by silver dirhams, 135–6 ended the experiments with figurative iconography, and choice of design was restricted to inscriptions. The principal reasons for the coinage reform are thought to be twofold. First, during the reign of the caliph Abd al-Malik, the sources say that a polemic took place between the Muslim caliph and the Byzantine emperor Justinian II. The ninth-century historian Baladhuri tells that the caliph began to head the Arabic papyri from Egypt to Byzantium with phrases referring to the 'Oneness of God'. This angered Justinian, who said, 'you have introduced an inscription which displeases us. Either you abandon it or you will find on the [Byzantine] dinars references to your Prophet which will displease you.' In reaction to this threat, Abd al-Malik chose to change the coinage. Secondly, and perhaps more importantly, there was a growing feeling among Muslim clerics against the portrayal of images in official or religious contexts, and an increasingly prevalent view that the portrayal of the ruler on coins was inappropriate. Along with the new design came a new Arabic weight standard for gold. The Byzantine standard of 4.55 grams was now adjusted to 20 Arabic carats – 4.25 grams – the weight also known as the *mithqal*. For silver, there was a variety of local dirham standards, but these early silver issues average about 2.8–2.9 grams. Copper coins, too, were affected by the reform, and coins inscribed simply with the text known as the *shahada* (see below) were struck. The new rules were not strictly adhered to, however, for by the eighth century there appeared a whole range of symbols – palm

137 Bronze fals struck at Baalbek in Lebanon. This post-reform issue is inscribed with the *shahada* and the mint. It bears no date but is part of a group now thought to have been issued by the Umayyad caliphate in the decade following the reform of 696–7.

138 Bronze fals struck at Hims in the late seventh to early eighth century, showing on the obverse an elephant and the beginning of the *shahada*, which is completed on the reverse. A few Umayyad fulus, like this example, retained pictorial designs after the reform.

139 Gold dinar of the Abbasid caliph al-Ma'mun (813–33), struck at Madinat al-Salam (Baghdad) in AH 212 (AD 827–8). Al-Ma'mun imposed uniformity on the diverse gold and silver coinage of the early Abbasid period. (× 2)

140 Silver dirham of the Umayyads of Spain, struck at the al-Andalus (Cordoba) mint in AH 154 (AD 770–71), during the reign of Abd al-Rahman I (756–88). The Spanish Umayyads established themselves as an independent dynasty in 750 and ruled for three centuries.

trees, candlesticks, even animals such as elephants and gerboa – associated with 138 particular mints.

Abd al-Malik's reforms were carried out by his powerful governor al-Hajjaj bin Yusuf, who was in charge of Iraq and Iran and who is credited with establishing the first Arab mint in Wasit in AD 702–3. Baladhuri recounts how 'al-Hajjaj inquired into the matter of coining dirhams of the Persians and then erected a mint and assembled men to do the stamping. He marked by tattooing or branding the hands of the coiners.' Indeed, it is clear from a number of sources that those working in the mint and also moneychangers were at various times closely supervised to ensure that no forging took place. When it did, the culprits could be punished by cutting off their hands.

Although many changes were to take place in succeeding centuries, the main elements that characterise Islamic coinage were now in place. The side generally called the obverse had a text stating the unity and uniqueness of God. The reverse initially bore a text controverting the Christian doctrine of the Trinity. This was replaced in AD 750 by a statement of Muhammad's role as the messenger of God. These phrases are known as the *shahada* or *kalima*. The mint and date were inscribed on most coins. The next major reform took place under the Abbasid caliph al-Ma'mun (AD 813–33) who imposed a uniformity on the 139 coinage that was to be maintained for several hundred years. Within the lands of the Abbasid caliphate, secular rulers kept the same coin type until the eleventh century, and in Iran and Iraq until the mid-thirteenth century, thereby displaying their continuing allegiance to the Abbasid caliphs as the religious heads of Islam. For, despite his limited territorial powers, as various provinces increasingly fell under the rule of independent dynasts, the caliph's importance, as 'God's lieutenant on earth', continued for several hundred years to provide legitimacy to rulers across the Muslim world, who generally went through the formality of obtaining sanction for their rule from him and placing his name on the coins alongside their own.

Although their primary function was monetary, it is clear that coins in the Islamic world were also important political and religious documents, containing in their inscriptions several complex messages. The striking of coins (*sikka*), along with the citing of a ruler's name in the Friday prayers (*khutba*), was one of the two primary public symbols of Islamic sovereignty. Rulers would often mark their seizure of power by striking coins in their own names, as would rulers who conquered a new piece of territory. Inscriptions could also be used to indicate the ruler's religious orientation. While Sunni dynasties continued to use the same religious messages as adopted after the reform, Shiite dynasties such as the Fatimids (AD 909–1171) made special reference with phrases such as *Ali wali Allah* ('Ali is the friend of God') to the Prophet's son-in-law Ali, whom they regard as the first of the Shiite *imams*. A ruler wishing to legitimise his

141 Copper coin of the Artuqid ruler Nur al-Din Muhammad (1167–85), struck in Hisn Kayfa (in eastern Turkey) in AH 578 (AD 1182–3) and showing a diademed head copied from a coin of Seleucus II (Greek king of Syria, 246–226 BC). The Artuqids were one of a number of Turkoman dynasties in the Jazira in the twelfth to thirteenth centuries to strike coins with a variety of images. Examples such as this one may represent an antiquarian interest in past civilisations. (× 1½)

142 Copper coin of the Artuqid ruler Husam al-Din Yuluk Arslan (1184–1201), struck in AH 596 (AD 1199–1200). It shows a helmeted figure seated cross-legged and holding a head thought to represent the planet Mars, one of a series of zodiacal images adopted in the Jazira in the last decades of the twelfth century. (× 1½)

position with a particular connection to the Prophet's family might, like Hussein Shah, the Arab ruler of Bengal (1494–1519), describe himself on his coins as *walad sayyid al-mursilin*, the descendant of the leader of the Prophets.

Islamic rulers referred to themselves in a variety of ways on the coins as in other contexts. Those who regarded themselves as leaders of the Muslim community, such as the Umayyads, Abbasids, Fatimids, Zaydis and others, styled themselves 'imam', 'caliph' and 'commander of the believers'. The secular rulers, who were, nominally, the agents of the caliph, used titles such as *malik* or *shah* (king) or *sultan* (sovereign). Such titles were often modified by adjectives such as 'the mighty' or 'the most glorious'. In addition to these titles of office, most rulers adopted individual personal honorifics that were not passed on, such as al-Mustansir or al-Zahir, and these usually became the names by which they were known in history. As in Europe, it became normal for a single ruler to have a panoply of titles, but only a few of these could fit on a coin.

While the use of figural imagery began to be discouraged in the late seventh century, the ban was to apply strictly only in religious contexts such as mosques or the illustration of Qur'ans, or on officially produced items such as seals and coins. However, there are a number of interesting exceptions on coins which illustrate the difficulties for Islamic rulers of adhering to the strict letter of their religious law. Many of the images represented were common to contemporary Islamic art and were designed for secular contexts such as metalwork and

ceramics. For instance, during the twelfth and thirteenth centuries in the region covered by present-day northern Syria, northern Iraq and eastern Anatolia, there appeared a fascinating and unique series of bronze coins struck by a number of dynasties of Turkoman origin, with designs coming from a complex and disparate range of sources. The earliest coins bear Byzantine Christian imagery such as an enthroned Christ and St George and the 141–3 Dragon. From the mid-twelfth century, coins with ancient Hellenistic and Sasanian portrait heads appeared concurrently with others showing various astrological symbols. The prototypes for these coins are in many cases followed so closely that they must have been readily available to the die-cutters, although only the Byzantine prototypes were actually in circulation. It may be that the appearance of these coins – at least those modelled on ancient prototypes – is evidence of a politically motivated antiquarian interest in the past civilisations of the region. The Saljuqs of Anatolia (1077–1307) under Kaykhusrau II (1237–46)

adopted on their silver coins the image of a lion and sun – an astrological symbol representing the sign Leo – and used ancient Persian names, features which have been ascribed to a revival of Persian interest at court at this time. Much later Iranian dynasties, the Qajars and the Pahlavis, were also to forge links with the glories of the ancient, pre-Islamic and specifically Persian past on their coins and in other very public ways, and the lion and sun motif went on to become 144, 146 the national symbol of pre-revolutionary Iran.

The Mughal emperor of India Jahangir (1605–27) also issued a remark- 145 able series of coins bearing signs of the zodiac and portraits, again images common in Islamic secular art. But as these were presentation coins and not for

143 Copper coin of the Artuqid ruler Fakhr al-Din Qara Arslan (1144–67). It shows the seated figure of Christ holding a book, a common image on late Byzantine coins during the tenth and eleventh centuries. Coins with Christian imagery were among the figural types struck in the Jazira, where previously the population had principally used Byzantine bronze coins. (× 1½)

144 Detail of a tile panel showing a lion and sun motif executed in tile mosaic on the portal in the Shir Dar madrasah built in Samarqand in 1619–36.

146 Silver 5-kran coin of Nasir al-Din Shah, Qajar ruler of Iran (1848–96), struck at the machine mint in Tehran in AH 1297 (AD 1879–80). The lion and sun is a popular zodiacal image which had been used by previous medieval Islamic dynasties such as the Saljuqs of Anatolia before it became the national symbol of Iran in the nineteenth and twentieth centuries. (× 1½)

145 Gold mohur, presentation coin of the Mughal emperor Jahangir (1605–27), struck at Ajmir, in northern India, in AH 1023 (AD 1614–15). It shows Jahangir seated cross-legged on his throne with a goblet in his right hand. The Persian inscription states: 'On the face of this golden coin, its ornament and beauty present the image of Nur al-Din Jahangir, son of Akbar Shah.' (× 4)

Calligraphy and ornament

The development of the Arabic script is principally associated with the need of the early Muslims to write down the Qur'an which was revealed orally to the Prophet Muhammad in the early seventh century. With its twenty-nine letters and written from right to left, it is based on the Nabatean script. The association with the Qur'an led to great efforts to beautify the script, and good calligraphers are still highly revered in the Islamic world. Kufic, with its elegant angular letter forms, was the main script used in the copying of Qur'ans and on coins until it went out of general use after the thirteenth century; from then on it was reserved for decorative purposes only. Cursive scripts had been in use since early Islamic times, principally on papyrus documents, but were not systematised until the reform introduced by the calligrapher Ibn Muqlah (886-940). *Naskhi* was one of the most commonly used of the cursive scripts and appears on coins from the twelfth century. Other forms of cursive script, such as *tughra'i* and *nasta'liq* were developed and echoed in the coin designs.

147c Silver dirham of the Mongol Ilkhanid ruler Abu Sa'id (1317-35), showing the *shahada* in Kufic in the form of a square, a style thought to be inspired by Chinese seal script. Around the margin are the names of the four Orthodox caliphs Abu Bakr, Omar, Uthman and Ali, inscribed in the cursive script *naskhi*.

147e Gold dinar of al-Kamil (1218-38), Ayyubid ruler of Syria and Egypt, inscribed in cursive *naskhi,* which was introduced on this gold coinage.

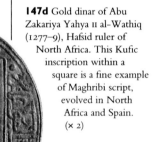

147d Gold dinar of Abu Zakariya Yahya II al-Wathiq (1277-9), Hafsid ruler of North Africa. This Kufic inscription within a square is a fine example of Maghribi script, evolved in North Africa and Spain. (× 2)

147a Gold dinar, dated AH 93 (AD 711–12), inscribed in early Kufic script with its characteristic elegant, angular letter forms. The development of Kufic is associated with the city of Kufa in Iraq.

147b Gold dinar of the Abbasid caliph al-Musta'sim (1242–58). Many different ways were found of ornamenting the Kufic script, such as the ends of the letters on this example, which are extended as foliage. (× 2)

147f Egyptian tombstone, dated AH 356 (AD 967), carved in relief in decorative Kufic script, 'In the name of God the merciful.'

147i Gold coin of Shams al-Din Ibrahim (1402–40), sultan of Jaunpur in India, inscribed in the cursive *tughra'i* script adopted in both Jaunpur and Bengal in the fifteenth century. (× 2)

147g Silver presentation coin of Shah Hussein I (1694–1722), Safavid ruler of Iran, inscribed in the cursive script *nasta'liq* evolved by Persian calligraphers in the sixteenth century.

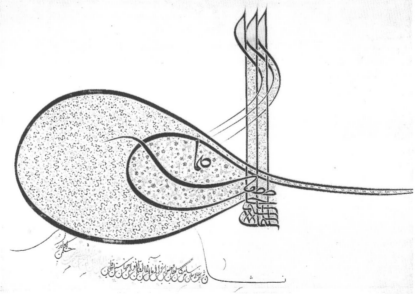

147h Gold sequin of Ahmed III (1703–30), Ottoman sultan of Turkey, showing his name and titles inscribed in the form of a *tughra*, first found on coins of the fifteenth century but not commonly adopted on Ottoman coins until the eighteenth century. (× 2)

147j Tughra of the Ottoman sultan Suleiman the Magnificent (1520–66), Istanbul, *c.* 1550. The gold and lapis loops are formed by the extension of the letters, the boldest one from the letter *nun* of the title *khan*. The tughra validated imperial decrees and, employed at first on written documents, its use extended to seals, coins, stamps and stone inscriptions. Various theories suggest that it represented the impression of Murad I's hand dipped in ink, or the fabulous *tughri* bird, the totem of the Ogus tribe, from which the Ottomans were descended.

circulation, the use of such images was acceptable. Moreover, this was a period of religious toleration. Jahangir's father, Akbar, had evolved his own religion, the *Din Ilahi*, proclaimed in 1582, which was an attempted synthesis of the many creeds of his empire. Jahangir's coins were apparently based upon a whim, which he recorded in his diary: 'Previous to this the rule of the coinage was that on the face of the metal they stamped my name, and on the reverse the name of the place and the year of the reign. At this time, it entered my mind that in the place of the month they should substitute the figure of the constellation which belonged to that month.' Jahangir and his father also struck presentation 145 coins with their portraits. One of Jahangir's shows him holding a cup of wine,

148 Silver dirham of Qilij Arslan IV (1257–67), Saljuq ruler of Anatolia, struck in Siwas (central Turkey) in AH 646 (AD 1248–9). Within the quatrefoil border is a horseman drawing his bow. The inscription around the margin gives the sultan's full name and his grand titles, 'The great sultan, pillar of the world and religion, Qilij Arslan, son of Kaykhusrau, partner of the commander of the faithful [i.e. the caliph in Baghdad].' (× 2)

which is quite unthinkable in a normal Islamic context. The Qajar ruler of Iran Fath Ali Shah (1797–1834) also struck portrait coins, full figure and seated on a throne, in the style of oil paintings of the Shah and the Persian aristocracy at this time.

Arabic is believed by Muslims to be the chosen language for the revelation sent by Allah to the Prophet Muhammad. Hence the Arabic script was greatly revered and its prac-titioners highly esteemed. A very important aspect of Islamic coins is the 147 changing style of the inscriptions, and as dated objects they provide us with an invaluable source for the study of Arabic epigraphy, mirroring as they do epigraphic developments on other materials. The quality of the epigraphic style on the coins depended of course on the standard of control at the mint. The early Muslim coins are in the Kufic style of Arabic script, a script associated with the city of Kufa in Iraq and characterised by angular letter forms. It was not until the Ayyubid period in the late twelfth century that the cursive *naskhi* script was employed on coins. Well balanced and elegant, the inscriptions in this series are often placed within stars or square frames. The cursive script evolved many different forms, a number of which appeared on coins, such as the elegant *nasta´liq* script on coins of the Safavid and Mughal dynasties from the seventeenth century onwards. The *tughra´i* script with its characteristically long upright letters was adopted in the Muslim Indian sultanates of Jaunpur and Bengal in the fifteenth century. Under the Ottomans a fine example of cursive script was the *tughra*, the imperial monogram, which was beautifully illuminated on Ottoman administrative documents and, since the sultans did not sign their decrees, it was the ultimate authentication. It is most commonly found on Ottoman coins from the reign of Ahmad III (1703–30) onwards.

The raw materials of money in the Islamic world

. . . and God created the two precious metals, gold and silver, to serve as a measure of value of all commodities . . .

IBN KHALDUN

149 Gold dinar of the Fatimid caliph al-Aziz (975–96), struck in Filistin (Palestine) in AH 383 (AD 993–4). The Fatimids, ruling first in North Africa and then in Egypt and Syria, struck · vast numbers of coins using African gold. They were commonly used in trade and were imitated by their Christian neighbours. (× 2)

150 Gold dinar struck in AH 105 (AD 723–4) at 'the mine of the Commander of the Faithful in the Hijaz' (*ma'dan Amir al-Mu'minin bi'l Hijaz*). This short-lived gold mine was located south-west of Medina. Gold was otherwise principally acquired from Africa (New York, American Numismatic Society). (× 4)

The metals used in Islamic coins were gold, silver and copper. The historian Baladhuri recounts a tale that the caliph Umar ibn al-Khattab (AD 634–44) suggested that coins could be made out of camel skins. He was told that if they were, there would be no more camels! Access to sources of gold was a problem for the first Islamic rulers. Under the early Umayyads the principal sources of gold were Byzantine coins and confiscated treasure. A gold mine in the Hijaz, south-east of Medina, is known to have operated briefly in the eighth century, 150 but the principal source of gold for the Muslim world was to be Africa. A slow but steady expansion in the availability of African gold can first be seen during the ninth century in the increased number of mints in the eastern part of the Muslim Empire striking gold dinars where previously they had struck only silver. Until the invasion of the North African dynasty of the Almoravids in 1062, the trans-Saharan gold trade had been largely in the hands of the kingdom of Ghana. Apart from a small amount that was cast into ingots in Timbuktu, it was carried in the form of gold dust and made into dinars in the North African mints. The regions that were most to benefit from the expansion of the gold trade were the cities of North Africa and Muslim Spain. At the end of the tenth century the geographer Ibn Hauqal estimated that the revenues of the ruler of Sijilmasa, a key city on the western route, were 400,000 dinars per year (1.7 metric tonnes of gold), the bulk of which came from the trade.

Egypt under the Fatimids 149 (909–1171) was greatly enriched as a result both of

151 Blue glass stamp of the Fatimid caliph al-Hakim (996–1021), bearing his name and titles. There has been much debate as to the purpose of these stamps in the Fatimid period: whether they were coin weights or a token currency to replace bronze coins is still not known for certain. (× 2)

152 Gold tari struck by the Norman king Roger II (1130–54) in Sicily in AH 535 (AD 1140–41). This coin, with both Latin and Arabic legends, is based on the quarter dinar struck by the Fatimids in Sicily. (× 2)

153 Gold morabetino struck by Alfonso VIII, King of Castille (1158–1214), imitating a gold coin of the Almoravids who ruled North Africa and Islamic Spain during the eleventh and twelfth centuries. (× 3)

its easy access to African gold and of its important role in international trade. From the flow of Sudanese gold, the mints of North Africa and Egypt struck such quantities of dinars that they became the most common coin of the Mediterranean. Gold also began to flow into the neighbouring Christian territories. By the end of the tenth century Muslim dinars were in common use in Barcelona, where they also later started striking dinar imitations. The Lombard princes of southern Italy and Sicily struck quarter dinars (*ruba'i*) which were known as *tari*. In northern Spain, Leon and Portugal they copied Almoravid dinars (1056–1147), called *morabetino*, but with Christian instead of Muslim inscriptions. In the mid-thirteenth century double-dinars of the Almohad type (1130–1269), called *doblas*, were struck. In England records from the reign of Henry III (1216–72) show that, while amassing gold in preparation for a projected Crusade, he collected much foreign gold including Muslim gold coins of the Almohads, which were known as *oboli* or *denari de musc*. Even the Christian kingdoms of the Crusader states in the Holy Land struck coins imitating Islamic Fatimid dinars of the eleventh and early twelfth centuries, such was the international prestige of the gold coins produced in Egypt.

The principal silver mines in the Middle East were in Transoxiana and the Hindu Kush. They were controlled by the Abbasid caliphs until those regions broke away in the ninth century. The main source was at Panjshir, north of Kabul, but by the mid-tenth century there were signs that the seams were being worked out and an acute silver shortage was imminent. From about 1000 to 1150 first the eastern then the western mints struck decreasing numbers of silver coins, and those that were struck began to suffer debasement. Another possible cause of the

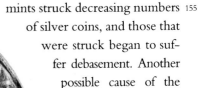

154 Gold dinar minted in one of the Crusader kingdoms in imitation of a Fatimid dinar of Tripoli in Lebanon, dated AH 463 (AD 1070–71).

155 Silver double dirham of the Ghaznavid ruler Isma'il (997–8), struck in Warwayliz (in northern Afghanistan) in AH 388 (AD 997). Under Ghaznavid and Samanid rule in Afghanistan, large low-grade silver coins, weighing about 12 g, were produced at mints in the Hindu Kush, where a large part of the silver was mined in this period.

silver shortage is thought to have been the Viking trade, which drew silver northwards away from the Islamic world. During the ninth century the Rus, whom we call Vikings, began venturing east down the Volga and Dnieper rivers across the Caspian Sea and into Persia. They brought with them into the Near Eastern markets slaves, furs, amber, honey and wax, which they exchanged for silver. That these Vikings treated the coins by weight as the Muslims did is indicated by the many hundreds and thousands of Islamic coins, mainly of the Abbasid and Samanid dynasties, that have been found in Scandinavia and Russia, sometimes in association with balances, jewellery and other precious items. They even reached as far as England, often cut into fractions to make up the weight or with cut-marks where they had been tested. With the virtual disappearance of silver for a century or more, the economies of the Islamic world were in different ways dependent on gold and copper. The Ayyubids (1171–1250), the dynasty founded by Saladin to succeed the Fatimids in Egypt, were the first Muslim dynasty to recommence coining in silver on a large scale, and by the mid-thirteenth century silver was again in plentiful supply. Some of the silver now seems to have come from Europe, initially as a result of the presence of the Crusaders, who brought quantities of silver with them and minted their own silver coins long before the Muslim states. Another source was silver mines in Anatolia, used from the thirteenth century by the Saljuqs of Anatolia.

Thus from the end of the twelfth century the reappearance of silver began to displace the gold that had been the basis of the Near Eastern currencies up to this point. The rarity of gold coins during the reign of Saladin (1169–93) is noted by Maqrizi (d. 1422), who remarked that 'to say the name of a pure gold dinar was like mentioning the name of a wife to a jealous husband, while to get such a coin was like crossing the doors of paradise'. From this period in Egypt gold became a commodity and a money of account, weighed rather than counted, unlike the standard Fatimid dinars, while silver supported by copper formed the state currency. With the arrival of the Mamluks in Egypt in 1250, economic decline set in, caused by a lethal combination of an unstable regime and the detrimental effects of foreign competition, in particular from the Byzantines, the Venetians and the Portuguese, who were steadily encroaching on Egypt's monopoly of the Indian Ocean trade. By the end of the fourteenth century Venetian ducats were circulating in the Mamluk Empire, and on account of their stability merchants preferred them to the unreliable gold dinars of the empire. Succeeding Mamluk sultans attempted to counter the power of the ducat, and after various attempts succeeded in introducing a gold coin to match it. This was the *ashrafi*, struck in 1425 by the sultan al-Malik al-Ashraf Barsbay 156 (1422–37) and named after him. It consisted of 3.41 grams of almost pure gold and was traded at par with the ducat. Thereafter *ashrafi* became the standard

156 Gold ashrafi of the Mamluk ruler al-Ashraf Barsbay (1422–37), struck at Cairo in AH 829 (AD 1425–6) to the same weight standard as the Venetian ducat. (× 4)

158 Silver coin of Termashirin (1326–33), the Mongol Chagatay ruler of Transoxania, struck at Tirmidh (Termez in Uzbekistan) in AH 729/ AD 1328–9 (the numerals 2 and 9 in the date are written backwards). Chagatay coins often use motifs resembling bows, thought to be tribal symbols.

157 Silver coin of the Mongol Ilkhanid ruler Abu Sa'id (1317–35). Coins of his reign are distinguished by a number of different designs, indicating progressive reductions in the weight standard.

term to describe an Islamic gold coin in Iran, in the Ottoman domains and in India.

In spite of this success, silver continued to provide the standard currency in Egypt and other parts of the Islamic world. In Iran, by the time of the devastating Mongol invasions in the mid-thirteenth century, no good silver coins had been struck for almost two centuries. Under the Mongols a definitive break 157–8 now took place in the style of Islamic coins, setting a pattern in the region for several hundred years. Although the types pre-existing in Transoxiana and eastern Iran were initially continued, new Qur'anic legends were adopted, Uighur script appeared and new weight standards were introduced. In an effort to remedy the dire financial situation that the Mongol Ilkhanid Empire found itself in at the end of the thirteenth century, Geikhatu (1291–5) tried to introduce paper

159 The Mongol Empire.

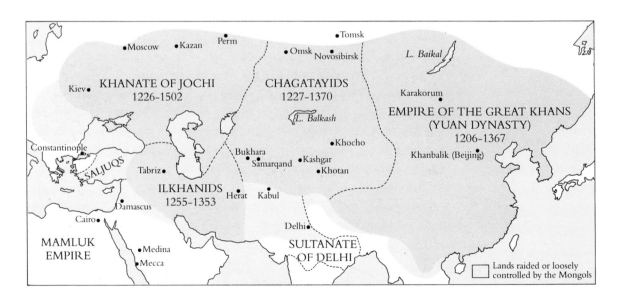

160 The thirty-fourth of the *Maqamat* (assemblies) of al-Hariri (d. 1122) illustrated by Yahya al-Wasiti in 1237. The *maqamat* are a collection of anecdotes featuring a narrator and a witty vagabond called Abu Zayd. This scene, set in Zabid in Yemen, involves the purchase of a slave. 'Here is the boy' (says Abu Zayd masquerading as a slave merchant), '. . . I wish to make you fond of the lad by lightening the price for him; so weigh out two hundred dirhams' (Paris, Bibliothèque Nationale).

money on the Chinese model. He attempted to ban the use of metal currency completely and force people to exchange their money for a paper note called a *ch'ao*, which was inscribed in Chinese and also bore the Muslim *shahada*, in order to fill the government coffers with precious metal. The attempt failed, however, and more successful currency reforms were carried out by Ghazan (1295–1304), whereby a standard silver coin weighing half a *mithqal* (about 2.16 grams) was struck all over the empire. Under Abu Sa'id (1317–35), who minted coins at over a hundred mints, a series of weight reductions in the silver coins 157 was marked by new designs, producing arguably some of the finest engraved Islamic coins.

Coins and money in daily life and trade

What do we know about the use and function of money in the Islamic lands? Copper coins formed the basic currency for everyday purposes, a point emphasised in Maqrizi's fifteenth-century treatise on coins, in which he says '*fulus*

[copper coins] were not used to purchase expensive items but only used for local transactions'. As elsewhere, there were in the Islamic world wide discrepancies between the earnings of the rich and the poor and their associated spending power. In eleventh-century Egypt, for example, a servant might earn one dinar per month while a judge might earn a hundred. A dinar at this time would have bought 100 kg of wheat, while an expensive embroidered coat from Damietta might cost up to 1,000 dinars.

On special occasions, such as the end of the Ramadan, the month of fasting, rulers might distribute coins amongst the people as largesse. In Fatimid Egypt the caliph specially minted 10,000 gold *kharubas* – tiny gold coins the weight of a carob seed – for distribution to state servants on a feast day known as Thursday of the Lentils. In present-day Iran coin-like tokens are frequently distributed at weddings. 162 Coins were often pierced and sewn onto women's 161 clothes or headdresses. The range and amount of these would be an obvious status symbol for the woman's family, but they were also the woman's own property which she could add to or dispose of at will.

The collection of taxes, principally the *kharaj*, or land tax, was the main source of revenue for Islamic states. It was this that enabled them to survive, and the main item of expenditure – at least in early Islam – was the payment of the army. The collection of *kharaj* was usually carried out by tax 'farmers' who would obtain a percentage of the amount for their trouble. In medieval times the coins once collected would be placed in sealed bags. The historian Mas'udi has a grim story about the people of tenth-century Isfahan refusing to pay their taxes. The officers cut off the heads of miscreants and put them in sacks which were then sealed, the sight of which proved sufficient encouragement to make other people pay up.

Trade was another source of wealth both for individuals and the state. The government could exact large sums from merchants in the form of harbour and customs duties, as happened in Yemen in the 1420s when the Rasulid sultan al-Nasir imposed such a high tariff on the goods coming in on the ocean-going vessels arriving at the port of Aden that they boycotted Aden and sailed directly to Jeddah. During the Abbasid period long-haul voyages across the Indian Ocean had regularly taken place between China and the Islamic world; at the key port of Siraf in the Persian Gulf Chinese coins have been excavated. Finds of hoards from this period can provide us with a fascinating insight into the ways in which coins were used in trade. The Sinaw hoard, for instance,

162 (*below*) Group of modern Iranian brass coin-like tokens inscribed 'good fortune'. These are scattered for good luck at weddings (V. Curtis). (× 1½)

161 Headdress from Samu'ah in the southern Hebron hills, dating from the 1840s but with later additions. In the nineteenth century, Palestinian women in some areas wore a bonnet to which coins were attached. Part of a girl's bridal jewellery, they belonged entirely to her and could not be touched by her husband. The majority of the coins in this example are Ottoman Turkish paras from the reign of Mahmud I (1730–54) to Mahmud II (1808–39). The headdress has clearly had a number of owners, each of whom has added ornaments or coins, including German coin-like reckoning counters.

which was buried in the Oman interior about AD 840, consists of 900 coins and fragments, the earliest of which are Sasanian coins of the sixth century. The rest of the coins, mostly Umayyad and Abbasid dirhams, represent a remarkable fifty-nine mints across the Islamic world from North Africa to Transoxiana. The hoard may have been the savings of a local inhabitant or, perhaps more likely, the property of a merchant involved in the lucrative Indian Ocean trade. This and other hoards of the period show that Islamic coins had a virtually unlimited circulation range as a result of their uniformly high silver content and also provide an image of a world uninhibited by political frontiers.

Under the Fatimids (909–1171) shorter segmented voyages between a number of leading maritime cities replaced longer voyages. The Red Sea supplanted the Persian Gulf as the main recipient of the trade, which then passed through Alexandria on the Mediterranean. European traders, particularly from Italy, were to be found trading on this route, and the Fatimid capital, Fustat, was called the treasure-house of the West and the emporium of the East. This was an age of free enterprise described as the 'golden age of the bourgeoisie', in which anyone with a small amount of capital could go into trade and make a fortune. A set of remarkable Judaeo-Arabic documents known as the Cairo Geniza, many of them the letters of eleventh-century traders, reveals in astonishing detail a complex system of banking and finance in operation at this time. Large sums could now be paid by bill of exchange, guaranteed by bonds and transferred by letters of credit – a system used by both merchants and government officials. Ibn Hauqal mentions a transaction in which a promissory note (*sakk*) for 42,000 dinars was sent from Sijilmasa to Audaghost, the southern terminus of the trans-Saharan route in West Africa. The eleventh-century Iranian traveller Nasir-i Khusrau says that in 1052 there were 200 bankers operating in Isfahan, while cities such as Baghdad had banking streets, rather like the streets of moneychangers that still exist in Arab suqs today. There were private and royal banks, and many of the banking families were Christians or, as in Christian Europe, Jews, because they belonged to communities that were not subject to the religious prohibition on money-lending which was imposed on Muslims.

The world of empires

The later Islamic period is dominated from the sixteenth century onwards by three major dynasties: the Mughals in India, the Safavids and their successors in Iran, and the Ottomans in Turkey and the Arab world.

The Safavids (1501–1765) believed in 'twelver Shiism', a form of Islam charac- 163 terised by a belief in the twelve infallible imams, the last of whom, Muhammad al-Mahdi, disappeared in AD 875 and is still expected to return. This belief is expressed on their coins, where the names of the imams are to be found amongst the inscriptions. Another distinctive feature of Safavid coins is the re-

163 Silver coin of the Safavid ruler Shah Tahmasp II (1722–32), struck at Isfahan (Iran) in AH 1142 (AD 1729–30). It is inscribed in Persian, 'In this world a royal coin has been struck by Tahmasp the second, by the grace of the True One (Allah).' From 1576 Iranian coins included Persian as well as Arabic inscriptions, the first time Persian had been used on Iranian coinage since the Arab-Sasanian dirhams.

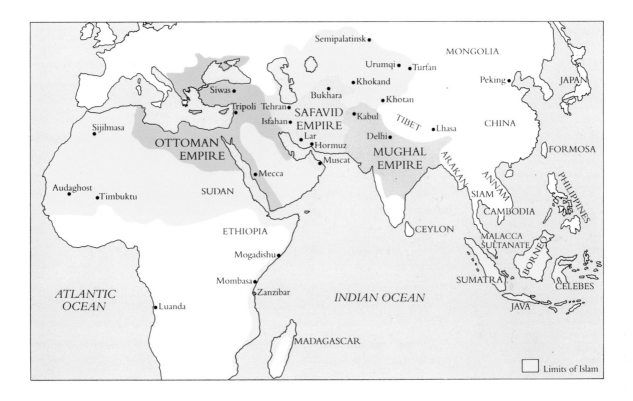

164 The Muslim world, *c.* 1700.

appearance during the reign of Isma'il II (1576–8) of the Persian language, replacing Arabic for the first time since the pre-reform silver coins of the seventh century. Monetary standards were expressed in terms of the *toman*, derived from the Mongol word meaning 10,000, which was a money of account originally indicating 10,000 dinars. The coinage consisted principally of the silver *shahi*, a coin struck in a number of denominations, and the gold ashrafi, which initially retained the Venetian ducat standard adopted by the Mamluks in Egypt in 1425. Gold, however, was struck only intermittently and, in the early sixteenth century at least, was reserved solely for presentation pieces. According to the reports of foreign travellers to Iran, there was great reliance on foreign gold coin. This came in the form of Venetian ducats, some of it in payment for silk exported by Armenian merchants. Father Pacifique de Provins, writing in 1628, says that 'when the Armenians brought with them sequins or piastres, they took them to the mint which paid them some interest. The coins received a Persian imprint and the king gained some benefit from this operation.' 'The king's coins', he adds, 'never left Persian territory and were nowhere accepted except by weight.' Foreign metal also came to Iran during this period through the port of Bandar Abbas on the Persian Gulf. In 1633 an Englishman reported: 'The Iranians will receive from foreigners no other money than Rix-dollars [probably Dutch *rijksdaalders*] or Spanish Ryals which they immediately convert to Abbasis.' (The *abbasi* was a four-shahi coin first struck in the name of Shah Abbas I (1588–1629.)

It was also during this period that the *larin*, the Indian Ocean trade coin pop- 165 ular between the sixteenth and eighteenth centuries, was invented. Named after the city of Lar in Iran (although it never seems to have been coined there), it was made of a length of silver wire bent in two and struck with circular or rectangular dies. The earliest examples were struck in Hormuz and under the Safavid Shah Tahmasp I (1524–76), but they were also produced in Arabia by the Ottomans, and in India and Ceylon. However, the most highly prized, particularly by Indian jewellers, were the Safavid larins, on account of the purity of their silver. Further monetary innovations were to occur in Iran during the reign of Nadir Shah (1736–47) who, following his conquest of present-day northern India and Pakistan, amalgamated the Iranian and Indian currency systems. The shahi coins were now called rupees, and the gold coin was based on the Mughal *mohur*.

165 Silver larin of Shah Tahmasp I (1524–76), Safavid ruler of Iran. These coins, made from bent silver wire and impressed with dies, were first struck by the rulers of Hormuz (southern Iran); between the sixteenth and eighteenth centuries they were a popular currency in Indian Ocean trade.

The Sunni Ottoman dynasty (1281–1924) did not come into prominence until the reign of Mehmed the Conqueror, who finally captured Constantinople from the Byzantines in 1453. The golden age of the empire began in the sixteenth century under the sultans Selim the Grim (1512–20) and Suleiman the Magnificent (1520–66) with a series of important conquests which resulted in a vast spread of territory and influence, including at its height Egypt and the Balkans and extending into Italy, North Africa, Arabia and into the lands of the Ottomans' arch enemies the Safavids of Iran. The Ottoman monetary system presents a highly complex picture which can only be hinted at here. Prices and wages were calculated in terms of small silver coins known as *akçe*. Suleiman's well-known architect Sinan received, for instance, 55 akçe as his daily wage. The dirham and its quarter and copper coins known as *manghir* were also in circulation.

166 Gold ashrafi struck by the Ottoman sultan Suleiman the Magnificent at the Serbian mint of Sidra Keysi in AH 926 (AD 1519–20). These coins are, with few exceptions, dated to 926, the year of Suleiman's accession. (× 4)

The main gold coin was the ashrafi, still based on the 166 Venetian ducat. It was under Suleiman III (1687–91) that silver *qurush* (derived from the German word *groschen* and, as *qirsh*, still a common term for a denomination) were introduced as a response to the Austrian *thalers* that were now monopolising European trade with the East. The demand for these coins was increasing to such an extent that the Ottomans began using Austrian and Dutch coins as blanks. An intriguing aspect of Ottoman coins is that the inscriptions on them lacked any religious content and included primarily the sultan's titles, one of which, adopted by Suleiman in reference to his military conquests, read 'sultan of the two lands and *khaqan* [lord] of the two seas'.

Striking by machine rather than by hand occurred in Turkey during the reign 167 of Abd al-Mejid I (1839–61) as part of his programme of modernisation known as the *tanzimat*, the principal purpose of which was to put into force European standards of law and administration. In Iran a mint producing machine-made coins was established in Tehran in 1876. Following the revolution in the manufacture of coinage, both the Ottoman and the Qajar coins maintained their traditional appearance: large-flanned copper coins with the tughra of Abd al-Aziz (1861–76) on the obverse and the mint and date on the reverse. With the increasing effects of colonialism in the twentieth century, Islamic coins became hybrid. A number of coinages began to be struck at mechanised mints in the West: Moroccan coins were struck in Paris and Berlin, coins of the cities of southern Yemen were struck in Birmingham. In southern Arabia and the Gulf, along with the popular trade coin the Maria Theresa thaler, coins based on East India Company issues were adopted. As in many other parts of the world, cupro-nickel as a metal began to be regularly used. Religious legends began to disappear, and the range of denominations expanded. Dates are often to be seen in the Christian rather than, or as well as, the Islamic era; inscriptions appear both in Arabic and Roman letters, and the ban on figural representation is now definitely a feature of the past: rulers' heads have even been depicted on twentieth-century coins.

Paper money was not adopted in the Islamic world until the mid-nineteenth century. During the 1850s the Ottomans issued notes in Turkey and other provinces of their empire. Iran followed closely, issuing banknotes from the late 1880s. Banknotes were also issued by the colonial powers and, upon reaching independence, most countries began issuing their own, although in the majority of cases these were actually printed for them in the West. Modern money in the Islamic world, although now a long way from where it started, retains links with tradition: there are still fine examples of Arabic calligraphy, and terms such as *fils* (from *fals*), dinar and dirham are still used for both coins and banknotes. The banknotes proclaim the identity of individual Islamic countries in a very conscious manner, now proudly exhibiting images of their most important antiquities. But in the end they are only paper: among the sanctions imposed on Iraq after the invasion of Kuwait in 1990 was a ban on the printing of banknotes by the British firm De La Rue. The Iraqis then produced their own notes, though this meant a reduction in quality and security devices.

167 Gold 500-piastre coin of the Ottoman sultan Abd al-Mejid I (1839–61), struck at the machine mint in Constantinople.

India and South-East Asia

Miss Prism: Cecily, you will read your Political Economy in my absence. The chapter on the Fall of the Rupee you may omit. It is somewhat sensational. Even these metallic problems have their melodramatic side.

OSCAR WILDE, *The Importance of Being Earnest* (1895), Act 2

The story of money in India and South-east Asia can be traced back over three thousand years. The region has its own monetary tradition firmly rooted in the culture of northern India. This tradition has been subjected to many outside influences from Iran, the Graeco-Roman world, Islam and the European colonial powers, but it has retained its own distinctive characteristics. Conversely, India's money and monetary practices have spread throughout the South Asian region to the lands surrounding the Republic of India, and at times in the past their influence has also reached into Central and South-east Asia.

In India today, and in the surrounding states, money circulates as coins and paper money, in the same form as it does in virtually every other country around the world. The currency of India and of many of its neighbours is denominated according to the *rupee* (divided into a hundred *paise*), the word 168 rupee being itself the English rendering of the Indian (Hindi) word *rupya*, meaning 'silver coin'. The same denomination system is used by the other states of the region. Pakistan, Nepal and Sri Lanka retain the name rupee, while other countries have given it a local name: *afghani* in Afghanistan, *taka* in Bangladesh, *ngultrum* in Bhutan, *rufiyaa* in the Maldives and *kyat* in Burma. The rupee is also the standard denomination of two Indian Ocean island states, Mauritius and Seychelles. A version of the rupee, called *rupiah*, is also now used in Indonesia.

The story of today's rupee in all its versions began in 1835, when the British 169 East India Company introduced a new standardised silver rupee for circulation throughout its Indian territories. The rupee denomination had already been in existence in India since the sixteenth century, but it was not a standardised unit and the reformed rupee was introduced to replace the three hundred different kinds of rupee that had previously circulated in India.

168 Nickel rupee of the Republic of India, dated 1950. The front shows India's national emblem, the lion capital erected by the third-century BC king Ashoka; the back names the denomination in Hindi and English. In the nineteenth century the rupee was a silver coin, but in 1940 its silver content was reduced to 50 per cent and from 1947 it ceased to be made of silver. The 'fall of the rupee' referred to by Oscar Wilde resulted when the value of silver halved between 1870 and 1895. India's currency was based on the silver rupee and this drastic fall was disastrous for its economy.

169 Silver rupee of the British East India Company, dated 1835 and struck at the Calcutta New Mint. This coin and its design were organised by James Prinsep. The front portrays the British king William IV; the back gives the denomination in Urdu and English.

James Prinsep and Indian money

We begin our story with a remarkable family of British administrators in early 170 nineteenth-century India. James Prinsep, the best-known member of the family, was heavily involved in the development of the 1835 East India Company silver rupee coinage, which became the first standardised coinage of India and developed into the rupee as it is now known. James's father, John Prinsep, a manufacturer of indigo under the patronage of the East India Company Government in Calcutta, had introduced modern coining machinery into India. He gained the permission of the company to open a machine mint near Calcutta to strike a copper coinage in 1780. He then tried in 1785 to persuade the company to allow him to reorganise its coinage for eastern India by also striking silver coins. His proposal was unsuccessful, but fifty years later his son James, working as Assay Master at the company's Calcutta mint, was able to introduce a Western-style coinage in the regions where the company held sway.

170 Silver medal of James Prinsep (1799–1840), designed by William Wyon R.A. as a memorial to the British administrator and scholar, pioneer of the study of the history of coins in India.

171 Watercolour of the New Mint, Calcutta, painted by Thomas Prinsep soon after the mint was opened on 1 August 1829. The mint was designed to have the capacity to produce coinage for the whole of India (London, India Office Library).

A year after James Prinsep had effectively redesigned India's coinage, his brother Henry, working as Secretary to the Calcutta Administration's Financial Department and later Secretary to its Government, was deeply involved in overseeing the good management of the Bank of Bengal. Henry helped keep 172 banking in India independent by resisting the proposal to set up a General Bank of India in London in 1836. He went on to become a government director of

172 One hundred-sicca rupee note of the Bank of Bengal, Calcutta, 24 December 1824, printed in London by Perkins and Heath. The Bank name and denomination were written in English, Hindi, Bengali and Urdu. This example was stamped CANCELLED and had its corner removed to prevent its reissue. The sicca rupee, meaning a newly struck rupee (no more than two years old), circulated at a premium over older coins. As the loss of value of old coins was a problem for the East India Company, from 1777 to 1835 the Calcutta Mint fixed the Mughal emperor's reign date on its rupees, so that they could not be discounted once they were two years old (Simmons & Simmons Ltd). (× ½)

the Bank of Bengal and then president of its board. Three other Prinsep brothers were involved in the running of the bank, two as directors and one as its solicitor. The bank subsequently became the Imperial Bank of India in 1921, then the State Bank of India in 1955. Between them, the Prinsep family did much to make India's money the way it is today.

James Prinsep had another role to play in the story of money in South Asia. Apart from his work at the mint, his chief passion was India's past. When he came to India in 1819, its early history was largely unknown. Prinsep revolu- 173 tionised the study of ancient India by deciphering Brahmi and Kharoshthi, the two ancient scripts of the subcontinent. Through reading Brahmi, Prinsep discovered the existence of the most important emperor of ancient India, Ashoka, the first great patron of Buddhism in the third century BC, and through the decipherment of Kharoshthi he was able to reveal the extent of the ancient eastern Greek kingdoms, ruling as successors of Alexander the Great in the territory now comprising Afghanistan, north Pakistan and north-west India. These discoveries allowed Prinsep to begin constructing a chronology for the ancient coins found in northern and north-western India. The telling of the history of money in South Asia could begin.

173 Silver 4-drachma coin of Menander I, Greek king of north-western India, mid-second century BC. The front shows the king wearing a helmet, with a Greek inscription 'of Menander King and Saviour'; the back shows the Greek goddess Athena, with an Indian translation of the Greek on the front written using Kharoshthi script. James Prinsep used coins such as this bilingual issue to decipher the Kharoshthi script in which the local Indian language of the ancient North-West (modern Pakistan and Afghanistan) was written.

When Prinsep began his study of ancient Indian coinage in 1832, he believed that the use of coins had come from the Greek world into India. He concluded that 'Coinage is certainly one of the improvements which has travelled and is still travelling eastwards', as he saw Greek-style coins in use in ancient India and, in his own day, European-style coins being adopted in Burma and China. The following year he again asserted, 'I . . . doubt whether any native coin, properly so called, had circulation in India anterior to the incursion of Alexander [the Great]'. In 1835, however, the coin collection of one Colonel Stacy gave him the first opportunity to examine a variety, the so-called punch- 174h marked coins, that made him change his opinion. He associated these newly discovered coins with ancient Buddhist communities and speculated that 'the antiquarian . . . will have little hesitation in ascribing the highest grade of antiquity in Indian numismatology to these flattened bits of silver', but was uncertain 'how far the antiquity of the first Buddhist groups of coins may have approached the epoch of the Buddha', which he put at 544 BC.

The beginnings of coinage in India

Prinsep's research and observations pointed the way and many eminent scholars have followed in his footsteps. These coins have since been confirmed as the earliest of Indian coins, datable to shortly after the death of the Buddha, which modern scholarship places around 400 BC. Latest research on the development of the designs on the punch-marked coins and on the hoards in which they are found suggests that they certainly began in the early fourth century BC at some point before the arrival of Alexander. The earliest coins in India therefore pre-date Alexander the Great's conquests in north-western India (329–325 BC). But they seem nevertheless to have developed as an adaptation of Greek prototypes, as they have been found in Afghanistan in association with Greek coins of the fifth and fourth centuries and with locally made imitations of Greek originals. It has been argued by some that the earliest coins in India should be pushed back as far as the eighth century BC, but it seems best to interpret them as derived from Greek models that reached India via the Achaemenid Empire, which ruled ancient Afghanistan and Pakistan before the invasion of Alexander.

The coins themselves are small pieces of silver (mostly weighing about 3.3 174 grams but with a range from 0.2 to 11.5 grams), decorated on one side with from one to five marks impressed onto the face of the coin with engraved punches. Some of the punch-marks can be recognised as representations of animals (bulls, elephants, turtles), plants (palm trees, fig trees), religious symbols (sacred hills, solar wheels, emblems of gods), and everyday objects (ploughs, pots, balances). There are also a few images of human figures who are probably Hindu deities (Krishna, Balarama, Karttikeya), but the majority of the marks are geometric patterns with no clear meaning.

The early development of coinage in India

Punch-marked and cast coinage

The first coins in the Indian tradition were made in the eastern provinces of the Achaemenid Empire of Iran. During the fifth and fourth centuries BC, Greek and Iranian coins issued in the western provinces of the empire circulated as far east as the Achaemenid territory now called Afghanistan and Pakistan. These coins were copied and adapted locally. The new local issues are known to historians as the punch-marked coinage, because the designs were applied to one side of the coin only by a set of punches, rather than by striking between dies. From Achaemenid territory this new coinage spread into northern India.

The development of silver coinage

The first local coins of the eastern Achaemenid Empire used the die-striking technology of Greek coins, but introduced new designs. The next stage of development placed the design on one side of the coin only, with two punches for the largest denomination and one punch for smaller coins. The earliest coins of cities along the Ganges copied this technology, but varied the number of punches and their designs.

174d–f Silver one, one-eighth and one-sixteenth karshapana coins of the Gangetic Plain (perhaps of the kingdom of Kosala), fourth century BC, with four, two and one punch-marks respectively. (× 1½)

174b Silver double shekel of Gandhara, early fourth century BC, with two punch-marks. The back of the coin has no design (× 1½)

174a Silver double shekel of the Kabul region, early fourth century BC. The front shows a flower; the back a circular symbol. (× 1½)

174c Silver half-shekel of Achaemenid Gandhara, early fourth century BC, with a single punch-mark. (× 1½)

174g Silver karshapana of the Gangetic Plain, late fourth century BC, with four punch-marks. (× 3)

174h Silver karshapana of the Mauryan kings, third century BC, with five punch-marks. (× 2)

Cast copper coinage

Alongside the punch-marked silver coins, Indians invented a new kind of coin made by casting copper in moulds. They were also decorated with a number of symbols, but on both sides. On later issues they were organised into an overall design, sometimes with an added inscription.

174i Copper coin of the Mauryan kingdom, third century BC. This cast coin has elephant, sun and moon, swastika and standard symbols. (× 1½)

174j Copper coin of the Mauryan kingdom, third century BC, with the same symbols arranged to stand on a river symbol. (× 1½)

174k Copper coin of the Mauryan kingdom, second century BC. (× 1½)

174l Copper coin of the city of Ayodhya in central northern India, first century BC, with the Brahmi inscription *Shivadattasa* (king of Ayodhya). (× 1½)

174m Copper coin of the city of Kausambi in central northern India, first century BC, with the Brahmi inscription *Sadevasa* (king of Kausambi). (× 1½)

Punch-marked to struck copper coinage

In some areas punch-marked copper coins were issued, but only after the issue of punch-marked silver had ceased. A further development was the use of a single punch on which all the symbols were assembled. By the first century AD the issuing of coinage had spread to south India and Sri Lanka.

174n Copper coin of the city of Eran, central India, first century BC, with five punch-marks. (× 1½)

174o Copper single punch coin of the city of Ujjain, central India, first century BC. (× 1½)

174p Copper single punch coin of the city of Taxila, north-western India, second century BC. (× 1½)

174q Copper single punch coin of the kingdom of Pandya, southern India, first century BC. (× 1½)

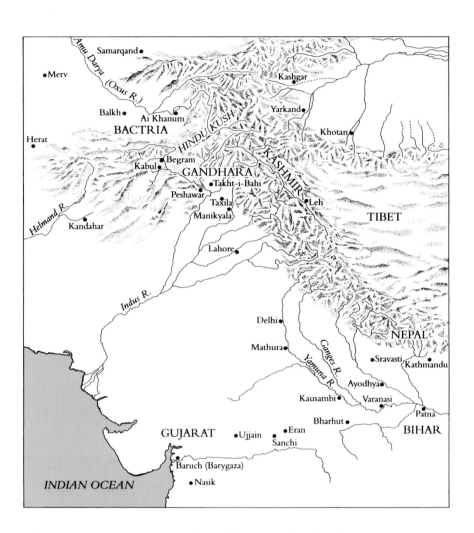

175 Bactria, Gandhara and northern India.

Two elements suggest that these objects can be identified as a circulating coinage: their adherence to particular weight standards, as mentioned above, and the fact that the punch-marks applied to them seem to follow a pattern of usage suggesting a regular system of production. Prinsep himself observed that all the pieces he saw had a sun symbol on them. The discovery of hoards of 174h punch-marked coins, sometimes including coins of the Greek kingdoms of Afghanistan and north-west Pakistan, indicates that they were used as coined money.

From excavations at Ai-Khanum, the site of an ancient Greek city in northern Afghanistan, there is now evidence that the silver punch-marked coins were called *karshapana* (Greek *kasapana*). A hoard of these coins, including coins of a Greek king called Agathocles (*c.* 180 BC), was found in the remains of a palace treasury destroyed by Central Asian invaders in about 140 BC. In the same treasury were found fragments of pots inscribed in Greek with records of the karshapanas they once contained. The same word was also used as a unit of money in ancient Indian literature. The earliest instance of its use is in the work of the grammarian Panini, writing in the fourth century BC, who refers to the karshapana as a unit of value in making purchases. The *Arthashastra*, a political treatise traditionally dated to the fourth century BC but containing later material, expresses all monetary values in terms of the *pana*, and Buddhist parables dating from the third to first centuries BC also make widespread references to a unit of money named the *kahapana*.

The earliest visual evidence for monetary use of punch-marked coins is a second-century BC relief carving on a Buddhist monument at Bharhut, near 176 Allahabad in northern India. The relief shows men covering the ground of a park with punch-marked coins being delivered in an ox cart. It is intended to represent the story of Anathapindika, a rich merchant who bought the Jetavana Gardens at Sravasti as a refuge for the Buddha and his monks for the price of covering it with karshapanas.

There are, however, some discrepancies between the evidence of art and literature and the surviving coins. The *Arthashastra* refers to half, quarter and eighth panas, whereas the only fraction of the 3.3 gram karshapana is a sixteenth weighing 0.2 grams. Early Buddhist texts also refer to gold karshapanas, but there were no gold coins in use in India before the first century AD. It is also quite possible that the karshapana was originally a unit of weight rather than a coin as such, and that the textual evidence refers anachronistically to coin use in a world where precious metal passed by weight as bullion.

176 Relief carving depicting the story of the purchase of the Jetavana Gardens by the merchant Anathapindika as a refuge for the Buddha and his followers. Punch-marked coins laid out over the gardens are the price of its purchase. The relief is from the Bharhut Stupa, a Buddhist monument in northern India, second century BC. The coins closely resemble late Mauryan punch-marked silver coins of the period (Calcutta, Indian Museum).

Further influences from the north-west

Whatever the dating and interpretation of the earliest stages of Indian coinage, it is clear that, ever since the invasion of north-western India by Alexander the Great in the 320s BC, coinage traditions from the West have continued to have an impact on India's monetary history up to the present day. From about 250 BC to the early decades of the first century AD, there was a succession of Greek kings ruling in the area to the north-west of the subcontinent. Initially these Greek kingdoms issued coins struck between dies, using Greek coining technology and with purely Greek designs of the type made by the successors of Alexander the Great elsewhere in the Greek world. From about 190 BC the

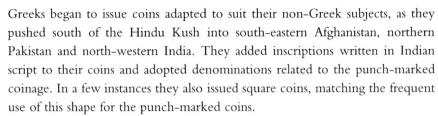

177 Copper coin of an unknown issuer, struck in the second century BC in the regions of Peshawar and Kabul. The front shows an elephant with a hill symbol; the back a lion with a hill symbol and a swastika. Although the content of the designs is Indian, the treatment of the animals is in the Greek tradition, and the coin was struck between dies using Greek technology.

178 Silver 4-drachma coin of Azes I, Scythian king of north-western India, mid-first century BC. The front shows the mounted king holding a lance; the back the Greek god Zeus, flanked by Greek and Kharoshthi monograms indicating the mint. Greek and Kharoshthi inscriptions state that it is a coin 'of Azes, King of Kings, the Great'.

Greeks began to issue coins adapted to suit their non-Greek subjects, as they pushed south of the Hindu Kush into south-eastern Afghanistan, northern Pakistan and north-western India. They added inscriptions written in Indian script to their coins and adopted denominations related to the punch-marked coinage. In a few instances they also issued square coins, matching the frequent use of this shape for the punch-marked coins.

The technology and designs of these adapted Greek coins were being copied by Indian coin issuers in northern India by the late second century BC and in 177 southern India by the first century AD. In some instances only the technology of die striking was borrowed, but in others the use of inscriptions and of Greek-style figurative art was also adopted. During the second and first centuries BC there had been a number of indigenous changes in coin design based on the punch-marked coinage, which did not develop towards either Greek-style technology or figurative art. Some Indian coins already had inscriptions, but these were invariably written in a straight line and treated as though they were another punch-mark. By contrast, Greek and Indian inscriptions used on Greek and Greek-style coins were placed in a circle as a border to the pictorial design. Hellenic influence extended also to denominations, as in the tenth century coins were still known as *dramma* or *damma*, the Indian word derived from the Greek *drachma*.

Greek rule in the north-west eventually disintegrated, but this did not terminate the influence of the Greek coinage tradition upon South Asia. The Greek kingdoms were overrun by a succession of nomad warrior peoples crossing the Hindu Kush to take control of the rich river plains of the region. Each of them also issued coins in the Greek tradition, sometimes drawing fresh inspiration from the Greek-style coinages of Iran and the Roman Empire. In turn the coinages of each of these peoples – Scythians (first cen- 178 tury BC to first century AD), Parthians (first century AD), Kushans (first to fourth centuries), Huns (fourth to sixth centuries) and 179–80 Turks (sixth to ninth centuries) – had its own impact in India. During the Kushan and Hun periods an additional injection of Western influence took place, as the Sasanian kings of Iran periodically conquered parts of the north-western region. Like the coins of the nomadic peoples, the Sasanian issues also ultimately derived their designs from the Greek coinage tradition. During the same period traders from Roman Egypt and Syria brought Roman coinage as bullion into the ports of western and southern India and Sri Lanka. In some areas these coins were put into circulation as local currency, augmenting or ousting the local coinages, and Roman coins of the first century AD have been found hoarded alongside punch-marked coins. In northern India during the Gupta period (fourth to sixth centuries) the 181, standard gold coin was named *dinar* after its Roman equivalent *denarius aureus*.

179 Gold coin of Kanishka I, Kushan king of Bactria and India, early second century AD. The front shows the king, surrounded by a Bactrian inscription written in Greek letters, 'the King of Kings, Kanishka, the Kushan'; the back the Kushan version of the Iranian sun-god Mithra, flanked by the royal emblem and his name in Bactrian, 'Miiro'. The Kushans extended the use of coins in the Greek tradition throughout Central Asia and northern India. The technology and overall composition of their coins were Greek, but the designs also reflect their Iranian cultural links. (× 3)

180 Silver drachm of Mihiragula, Hun king in north-western India, early sixth century AD. This Sasanian-style coin shows the king flanked by trident and bull standards of the Hindu god Shiva, with a Brahmi inscription: 'the victorious King Mihiragula'. (× 4)

The variety of influences exhibited in the Gupta dinar coinage exemplifies the way in which the Indian coinage tradition absorbed and enriched itself through Western contacts. The use of a gold coinage by the Guptas was a borrowing from their western neighbours, the Kushan kings who ruled former Greek territory in Afghanistan, Pakistan and north-western India. The designs, a standing king on the obverse and a seated goddess on the reverse, were also borrowed 181

117

181 Gold dinar of Samudragupta, Gupta king of India, about 335-70. The front shows the king sacrificing at a small altar before a Garuda standard of the Hindu god Vishnu. The king's name appears in Brahmi script below his raised arm; the back shows an enthroned image of the Hindu goddess Shri, with another title of the king in Brahmi. This coin uses Kushan designs, but the Indian style and emblem were typical innovations of the Gupta coinage. (× 3)

from the same source, but these images were remodelled by Indian artists according to their own sculptural style. The inscriptions were written in Indian using Brahmi script, but were positioned in the same way as the Greek inscriptions on Kushan coins. Next to the king was a standard topped by the image of the Indian man-faced bird deity Garuda, a symbolic emblem like those used on Indian coins from the first century BC. The designs borrowed from the Kushan coin were derived from three different sources. The circular inscription on the obverse can be traced back to the Greek coinages of the north-west. The standing figure of the king was taken from Iranian coinage and the seated goddess on the reverse recalls the early gold and silver coins of the Roman Empire. It is also likely that the idea of using gold coins came to the Kushans from the Roman gold coins being traded into their territories.

Despite these developments, many elements of the Indian tradition based on the punch-marked coinage survived, but they were continually being transformed. The most enduring elements were the use of symbolic marks and of the square 182-5 shape, and these could still be seen in Indian local coins until the nineteenth century. The symbols used during this period became as unintelligible to the uninitiated as the use of marks on the ancient punch-marked coins. We have no clear idea of the precise meaning of the early punch-marks, but for the nineteenth-century symbols we can again turn to James Prinsep. He had the foresight to record the symbols used on 125 different coins in circulation in his day, and he identified the mints to which they referred.

In addition to the continuing influence of Greek and Indian traditions on Indian money, we must also look briefly at the contribution of the Islamic

182 Silver rupee of the French settlement at Pondicherry in southern India, in the name of the Mughal emperor Shah Alam II, dated 1219 (AD 1804). Although struck at Pondicherry, the mint name on the coin is that of the Mughal district of Arcot. The crescent symbol identifies the Pondicherry mint.

183 Plate from James Prinsep's *Useful Tables illustrative of the Coins, Weights and Measures of British India*, Calcutta 1834–6, showing symbols in use as mint marks on contemporary Indian coins.

184 Silver rupee of the kingdom of Awadh, struck in the name of the Mughal emperor Shah Alam II, dated 1226 (AD 1811/12), and year 26 (a fixed date). The front of the coin has the fish, ear of wheat, star and flag symbols (Prinsep no. 81) of the Lucknow Mint.

185 Silver rupee of the state of Kotah, struck in the name of the Mughal emperor Akbar II, dated 1245 (AD 1829/30) and year 24 (of his reign). The back of the coin has the tree (Prinsep no. 57) and leaf (Prinsep no. 56) symbols of the Kotah City Mint.

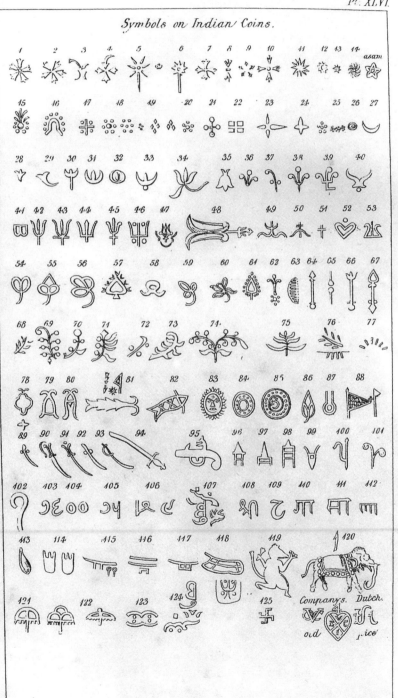

Pl. XLVI.

Symbols on Indian Coins.

after J. Prinsep.

West & Co. Lith.

Published by Stephen Austin, Hertford.

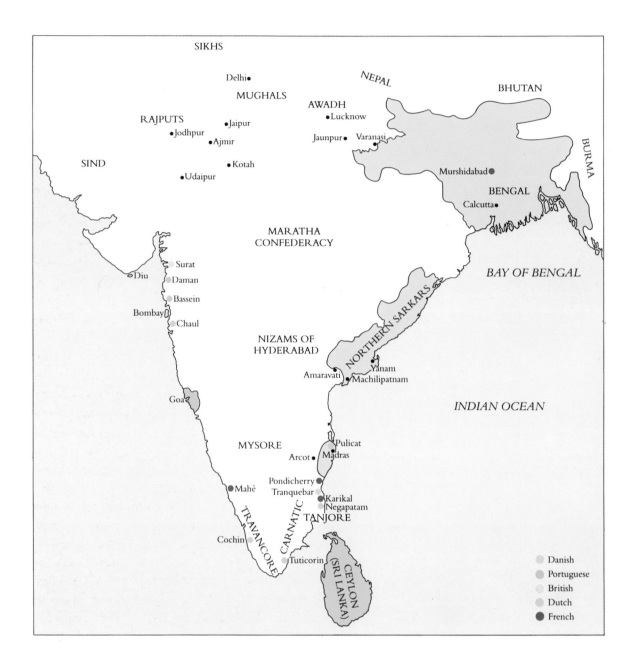

186 India, *c. 1790*.

tradition, which, though quite distinct, was also ultimately descended from Western forebears. Before the reform of 1835 the majority of coins in circulation in northern India, whether issued by Mughal emperors and local princes or 187 by French and British possessions, were essentially modelled on Islamic prototypes with inscriptions in Persian. The Mughals, descendants of the Mongol conquerors Ghengis Khan and Timur (Tamberlaine), had invaded India from the north-west in the sixteenth century, bringing with them the Persian language, but even prior to this northern India had been subject to Islamic rulers. Mu'izz-ad-Din Muhammad bin Sam (1173–1206), the Ghurid ruler of Afghanistan, had brought the whole of northern India under Islamic rule and introduced an Islamic coinage with Arabic designs which were grafted onto the indigenous denominational system.

The impact of the Islamic tradition on South Asian coinage was widespread. Only in the far south of India and Sri Lanka did traditional Indian designs continue to be used, until they were eventually replaced by types introduced by the European imperial powers: the Portuguese, British, Dutch, French and Danish in south India; and the Portuguese, Dutch and British in Sri Lanka. In the rest of India the influence exercised on the coinage by the European powers was much weaker and took a long time to make itself felt, and the Europeans had significantly to adapt their systems to suit the local standards.

The Portuguese were the first Europeans to issue coins in India in the late sixteenth century, but they adopted the Mughal system, issuing silver rupee and copper paisa denominations for the Portuguese settlement at Goa in western India with European designs: coats of arms, crowns and representations of kings and saints. The Portuguese also issued similar coins at their other settlements and in Sri Lanka, but they were not intended for circulation outside the settlements and had little impact on Indian coinage. In the seventeenth century the British tried to follow the same pattern, issuing Indian denominations but with European designs such as crowns, coats of arms and the East India Company emblem. But these coins also had only a limited circulation and, as more and more of India came under British rule, it became necessary for the company to issue coins with Mughal designs. These Mughal-style issues continued to be issued by the company until Prinsep's reform. The coins made by his father, 188

187 Mughal miniature depicting an Indian minting scene, seventeenth or eighteenth century. Two moneyers are hand-striking coins in the traditional manner. One holds the punch die while the other prepares to strike it with a hammer. Struck coins are on the floor, and blanks are placed in a tray ready for striking. Two officials check the weight of the coins, while attendants hold bags of coins or store them in a chest.

188 Copper half anna of the British East India Company, Bengal Presidency, minted in 1781 by John Prinsep at his machine mint at Falta, 35 kilometres outside Calcutta. The inscriptions state that the coin was struck in 1195 (AD 1780/81), year 22 of Emperor Shah Alam II. This coin was valued as legal tender at $\frac{1}{32}$ of a silver rupee or 160 cowries, but, unable to compete with the cowries in local currency, it ceased production in 1784.

John Prinsep, for example, were struck in the name of the Mughal emperor Shah Alam II (1759–1806). So pervasive and lasting was the influence of the Islamic tradition established by the Mughals that the British had to adapt themselves to its system in order to maintain a successful coinage.

Money and the state

The wholesale adoption of the Mughal system meant that the East India Company was not identified in any way as the issuing authority on its coins. This might appear somewhat surprising, accustomed as we are to the practice of modern states which clearly express their sovereign monetary authority through the choice of appropriate designs on coins and banknotes. But the situation in early nineteenth-century India was very different, in three ways.

First, the company's coins were not those of a sovereign nation as such, but were manufactured by a private merchant and issued by the British government for circulation in India through the agency of its trading company. Second, by this period the Mughal Empire itself had largely been divided up into foreign possessions and princely states, and coin production was no longer solely in the control of the emperor. And yet, to be acceptable in most areas, coins still had to bear the name of the current Mughal emperor, Shah Alam II. Coins were issued by many different states, but the presence of the Mughal emperor's name was considered a necessity if they were to act as coinage. The relationship between political authority and coin design was therefore quite different from what we might expect. Third, coin circulation and use were not controlled either by the Mughal emperor or by the actual issuer, but were in the hands of the *shroffs*, the local moneychangers. These important merchants specialised in the buying and selling of coins and regulated the use of money in virtually all payments. When John Prinsep first made his coins in 1780, there are thought to have been between thirty and forty thousand shroffs working in Bengal alone. Whenever large payments were being made, they were asked to examine each coin, to identify its place and time of issue and to assign the discount appropriate to the type of coin, together with a further discount if the coin was worn. Without the expertise provided by a shroff it was impossible for coins to circulate. This was one of the main problems addressed in 1833 when James Prinsep was advocating reform. Old coins issued in the name of Shah Alam II's predecessors could only be used at a large discount, with a loss of value often over 10 per cent.

John and James Prinsep's intention was to transfer control over the monetary system from the native shroffs to the company. Furthermore, in the local mints of the princely states merchants were invited to buy the right to coin from the local ruler, and many of the coins they made were commissioned from them by other merchants. The merchants who ran the mints often had the freedom to

189–91 Silver drachm of Piruz, Sasanian emperor of Iran, AD 459–84, and (*below*) two Indian imitations with stylised copies of the portrait of Piruz. The dramma of the Chaulukya kings of Gujarat, seventh to eighth century (*left*), has no inscription, but the dramma of the Pratihara kings of central northern India, eighth century (*right*), adds in Nagari script the honorific name of the Hindu god Vishnu, 'Sri Vigraha'. Piruz coins were originally brought into India by the Huns. Local rulers in western India were still making coins with the stylised Piruz portrait design until the thirteenth century.

adjust the silver content and weight standard of the rupees they struck in response to market forces. This activity was one of the main causes of the proliferation of the three hundred rupee types recorded by James Prinsep.

When the early Mughal emperors had begun to issue coins in the sixteenth century, a different attitude to the state's role in coinage applied. As Islamic rulers, they saw the right to issue coins as an important symbol of their political authority. Traditionally two events marked the accession of a new Islamic ruler: *khutba*, the inclusion of his name in the public prayers at the mosque each Friday, and *sikka,* the right to issue coins and place his name on them. Islamic custom was thus substantially the same as the attitude towards the political implications of coin design in nineteenth-century Britain. Accordingly, James Prinsep's new rupee coinage of 1835 prominently depicted the portrait and name of the British king William IV on the obverse, to be replaced by those of Queen Victoria on the next rupee coinage in 1840.

The traditional Indian attitude to the concept of the royal right to issue coins was apparently very different, as we can see from the coins themselves. It was clearly not thought necessary in India for coinage to express the identity of the issuing authority. Consequently, coinage in India did not serve as a symbol of state authority, as it generally had in both Islamic and Western traditions. Conversely, the currency of coinage in general seems rather to have been guaranteed by its resemblance to a generally accepted prototype rather than by the authority of the state or ruler. This curious non-political attitude to coin design is best exemplified by the coinage of northern India from the eighth to tenth centuries.

During this period the dominant coinage in western India was an anonymous 189 dramma, with designs copied from Iranian silver drachms of the Sasanian king Piruz (AD 459–84). The coins simply bear a crude copy of the king's head on the obverse and an equally crude representation of a Zoroastrian fire-altar on the reverse. The original Persian inscriptions were not copied, and the dramma bear no indication of who issued them. Local stone inscriptions provide evidence that the Chaulukya kings of Gujarat had a mint and were therefore prob- 190 ably the issuers of these coins, but they were clearly unconcerned with identifying themselves on their coinage.

The Pratihara kings, who ruled central northern India and were the north- 191 eastern neighbours of the Chaulukyas, are also known from stone inscriptions to have issued coins. Modern research has identified as their coinage another kind of Sasanian Piruz imitation. These coins are clearly distinguishable from the western Indian versions because they are only found within the Pratihara kingdom and because their inscriptions name Indian divinities rather than the kings themselves.

Further to the east the regions of Bihar and Bengal were ruled by one of

India's most renowned dynasties, the Palas. This was a rich domain in which art and religion flourished, but to this day no coins issued by its kings have been discovered. It appears that from the seventh to the eleventh centuries the Pala kings did without coins. They must have been aware of the possibility of using them, as amounts of money are frequently found mentioned in the stone inscriptions of the region during this period, and coins were in use on its western borders in Pratihara territory and to the east in the kingdoms on the border with Burma, but they still refrained from their issue. They had clearly found a different kind of monetary system which suited them better than coinage, as, apparently, gold dust and cowrie shells (Hindi *kauri*) were used to make payments.

The Islamic invasion of 1205 under King Muhammad bin Sam brought gold and silver coinage back to the area. His Islamic successors in the east continued to issue coins with their names inscribed in Arabic, according to their custom, but the indigenous preference for cowrie shells as small change did not diminish. The issue of low-value copper coins in the area was rare, and even at the time of John Prinsep's 1780 coinage the use of cowries was still common. In the advertisement circulated by the Calcutta Administration announcing the issue of his new coinage, values were also given in terms of cowrie shells, at the rate of 5,120 cowries to the rupee.

Both the Islamic right of *sikka* and the European concept of coinage as a royal prerogative were alien to Indian practice by the medieval period. But the situation had been rather different in earlier centuries, as we see from the evidence of the *Arthashastra*, the only ancient Indian text that addresses the relationship between the state and coinage. The *Arthashastra* is a manual on statecraft attributed in its text to Kautilya, the chief minister of Chandragupta Maurya, Ashoka's grandfather (c. 310–285 BC), but it was probably compiled several centuries later. Nevertheless, it forms a valuable source for political attitudes in ancient India. The impression it gives is that kings in this period were deeply interested in their coin and monetary systems for their own benefit.

Money is understood by the author of the *Arthashastra* as an instrument by which the state secures income in order to establish stable government. The king should have one officer to make coins according to the official weight and quality standards and another to make sure that coins are used properly. The second officer can also allow others to make coins for a fee. The functions of coinage mentioned are for use in trade and for royal income, and the text makes it clear that the role of these officials is to secure income for the king. Income meant profits from trade conducted by state officers as a monopoly or fees and taxes paid by foreign traders. Royal income should include trade revenue, land taxes and fines. According to the *Arthashastra*, the king can only rule if he controls the state through his army, his officials and his treasury. He can only do this if his treasury is full so that he can pay his army and officials. The salary of each rank of soldier and official, from the commander-in-chief and prime minister down to spies and servants, is stipulated, and each of the king's officers has orders to fine people committing offences liable to deprive the treasury of income. 'Looking after income and expenditure in this manner, he does not suffer a calamity of the treasury and the army' (*Arthashastra*, 5.4.45).

For the author of the *Arthashastra*, this view, that money is primarily a means for the state to ensure sound and stable government, is ethically correct, and he contrasts his own ideas with those of a more mercenary teacher of statecraft:

> 'As between violation of property and physical injury, violation of property is worse,' say the followers of Parashara. 'Spiritual good and pleasures are rooted in money, and the world is tied up with money. Its destruction is a greater evil.'
>
> 'No,' says Kautilya. 'Even for a very large sum of money, no one would desire the loss of his life.'
>
> *Arthashastra*, 8.3.30–35

This understanding of money is very closely related to the ancient Indian concept that a good king ought to be prosperous in order to bring prosperity to his subjects. A sculptural relief from the Buddhist shrine at Amaravati (first to

192 Relief carving depicting the Indian idealised king, or *Chakravartin*, in his role as the source of national prosperity, causing coins to fall from the heavens. The coins to the right of the king are carved as a square, a circle and a triangle, reflecting the varied shapes of punch-marked coins. This panel is from the Amaravati Stupa, a Buddhist monument in southern India, second century AD.

193–5 Silver drachma of Apollodotus II, Greek king in the Punjab, first century BC, and two Indian drammas copying the Indo-Greek design. The dramma of Jivadaman, Shaka Satrap in western India, AD 197–8 (*left*) retains a semblance of the Greek inscription, but without meaning. The dramma of Chandragupta II, Gupta king of India, 376–414 (*right*), simply copies the satrapal version of the Greek original. Coins using this type of portrait were still being made by local kings in the Punjab in the eighth century AD.

second century AD), now in the British Museum, shows the same conception of 192 the relationship between the king and money: it depicts a supreme king, the idealised world-ruler, *Chakravartin*, scattering coins to his subjects.

This relationship is not apparent in the punch-marked coinage produced in the period when the *Arthashastra* was reputedly written. Later, however, the Greek use of royal portraits on coins was copied by the Kshatrapas and Satavahanas in western India on their dramma coinages (first to fourth centuries AD). On their coins with traditional symbolic designs they also adopted the Greek practice of marginal inscriptions giving royal names and titles. The Gupta kings of northern India (fourth to sixth centuries AD), who invaded and captured western India from the Kshatrapas, also issued Greek-style dramma coins 193–5 with stylised portraits modelled on those of the Kshatrapas. In their own territory they also issued coins reflecting Graeco-Roman attitudes to royal coinage. Their gold coins were modelled on those of the Kushan kings of the northwest, and feature the most splendid idealised depictions of Indian kings to survive from ancient Indian art, showing the king in a variety of postures but 196 always identifiable as the *Chakravartin*, with inscriptions to match. On one coin the king is replaced by the tethered horse symbolically sacrificed by Indian kings 197 who sought the status of *Chakravartin*. The iconography of these coins introduces a further element into our consideration of the meaning of money and coinage in ancient India, the significance of religion.

196 Gold dinar of Samudragupta, Gupta king of India, *c.* 335–70, showing the king killing a tiger. This represents the king as all-powerful, a *Chakravartin*, and the inscription states that he is 'valiant as a tiger'. (× 5)

197 Gold dinar of Samudragupta showing a tethered horse. The Gupta kings revived an ancient Hindu ritual which identified them as *Chakravartin*. A horse was released to roam for a year. Wherever it went was counted as part of the king's domain. At the end of the year the horse was sacrificed. The officiating priests, Brahmins, were given *dakshina*, a ritual payment of gold, probably in coins like this one. The Sanskrit inscription also refers to the *Chakravartin* status of Samudragupta: 'The king of kings, of irresistible prowess, having protected the earth, wins heaven.'

Money and religion

It has been suggested that one of the main reasons for the Gupta gold coinage was to enable the kings to perform the religious rituals associated with their role as *Chakravartin*. In order for an Indian monarch to perform the horse sacrifice and other rituals involved in establishing his identity as world-ruler, he had to make large payments to the Brahmin priests who conducted the ceremonies. In the traditional texts of the Hindu religion, the sacred *Vedas*, it is stated that priests are paid in gold. Perhaps this is not the only motivation behind their gold coinage, but it is clear that they were not issuing coins for the convenience of their subjects. In northern India they made little effort to issue coins for every-

198 Votive deposit and four copper coins from the Sonala Pind stupa, a Buddhist shrine at Manikyala in the Punjab (modern Pakistan), late first century AD. The reliquary, in the shape of a stupa, contained a small crystal vessel with a stopper, a sheet of gold marked with an inscription, four precious beads, a silver coin and a copper ring – the seven precious things normally buried with a relic, in this case a small piece of bone.

199 Relief of the Buddhist deities Panchika and Hariti, with their feet resting on bags of coins. Over the shoulder of Panchika, an attendant offers another bag of money. The statue was originally part of the Buddhist stupa at Takht-i-Bahi (in modern Pakistan), second to third century AD. Greeks living in the region would have recognised these deities as Hermes, the god of commerce, and Tyche, the goddess of good fortune, while on Kushan coins they were named as Pharro and Ardochsho, the Zoroastrian deities of royal good fortune.

day use; their copper coins are rarer than their gold issues, which are themselves uncommon.

The descriptions of gold paid to priests in the Vedic texts are the earliest references to metallic money in India, and it is significant that the earliest context for its occurrence is religious and social rather than commercial or political. These scriptures survived into the first millennium AD only through oral transmission, so their original date is uncertain, but they are generally thought to have been composed in the late second to early first millennium BC and to have been contemporary with the Iranian *Avesta*, a comparable body of texts.

The gold mentioned in the Vedic texts is either of unspecified form or in the shape of a neck ornament called a *nishka*. Typical payments are royal gifts of 100 up to 40,000 nishkas to poet-priests. The Vedas and later legal texts, such as the *Laws of Manu*, also refer to payments and valuation in terms of cattle, a custom paralleled in the *Avesta* and in certain early Greek and Roman texts.

Fees to priests could be in cattle or in nishka and cattle. Such practices cannot be verified from archaeology, and the texts do not provide accurate enough descriptions of the form of the nishka to identify them among the few surviving examples of prehistoric gold jewellery from northern India.

The nishka as a unit of gold money continued to be used into the historical period and reappears, with the name *nikkha*, in the *Jatakas*. These religious texts were composed during the period from the fourth to the first century BC and recount legends of the earlier lives of the Buddha. The nikkha seems to have been used in payments to teachers and in ransom payments, but not in commercial transactions. This may perhaps reflect the bias of the texts themselves rather than the full reality of monetary usage in ancient India. Nevertheless, it reveals the genuine importance of non-economic cultural factors in determining attitudes towards the function of money within Indian society, in particular in relation to religion and ties of social obligation.

Money and the market-place

The majority of occasions on which monetary payments are mentioned in the *Jatakas* involve religious or social payments. There are, however, about twenty references to commodity purchases, suggesting that by the second century BC market transactions were becoming normal. What was the relationship between religion and the market in ancient India? A story from the Kshatrapa territory in western India during the first century AD provides some evidence. Rsabhadatta, the son-in-law of the Kshatrapa king Nahapana (*c.* AD 40–78), recorded in two stone inscriptions at Nasik that he had given a cave to a community of monks and bought a field for 4,000 karshapanas, so that the food from it would feed the community. He also donated 2,000 karshapanas for their benefit. The money was to be deposited with the guild of weavers in the city of Govardhana, who would pay 1 per cent interest per month to buy clothes for the monks. This story perhaps suggests that religion and money had a less troubled relationship with one another in ancient India than, say, in the Islamic or Christian worlds.

One of these inscriptions also records a payment of 3,000 head of cattle by Rsabhadatta to the priests as the fee involved in his ritual purification after battle. The survival of cattle payments is not surprising, as ancient Indian rulers were enthusiastic in maintaining the antiquarian traditions recorded in the Vedic texts. The term *dakshina*, still used in India for the fee paid to priests for performing religious ceremonies, originally meant 'a cow on the left', that is, a cow set aside for the priest.

Both the accounts of buying and selling in the *Jatakas* and the complex deposit and interest arrangement made by Rsabhadatta demonstrate that major commercial transactions in ancient India could be conducted with money.

Trade also had an impact on developing the complexity of monetary practice. For instance, the *Cullaka-Setthi Jataka* story illustrates the extent to which money was considered to have penetrated all levels of society, and suggests the range of activities that could involve monetary payments, together with various sorts of payment in kind. It tells of a young man's rise from rags to riches. First he found a dead mouse and sold it for a copper coin to a tavern to feed its cat. He used the coin to buy molasses and sold sweetened water to flower pickers, who paid him in flowers; then he sold the flowers and used the proceeds to repeat the bargain until he had 8 karshapanas. His next venture was to gather firewood, using children paid with molasses, selling the wood to a potter for 16 karshapanas and some pots. He then returned to selling water, this time to grass-mowers, taking payment in bundles of grass which he sold on for 1,000 karshapanas as fodder to a horse trader. His business activities were now on a grand scale and he hired a carriage for 8 karshapanas and went to the port where he used credit to buy the cargo of a newly arrived ship. When the usual merchants arrived to buy the cargo, they had to buy it through the young man, who thereby raised 200,000 karshapanas.

This parable is reported in the *Jatakas* as told by the Buddha himself, and shows clear approval of the actions of the young man: 'With the humblest start and trifling capital, a shrewd and able man will rise to wealth.' There was, however, a diversity of attitudes towards money and wealth in Buddhism. In its earliest teachings to the monastic community, the *Vinaya*, Buddhist teaching strongly condemned contact between any member of the community and gold and silver above the value of a quarter karshapana.

As a result, it was the followers of another Indian religion who apparently learnt from the Buddha's lesson. The Jains, followers of Mahavira, the Buddha's contemporary, took on the role of India's bankers. From the twelfth century we hear of the exploits of wealthy Jain bankers. As well as lending money, they were also experts in exchange and played a similar role to that of the shroffs who controlled money in the time of the Prinseps. In the fourteenth century the Delhi Sultans relied on their Jain bankers to organise army pay in remote regions. One Jain moneychanger, Thakkura Pheru, was employed as mint master by three successive sultans, and a record of his valuations of all coins current in northern India in 1318 has survived.

The biography of Banarasi Das (born 1586), a Jain merchant during the early Mughal period, shows how information such as that compiled by Thakkura Pheru was put to use. As a child of eight Banarasi Das's father was sent to school to learn 'the art of testing precious metals such as gold and silver for impurities. He became skilled in distinguishing good coins from bad and was efficient in drafting bills for the family business of money lending.' Banarasi Das also tells us that his father kept his money buried underground and that when he was old

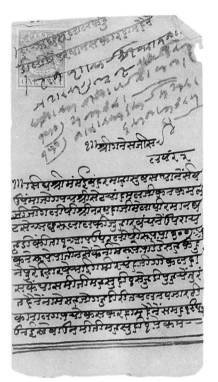

200 A hundi (a native bill of exchange) requesting a payment of 300 rupees, made by a Bombay merchant in the late nineteenth century, with a revenue stamp of Queen Victoria for one anna (one-sixteenth of a rupee). (× ½)

enough to enter the family business his father gave him a bill, known as a *hundi*, for 200 rupees to enable him to borrow money and start trading in another city. In wording it was a very polite request from a banker in one city addressed to another in a distant city to pay money to the bearer of the hundi.

Like the bill of exchange in European banking, the hundi remains in use in India to the present day, even though the resources of modern banking are available for most commercial transactions. The traditions of native banking are preserved to maintain the strong family connections still involved in business.

Although hundis were widely used in the early nineteenth century, they were soon replaced as the most widely used form of bank money by the introduction of British style banknotes, issued by the Bank of Bengal and its predecessor the Bank of Calcutta. From 1806 to 1815 they issued more than 20 million rupees' worth of notes. Soon other European-style banks joined in the issue of notes until the Imperial Government took over the role of note issuer in 1861.

The spread of Indian monetary systems

The strong and unified traditions shaping the history of money in India have carried the Indian monetary system beyond the subcontinent. Northwards, Indian-style coinage was carried into Central Asia. In the period of Greek and nomad rule in the north-west, the regions now represented by Afghanistan and its northern neighbours were part of a geographical unity. Kushan coins, for example, have been found at sites excavated in Uzbekistan and Chinese Central Asia. Trade also carried Kushan coins as far as Iran, Iraq and Ethiopia.

In Tibet Chinese authors report the use of silver money ingots from the fifteenth century, but coinage was not used until the sixteenth century, when coins copied from Indian issues entered from Nepal. During the late nineteenth and early twentieth century the British Indian rupee became very popular in Tibet and the neighbouring area of western China, prompting the Chinese mint at Chengdu in Sichuan Province to make imitation rupees for trade across the Tibet border. British Indian rupees also strayed into China's Yunnan Province and its southern neighbour, Burma.

Burma was not unfamiliar with Indian-style coinage and the king of Burma had commissioned the Calcutta Mint to strike rupee-sized coins for him in 1796 and to sell him some coining machinery to continue their production. These coins recalled an earlier expansion of Indian-style coinage, as their designs were

Ingot currency in South-east Asia

Silver ingots

The issue and use of coinage in mainland South-east Asia, introduced from India during the seventh to eighth centuries, had disappeared by the eleventh century. The Burmese and Thai peoples who came to dominate the mainland during the eleventh to thirteenth centuries brought new monetary traditions based on the use of silver ingots into the area.

Burma

There is little evidence, other than from inscriptions, of the types of ingots used by the Burmese before the seventeenth century when European travellers and traders began to describe the use of ingots cast by merchants, weighed out in payments according to standards regulated by royal decree.

Thailand

Three different types of silver ingot were used as money by the Thai people. The ingots normally had stamps to indicate the authority responsible for their regulation. They were all bar-shaped, but in different regions they were given a particular form: a flat bar in Laos, a bent ring in northern Thailand, and bent into a sphere in southern Thailand. The sphere-shaped ingots were issued and used as though they were coins.

201f Silver bullet coin of the southern Thai city of Sukhotai, sixteenth century. (× 2)

201d Silver bar from Laos, eighteenth century.

201a Silver snail-shell ingot from northern Burma, nineteenth century.

201b (*below left*) Silver flower-pattern ingot from Burma, eighteenth century. According to Alexander Hamilton, a British traveller (1688–1723), flowered silver was the currency of the city of Pegu, made by merchants under licence from the king.

201e Silver bent ring of the northern Thai city of Chiang Mai, sixteenth century.

201c Bronze official weight in the form of a mythical lion, eighteenth century. A flower-shaped royal mark was stamped on the base of each weight (J. Cribb).

201g Porcelain token valued at 1 silver salung, issued by the Lifa gambling house, Bangkok, mid-nineteenth century. The inconvenience of using ball-shaped coins in the Chinese gambling houses of Bangkok prompted the introduction of ceramic tokens, made in China. (× 2)

201h Tin crocodile-shaped ingot, Pahang, eighteenth century. (× ½)

Tin ingots

Chinese accounts of the Malay Peninsula report the use of tin ingots as money during the fifteenth century. Many of the ingots which survive are in the form of animals. In the Pahang Sultanate pyramid-shaped ingots became popular, and in the nineteenth century versions of them were made to circulate as coins. These coins had the shape of the ingots, but were hollow, earning them the name of 'tin hat money'.

201i Tin cockerel-shaped ingot, Pahang, eighteenth century.

201j Tin hat-shaped coin, Pahang Sultanate, valued at 4 cents, issued about 1890.

202 Silver tanka of the Pyu kingdom of Shrikshetra in central Burma, eighth century. The back shows the Indian *shrivatsa* emblem representing the Hindu goddess Shri. It contains a mountain representing the Hindu god Shiva and is flanked by the conch of the god Vishnu and the thunderbolt of the god Indra, with sun and moon symbolising the heavens and a wavy line symbolising the ocean. Silver coins with *shrivatsa* emblems were issued by various kingdoms from south-eastern Bengal to Thailand, and circulated further east into Cambodia and Vietnam until the tenth century.

copied from an earlier coinage issued in Burma more than a thousand years before, in the seventh century, which had been modelled on base-gold coins from Bengal. Burma had rich resources of silver, and accordingly the use of Indian-style silver coinage spread from Burma to Thailand, Cambodia and southern Vietnam, wherever Indian religion and culture had been adopted. The Indian coinage tradition was dominant in South-east Asia until the eleventh century, by which time Burma and Thailand had been overrun by migrant peoples from south-western China, who imported their own monetary traditions. The Indian tradition of gold and silver coinage also spread to the area of present-day Indonesia and the Philippines from the ninth to the thirteenth centuries. Stone inscriptions in Java provide plentiful evidence of monetary transactions from this period, such as religious offerings and land purchases, which use Indian monetary terms.

In the modern period the influence of Indian custom on surrounding regions has been equally strong. The success of the rupee, particularly after its standardisation following Prinsep's reform in 1835, prompted many other regions to circulate this Indian denomination. In the eighteenth century rupees were already being issued in Burma, Afghanistan and Indonesia. To the west the rupee became the standard unit of currency in the Persian Gulf and in southern Arabia (Oman and Aden). As British imperial expansion brought parts of East Africa into the empire (see fig. 303), rupees also began to be used in Somalia and British East Africa, with a rupee coinage struck for Mombasa in 1888 and the rupee adopted as the standard denomination as far south as Natal in South Africa. Italian Somalia and German East Africa also issued their own rupees and Portuguese Mozambique countermarked British rupees for local use.

Conclusion

During the early years of the present century, as a consequence of its adoption by Western imperial powers, the Indian coinage system achieved its most widespread use in all the lands which border on the Indian Ocean. But this was merely the latest in the long series of foreign influences on India's money which had such profound effects on the monetary history of the subcontinent. Despite India's susceptibility to invasion and cultural influence from without, the distinctiveness of its traditions is clear, both in the coinage itself and in the

other aspects of monetary practice we have looked at, and particularly when contrasted with its most immediate neighbours in the Islamic world and China. We now turn to China, to look at its long and independent tradition of money and coinage.

203 Silver tanka (reduced weight) of the Mon kingdom of Dvaravati in central Thailand, ninth century. The back shows a *shrivatsa* emblem containing Indra's thunderbolt, flanked by an elephant goad and flywhisk, symbols of kingship.

China and the East

They asked, 'Why must you die?' He replied, 'My death is fated by heaven, but I have been cheated by Lu Jin. Previous to this, when we were bargaining over the price of the ox, did we set the price in heavy silk or in silver?'

YUAN HAOWEN (1190–1257), *Accounts of Yijian, continued*

Small, round bronze coins with a square hole in the middle are instantly recognisable as coins of East Asia. The basic design of this tradition of coinage originated in China in the fourth century BC and became a familiar form of currency over a vast geographical area, stretching from China to Central Asia, Japan, Korea, Vietnam and South-east Asia. Hoards of these coins have also been found, showing trading links with the Middle East, South Asia, Australia and Africa. The latest coins to be made in this form date to the early twentieth century, when a more Western style was adopted, with pictorial images in place of the square hole, on struck, rather than cast, coins. The East Asian coins in circulation today look like modern coins found all over the world, yet the distinctive form of the traditional East Asian coins, known by Chinese writers as 'little brothers', has persisted over two thousand years to remain to this day a popular form for amulets and temple souvenirs.

The origins of money and development of coins

The earliest record of money in East Asia is found in the *Guanzi*, or *Book of Master Guan*, attributed to a Chinese minister who died in 645 BC, although it was compiled over six centuries later (*c.* 26 BC):

> The early kings put a value on things from the farthest distance that were difficult to find. They saw pearls and jade as superior money, gold as medium money, and spades and knives as inferior money. You cannot wear money but you can be warm; you cannot eat money, but you can fill your belly. The early kings amassed stores of wealth with which they ruled the people, thereby bringing peace to the world.

Rare natural products, grain, cloth, animals, ornaments and metals were exchanged from the earliest times. Certain items, such as cowrie shells, were regarded as symbols of wealth, and Chinese inscriptions from about the thirteenth century BC refer to cowrie shells as treasures being used as gifts. But the first pieces that can be called 'coins' and were used as a means of payment 204 are the bronze spade and knife money, issued in the late seventh or early sixth century BC by the Zhou kings. They are approximately contemporary with the first coins in the West, which were discussed in the first chapter. They

The development of bronze money in East Asia

Phase 1: When coinage was invented by the kings of the Zhou state in the late seventh or early sixth century BC, China consisted of several independent states. By the time of the violent Warring States period (475–221 BC) all the states were issuing shaped money, in the form of knives or spades, imitation cowrie shells, or round discs with a hole in the centre. The next three major phases of development all coincide with strong rule over a unified empire, by the Qin, the Han and the Tang dynasties.

Phase 2: The Qin state established supremacy in 221 BC and made its own money standard throughout the new empire. It was round with a square hole in the centre and had a two-character inscription reading, from right to left, *banliang* ('half-ounce'). The form of Chinese money was now established, but the actual weight of the banliang coin continued to vary.

Phase 3: The Han state replaced the banliang with the wuzhu ('five grain') in 118 BC. The form of the coin was advanced by the addition of outer and inner rims on the obverse and reverse. The wuzhu was the major coin type for over 700 years.

Phase 4: In AD 621, three years after the founding of the Tang dynasty, the wuzhu was replaced by the Kaiyuan tongbao ('new beginning, circulating treasure'). The new dynasty had a new style of inscription: no longer did it refer to weight. Instead, it was expanded to four characters, two indicating the period of issue and two indicating the concept of money for circulation. The Tang dynasty was a golden age in China's history and, as China's influence grew, neighbouring countries began to issue their own coins imitating the Tang coins. The earliest was the Wado kaiho ('beginning treasure of the Wado period') issued in Japan in AD 708. *Wado* means soft copper, and was used in the coin inscription following the important discovery of copper in Musashi (modern Tokyo). In Central Asia the Jianzhong tongbao ('circulating treasure of the Jianzhong period') was issued in Xinjiang (Chinese Central Asia). These coins were made as a new issue of the Jianzhong reign period (780–83) by loyal officials in this region during its isolation from the rest of China. They apparently did not know that although there was a new reign name, no coins with this name were being made elsewhere. Local Central Asian imitations of this coin were also made, both in Xinjiang itself and in Sogd (modern Uzbekistan). During the Song dynasty (960–1279), China's coinage in the Tang style continued to spread throughout the Far East, with the Thaibinh hu'ngbao ('beginning treasure of the Thaibinh period') coin issued in Vietnam in AD 970, and the Haedong t'ongbo ('circulating treasure of Korea') issued in Korea in AD 1097.

PHASE I

204a Bronze spade money from the state of Zhao.

204c Bronze round money from the state of Wei.

204d Bronze imitation cowrie money from the state of Chu.

204b Bronze knife money from the state of Qi.

PHASE 2

204e Bronze banliang coin issued during the Qin and early Han.

PHASE 3

204f Bronze wuzhu issued by the Han emperor Wudi from 118 BC. (✗ 2)

PHASE 4

204g Bronze Kaiyuan tongbao coin of the Tang dynasty, AD 621. (✗ 2)

204h Bronze Wado kaiho coin of Japan, AD 708.

204i Bronze Jianzhong tongbao coin of Xinjiang, AD 780–83.

204j Bronze local imitation of the Jianzhong tongbao coin, with the single character, 中 Xinjiang, late eighth century.

204k Bronze coin of Sogd, with a Sogdian inscription, in the shape of a Chinese coin, eighth century.

204l Bronze Thaibinh hu'ngbao coin of Vietnam, AD 970.

204m Bronze Haedong t'ongbo coin of Korea, AD 1097.

205 Bronze knife money and stone mould of the Warring States period (475–221 BC). Like the contemporary spade coins, and later cash coins, knife coins were cast in moulds. The moulds could be made in stone, clay or in metal. The inscription on this knife coin identifies it as 'legal money of Qi', i.e. the state of Qi in north-east China. (× ¾)

were modelled on agricultural tools, but made to a much smaller size, of thinner metal and with an inscription indicating a clan-name, place-name or weight. Within three hundred years most states in China were issuing spade coins, except for Chu in the south which issued bronze money in the form of cowrie shells, and Qi in the east which issued bronze money in the form of knives. In the third century BC Qin shi huangdi unified the Warring States, and made the existing Qin currency the standard throughout the new Qin empire. This was a round coin with a square hole and a two-character inscription, *banliang* (literally 'half-ounce' in weight).

The *banliang* survived, albeit in coinages of varying weights, until 118 BC when a new and historically important coin type was introduced by the Han emperor Wudi. The Han coin, with the inscription *wuzhu* (literally 'five-grain' in weight), was used widely in the interior of China, and followed imperial expansion far off to the border regions. The *wuzhu* continued to be the major coin type after the demise of the Han

206 Bronze coins of the Eastern Han dynasty (AD 25–220) and later, found at the ancient site of Rawak, Xinjiang. In the north-west of China, archaeologists have found wuzhu coins corroded together on a string. When separated, the corroded coins proved to be standard wuzhu coins, good local imitations, sub-size imitations and clipped wuzhu coins.

207 Bronze Sino-Kharoshthi coins from Khotan, Xinjiang, first century AD. Chinese tradition met Western tradition in the form of the Sino-Kharoshthi coins of Khotan. These coins had a Chinese inscription on one side stating the denomination in terms of weight (6 grains or 24 grains: the equivalent of the north-west Indian drachm and 4 drachm respectively), and an Indian (Kharoshthi) inscription giving the name of the king around an image of a camel or horse on the other. This example is a bronze coin of Gurgamoya, king of Khotan, mid-first century AD. The obverse Indian inscription identifies the coin as an issue 'of the great king, king of kings, king of Khotan, Gurgamoya'. The reverse inscription is in Chinese: 'Copper coin, weighing 24 grains'.

dynasty, when the empire fragmented into a number of smaller states (AD 220), some of which continued to issue coins. Only when the empire was unified once more at the end of the sixth century did the Tang emperor Gaozu declare the wuzhu obsolete, replacing it in AD 621 with a new coin design, the *Kaiyuan tongbao*.

The new coin was still round with a square hole, but where there had formerly been an inscription indicating the weight, usually in two characters, there was now a four-character inscription indicating the period of issue and designating the coin as money. Thus, the new inscription reads from top to bottom and from right to left around the hole: *Kai yuan* (literally 'the new beginning') *tong bao* (literally 'circulating treasure').

The influence of the Tang Empire (618–907), the 'Golden Age', is renowned worldwide and was phenomenal throughout East Asia. Chinese culture, including coinage, spread throughout the region. The first Japanese coins were made in 708, the first Vietnamese coins in 970 and the first Korean coins in 996. All are modelled on the Kaiyuan and, significantly, all their inscriptions

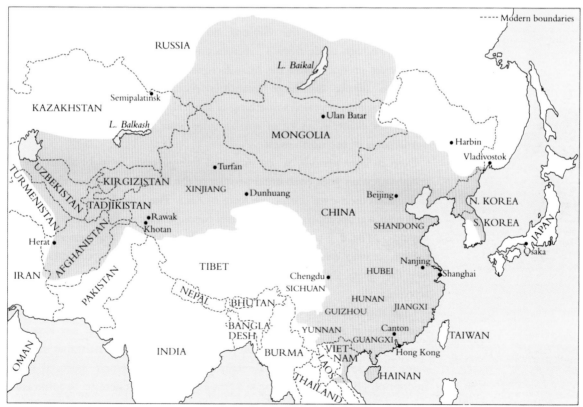

208 The Tang Empire, AD 669.

are written in the Chinese script, which had been adopted for official use in these countries. The physical form of Chinese coins was also adopted in Central Asia, but the legends were written in a different script.

The Kaiyuan became the model for all East Asian coins until the expansion of the coins of European nations, particularly in the nineteenth century. The last coins to be made in the East Asian tradition were the imperial *Xuantong tong-bao* ('circulating treasure of the Xuantong reign', China 1909–11), the republican *Minguo tongbao* ('circulating treasure of the Republic', China 1912), and the *Fujian tongbao* ('circulating treasure of Fujian', China 1912); in Japan, the *Bunkyu eiho* (1863–7); in Korea, the *Sang p'yong t'ongbo* ('circulating treasure of the stabilisation', 1633–1887); and in Vietnam, the *Baodai thongbao* ('protect the great, circulating treasure', issued by the French from 1926 to 1945).

209 Gold imitation of a Byzantine coin, sixth century AD. The archaeologist Sir Aurel Stein found this imitation used as a personal ornament on a corpse excavated from a tomb at the Astana cemetery near Turfan, Xinjiang. (× 2)

The form of the East Asian 'cash', as these coins are known, thus persisted for two thousand years. Although the Chinese knew of Western coins made of precious metal and with pictorial images on them – Byzantine gold solidi and Sasanian silver drachms have been found in China – such coins have been discovered mostly in tombs or in the western regions. In ancient China, before the appearance of coins, bronze was regarded as a precious metal and was particularly used for making highly elaborate ritual vessels for ancestral worship on the part of kings and dukes. The choice of bronze as the appropriate material from which to make coinage may have cultural associations, however ancient, with the religious and social prestige of these early bronze vessels. Though made from a precious and highly regarded metal, coins had to be mass-produced and the manufacturing process needed to be simple in order to supply the huge quantities required throughout the empire. Archaeology has revealed something of the scale of coin production in ancient China: for example, 45 kg of wuzhu coins were found at a single site in the borderlands of the north-west.

Even in later periods, when increased foreign trade brought about greater communication with coin-using peoples of the Western tradition, the Chinese maintained their own distinctive form of coin. The low-denomination bronze cash coin was appropriate to its primary function: to circulate and to be used in payment. The day-to-day business of 'stinking coppers' was generally left to merchants who were often despised as amoral for seizing opportunities wherever they arose, and as long as the monetary system worked, there was no need to change it.

Gold and silver were occasionally used to make coins. The first coins made in Japan were of silver, but very soon these had to be made in less expensive bronze. The discovery of copper in Japan in 708 was so important that the reign name was changed to *Wado* (literally 'soft copper'), which appeared in the inscription (*Wado kaiho*) on Japan's first copper coins. There were some issues

210 Coin tree, early twentieth century. Until the late nineteenth century Chinese coins were cast in moulds rather than struck. Master coins were used to make impressions in sand moulds. The moulds were stacked together and molten brass was poured into the openings. The brass flowed along the gullies between the coins, thereby making the tree. Once cooled, the coins were normally broken off the tree and their edges filed down to remove traces of the gullies. The coins on this tree are 10-cash coins of the Guangxu period (1875–1908) from the Board of Revenue Mint, Beijing, cast c.1905. (× ⅛)

of Chinese gold and silver coins, but these were mainly presentation pieces for those working at the imperial court and were not intended for circulation.

Coin design

'In one coin we can see both heaven and earth': the shape of Chinese coins was symbolically very important. In ancient times the Chinese believed that the earth was square and heaven was domed. Heaven communicated with earth through the Mandate of Heaven and its agent, the emperor, who governed and issued coins for the people. In making coins that reflected the shape of both heaven and earth for the people, the emperor was thereby completing the symbolic link between the two regions. A number of ritual objects, such as the jade *cong*, also employ the same round and square features in their design. From Han times onwards (206 BC to AD 220), ancient Chinese philosophy also centred on the *yin-yang, wu xing* theory. Coins were regarded as perfect in the terms of this theory, each one having two sides (*yin* and *yang*) and embodying the five directions (*wu xing*): north, south, east, west and centre.

But the square hole was also functional, both in manufacture and in circulation. Thousands of coins were cast at once in multi-layered moulds, and when the finished coins were removed the rough edges had to be smoothed down. A four-sided metal rod was pushed through the square holes to hold the coins in place, thereby making filing quicker. Once the coins had been issued for circulation, the hole allowed them to be used threaded together in strings of 100 or 1,000 coins.

The inscriptions on coins are important, as they indicate the reign period, the value and sometimes the range of circulation. The basic unit of account is called *wen* in Chinese, *mun* in Japanese and *mon* in Korean, which are different pronunciations of the same character, meaning 'writing', used in all three languages. The Western term for East Asian bronze coinage, 'cash', has no connection with Chinese tradition, as it is derived from the Indian word *karsha*, meaning 'copper coin'.

Inscriptions on Chinese coins were written in the traditional calligraphic styles and generally belong to one of the four main scripts: pattern, clerk, seal 211–13 or running. Chinese historical records often name the calligrapher who designed the inscriptions, especially when they were in the emperor's own hand. Calligraphy is one of the highest art forms in East Asia, and in the Song dynasty (960–1127) famous calligraphers such as Ouyang Xiu and the poet Su Shi were invited to provide calligraphy for coin inscriptions. The Huizong emperor provided the calligraphy for the coins he issued. As the Kaiyuan coins show, the Chinese script was known and used throughout East Asia.

Subtle differences, easily overlooked, were sometimes made to a character to indicate the place of manufacture, and small identifying marks were often added

211–13 Bronze coins of the emperor Huizong of the Song dynasty (1101–25). Huizong is renowned for his attention to the arts, in particular for his 'slender gold' style of calligraphy. The emperor himself supplied the calligraphy for many of the coins issued during the five periods of his reign. He was in his early twenties when he wrote the inscription for the Chongning coin (*left*), almost thirty when he wrote for the Daguan coin (*centre*), and by the Xuanhe period he was over forty (*right*). The two characters *tong* and *bao*, usually found to right and left of the hole on each coin, show especially well how the bold tension of the early calligraphy gives way to a gradual softening and roundedness over these twenty years. (× 1½)

to the front or back of a coin. Chinese legend has it that one of the first of these small marks was a fingernail impression by the most famous concubine, Yang Guifei, during the Tang dynasty. The most obvious marks are those found on the reverse of coins, in particular the mint names given in Manchu and Chinese scripts on coins of the Chinese Qing dynasty (1644–1911). In Korea a very elaborate system of markings was developed for the Sang p'yong t'ong bo coins mentioned above. These coins had a blank reverse when first issued in 1633. Then, in 1678, when authority to issue coins was given to over fifty different offices, the first or second character of the name of each office was put on the reverse, and from 1742 furnace and series numbers were also added.

The Six Dynasties period in China (AD 222–589) was a watershed for calligraphy in coin inscriptions. Before this time, seal script alone was used on coins, whereas afterwards other scripts were used as well. During the Six Dynasties Chinese art was heavily influenced by Buddhism from India and Central Asia. Its effects can be seen in the curving strokes in the calligraphy on *Xiaojian sizhu* coins ('four-grain coins of Xiaojian'), which have been compared with the human figures in flowing robes and ribbons found in Chinese Buddhist wall-paintings of the period. In a sense, Buddhism was also partly responsible for the beginning of coinage in Japan: the tremendous Japanese interest in Buddhism and demand for Buddhist statues, bells, etc. from the mid-sixth century AD onwards led to an increase in communications with China of all kinds, and coins proved to be a more convenient means of payment than the traditional Japanese custom of making payments in rice.

It should be clear by now that, unlike Western coins, traditional Chinese coins did not bear any form of pictorial image. The inscription formed the design and the means of identification. In the early history of Chinese art there is an absence of representations of royals and nobles. Indeed, the first portrait to appear on an East Asian coin was that of Sun Yat-sen, the first President of China, on the dollar coins of Nanjing made in 1912, the year the Republic of China was founded. That the Western tradition of ruler portraits had been resisted for so long is vivid testimony to the continuity and integrity of the Chinese monetary tradition.

214 Silver Chinese good luck charm, nineteenth century. This charm, representing a coin resting on a silver ingot, wishes the owner long life, riches and honour. The holes around the edges indicate where it was once joined to a chatelaine, from which tweezers, ear-scoop, toothpick and tongue-scraper may once have hung.

The use of money

After their invention, coins became an important form of money in ancient China, and they served a wide variety of monetary functions. Much as in the West, coins were used in commercial transactions, and prices for goods were commonly expressed in terms of coin. The Chinese imperial histories make special mention of prices at times of exceptionally good harvests and in times of shortage, such as droughts, floods or during wartime, when prices were unusually high or low. Although the '1-cash coin' remained the basic denomination in East Asia, its purchasing power varied over time and according to local circumstances. The recorded prices for horses, for example, show a considerable variety. In the Han dynasty (206 BC to AD 220), a horse cost around 4,500 cash; in AD 636 (Tang dynasty) around 25,000 cash; in the Northern Song dynasty (960–1127) 20,000 cash; during the Mongol Yuan dynasty (1206–1367) about 90,000 cash; and in 1362, in the early Ming dynasty, 10,000 cash. Other evidence, however, suggests that payment for horses could actually be made in a medium other than coin. A horse in the Western Han dynasty (206 BC to

AD 24) could be exchanged for three head of cattle; in AD 653 (Tang dynasty) for two head of cattle; in 1362 (Ming dynasty) for one head of cattle. It is possible in any context that the practical realities of buying and selling lying behind the literary evidence for prices stated in coin did not always involve the use of coin. But the common existence of a money of account expressed in coin denominations is in itself evidence of the importance of coins in commercial transactions.

Although the state took on general responsibility for money and coinage, the earliest coins in China were not issued by central government but by private enterprise, and even in later times local and private manufacture of coins was sometimes encouraged. As long as the coins were up to weight people would trust them and it was not so important who issued them.

> The law requires that those publicly hired to do so use copper and tin [i.e. bronze] to make coins. Those who dare to adulterate them with lead and iron for their illicit profit, should be punished by tattooing of the face.
>
> Treatise on Food and Money in the *Hanshu* (History of the Han)

Naturally, illegal private casting happened when it was profitable. During the Xianfeng period (1850–61) when 1,000-cash coins were issued, a forger could make easy money: there was enough copper in one thousand 1-cash coins to make thirty 1,000-cash coins. Even in less extreme circumstances, local and private casting made it difficult to achieve a true standardisation of coins, and for some types, e.g. the Song dynasty *Yuanfeng tongbao*, there are hundreds of variations. This flexibility between central and local, official and private continued: the Qing government (1644–1912) even made use of the remittance facilities offered by the Shanxi banks. These were private banks whose status was enhanced by government patronage, and which were at one time the main medium of interprovincial trade.

This regional factor is crucial to understanding Chinese monetary history. Even the Kaiyuan coins of the Tang dynasty were cast and issued regionally. In Song times some provinces used bronze cash coins, others iron, some both bronze and iron. The local currency was often determined by the economic strength of the region. For instance, it was in the interests of a fertile and wealthy province, such as Sichuan, to have a different currency from its poorer neighbours, so that it could control the flow of its coins outside its borders.

Coins were not always the sole form of money. In China, Korea and Japan cloth and grain also played key monetary roles. Silk, especially, was a measure of value and a means of payment, as well as a store of value. For example, during the Tang dynasty the Chinese monetary system was based on a dual coin–textiles standard, and the price of rice, as well as debt contracts, was calculated in numbers of rolls of heavy silk cloth. In 734 the government ordered that purchases of manor houses, bondservants and horses should be made solely in silk or cloth, whereas all other goods costing at least 1,000 cash could be bought in cash or goods.

Another important function of money was for the payment of taxes. Here, too, coins were by no means the only acceptable means of payment. Taxes were also payable in textiles and grain. In Japan taxes were still being paid in rice up to the time of the Meiji restoration (1868). In the Chinese Qing dynasty, silver was made the medium for tax-payment, indicating its increasing role in the Chinese monetary system. From the Tang dynasty until the twentieth century silver ingots were the predominant form in which precious metal circulated as money in China and, especially in the eighteenth and nineteenth centuries, they were the most important medium of payment for large transactions. The ingots 215 passed as a bullion currency, with the value determined at every transaction between payer and payee as to the fineness and weight of the silver, as described by J. R. Morrison in 1834:

> The refined silver is cast into ingots, and stamped with the names of the 216–21 banker and the workmen, the year and district in which it is cast, and sometimes the kind of tax for which it was to pay. Should any deception be afterwards discovered, at whatever distance of time, the refiner is liable to severe punishment.
>
> J. R. MORRISON, *Chinese Commercial Guide* (1834)

215 Shroff at work at the Shanghai Office of the Hongkong and Shanghai Banking Corporation, 1936. The Hongkong and Shanghai Banking Company (Corporation from 1866) opened in Hong Kong and Shanghai in 1865 with branches throughout the Far East. Silver was the main means of payment for large transactions in China at that time, and shroffs were employed by the Bank to test the fineness of the silver. Here, the shroff is examining a case of 50-ounce Shanghai City '27' ingots in the vaults of the Bank's Shanghai branch.

216–21 Silver currency ingots from different regions of China, 1840s–1930s. As well as being the main form of currency, by the end of the late nineteenth century silver was also used for paying taxes. People would take their silver bars, dollars or jewellery to a silversmith to have them cast into ingots. The smiths cast and stamped the metal in such a way that the fineness of the silver would be immediately recognisable to the public assayer. Different shapes and sizes of ingots were made in each region of China. (All × ¾)

218 Sichuan Province certified ingot: 11-ounce local tax ingot cast by smith Xing Yonglong, dated 1883.

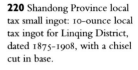

220 Shandong Province local tax small ingot: 10-ounce local tax ingot for Linqing District, dated 1875-1908, with a chisel cut in base.

216 Yunnan Province 3-stamp remittance ingot: 4.5-ounce bank ingot of the Tongfusheng Bank.

217 Hunan Province square trough ingot: 10-ounce local tax ingot cast by smith Qian Gongshen, Liuyang county.

219 Shanghai City '27' ingot: 50-ounce bank ingot cast for an unidentified bank at foundry no. 9 by smith Gong Chengchang, with black assayer's mark in ink on face. This is the type being checked by the shroff in **215**.

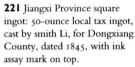

221 Jiangxi Province square ingot: 50-ounce local tax ingot, cast by smith Li, for Dongxiang County, dated 1845, with ink assay mark on top.

Foreign silver coins and silver trade dollars, issued by Western nations specially for use in East Asia, were also treated as bullion:

> It would not be so bad if this tinkering and tampering with the money circulating was confined to foreign coins; but as we have seen, the Chinese constantly 'chop' and frequently break any silver coin or dollar which comes into their possession.

> W. F. SPALDING, *Eastern Exchange, Currency and Finance* (1918)

Chinese handbooks exist with crude drawings of these and other foreign coins, with notes as to their fineness, and examples such as Mexican dollars (known in Chinese as 'eagles') with Chinese chop-marks stamped into them have survived.

222–6

222 Moneychanger's handbook from south-east China, printed in 1836. This handbook is filled with sketches of coins, detailed drawings and notes to help the moneychanger recognise foreign silver dollars in circulation in south China. This page illustrates a Mexican dollar, of the type issued by the Republic of Mexico from 1825 until 1909, known to the Chinese as the 'eagle' coin.

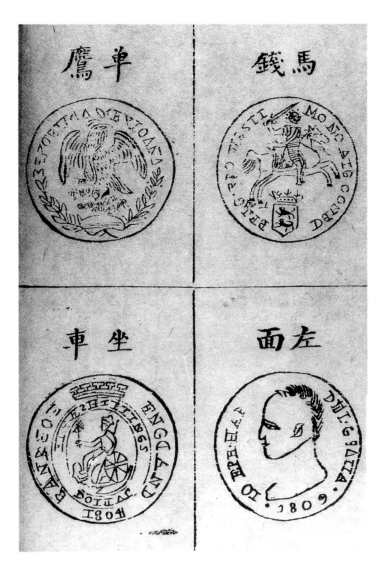

223 Mexican silver dollar taken from circulation in China. Mexican dollars and other foreign silver coins were treated like any other kind of silver in China. This example has been 'chopped' to indicate that a Chinese money-changer has checked it to ensure it is solid silver, because of the high incidence of plated forgeries in circulation. (× 1½)

224 Plated copy of a Mexican silver dollar collected in Shanghai in the 1930s. This forgery was made by a highly technical method known as electrotyping. An outer skin of silver was made in two halves by electro-plating, and this was then filled with a tin core and soldered together. (× 1½)

226 Silvered cardboard 'eagle' made for offering to the ancestors at Chinese New Year, for use in the other world. (× 1½)

225 Mexican dollar adapted to perform the traditional role of silver as a wedding gift; the red character 囍 wishes for 'double happiness'. (× 1½)

Paper money

Of the iron coins used in Shu [Sichuan], the larger weigh 25 catties per thousand, and the middling ones weigh 13 catties per thousand. Carrying them on a journey is inconvenient. Therefore, the certificate of account of those times arose from the inconvenience of iron coins, because their weight kept them from being carried along with one. The exchange note system arose from the initiatives of the people, and was entrusted to the officials so that it could be maintained.

MA DUANLIN (*c.*1228–1322), *Investigation of Literary Documents*, quoting Lü Zuqian

The Chinese scholar Peng Xinwei suggested that the following factors led to the development of paper money during the Song dynasty (960–1279). When the Song dynasty opened up 'free markets', commerce developed and there was a greater demand for money in circulation. But China was divided into regions using different, sometimes incompatible currencies. Some regions even forbade the export of bronze coins. Paper money, in the form of exchange notes, was a way of solving this problem of interregional exchange. Moreover, a number of the regions were using large, low-value iron token coins, which were very inconvenient to use in great numbers. Foreign military pressure during Song times was also stretching government finances; paper money could be used to supplement official expenditure.

Prices soon came to be expressed in terms of paper money, and bronze coins virtually became a commodity. Furthermore, as sales of tea and salt were very profitable, the vouchers that merchants received as proof of payment of tolls on the way to the capital for redemption at the tea and salt warehouses themselves became a form of money. All these early forms of paper money were privately issued remittance, credit or exchange notes with a date limitation. The first paper money as we know and use it today (i.e. officially issued exchange notes, with no date limitation) were the Exchange Certificates issued by the Jin in 1189. During the Mongol Yuan dynasty (1206–1367) paper money was used exclusively, as gold and silver as well as copper cash were not permitted in circulation. It was during this time that Marco Polo wrote his famous account of Chinese paper money:

When these papers have been so long in circulation that they are growing torn and frayed, they are brought to the mint and changed for new and fresh ones at a discount of three percent. If a man wants to buy gold or silver to make his service of plate or his belts or other finery, he goes to the Khan's mint with some of these papers and gives them in payment for the gold and silver which he buys from the mint master. All the Khan's armies are paid with this sort of money.

The Travels of Marco Polo, trans. R. E. Latham (1958)

In the thirteenth century the Mongols subjugated Korea and forced paper money on the region. It is an interesting point that, while the Mongols were successful in issuing paper money where cash coins had previously been in use, their attempts to circulate paper money in western countries, such as Iran, were not so effective.

The effect of the growing acceptance of paper money in China was to drive cash coins out to Japan, Korea, Vietnam and South-east Asia. In 1074 the ban on exporting Chinese coins was lifted (previously export of even one string brought the death penalty):

> Since 1074, when the new regulation was issued, and the old one forbidding removal of coins was abolished, heavy carts have gone out through the frontier passes, and heavily loaded ships have returned from overseas. I have heard that when coins are being exported, the border areas simply collect a tax on each string. Officials everywhere are involved in secret departures.

LI TAO (1115–1184), *Long Summary of the Comprehensive Mirror to Aid the Government, continued*

The greatest demand for Chinese coins came from Japan where, by the late tenth century, people had lost confidence in Japanese coins, preferring to use imported Chinese currency. With extensive official and private importing going on, often involving an illicit trade conducted by pirates, it was difficult for the Japanese government to maintain its authority over money. In 1179 the government tried to fix prices in terms of Chinese coins, and fourteen years later, in 1193, they were forced to ban all use of Chinese coins, since they could not control the amount and types of coins in circulation in Japan. By the early fourteenth century some of the Japanese purchases of Chinese coins were being paid for by shipping swords and sulphur to China in a form of tribute trade.

The export of coins to Japan and elsewhere also had repercussions in China: in the Southern Song period (1127–1279) prices expressed in paper money increased, and it became profitable to melt down copper coins to make objects such as copper utensils and musical instruments. The reduced quantity of copper coins of this period also reduced the purchasing power of paper money.

When the Korean Yi dynasty copied Chinese Ming dynasty paper money in 1401, the effect was disastrous. Once again, paper money drove coins out of circulation, mostly to Japan, and the Koreans had to resort to using cloth as money.

Amulets and money not for use

Coins in East Asia have often been used for purposes other than strictly monetary. This aspect also deserves a brief mention in a history of money, as it serves to illustrate something of the broader cultural context within which coins circulated in China and East Asia.

Certain types of Chinese coins were regarded as lucky, and the historical facts associated with the inscription in each case explain why these types came to be used as lucky charms. A good example of this interesting phenomenon is the *Zhouyuan tongbao* coins from the late tenth century, which still survive in large numbers. The original Zhouyuan coins were finely made from bronze taken from the statues of over three thousand Buddhist temples. Their inscription

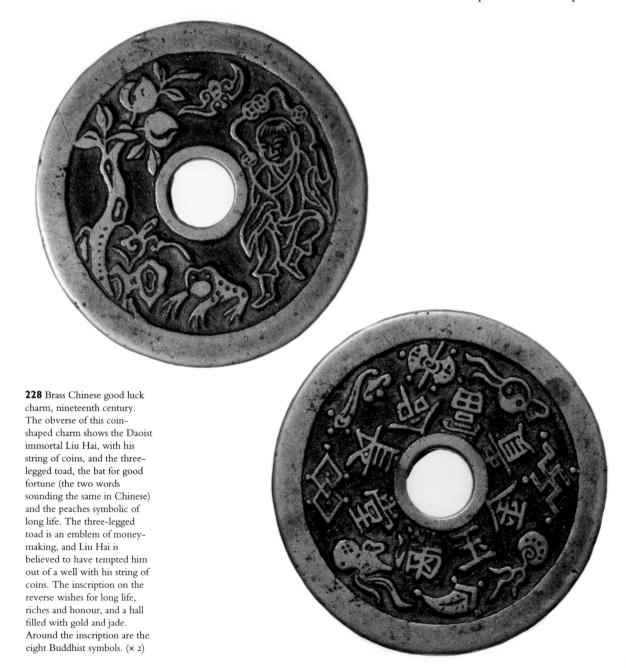

228 Brass Chinese good luck charm, nineteenth century. The obverse of this coin-shaped charm shows the Daoist immortal Liu Hai, with his string of coins, and the three-legged toad, the bat for good fortune (the two words sounding the same in Chinese) and the peaches symbolic of long life. The three-legged toad is an emblem of money-making, and Liu Hai is believed to have tempted him out of a well with his string of coins. The inscription on the reverse wishes for long life, riches and honour, and a hall filled with gold and jade. Around the inscription are the eight Buddhist symbols. (× 2)

152

literally means 'everywhere – new beginning, circulating trea-sure', and they were issued in the Xiande reign, which means 'noticeable virtue'. People believed that these coins could help cure illness and aid in childbirth, and they became so popular that they were extensively copied later.

Good luck charms (with inscriptions or pictures) were made for all kinds of purposes: for New Year, weddings, long life, 214, 228 baby's first bath; coin-shaped pieces were also used for playing chess, gambling and in drinking games. Other coin-shaped 230 charms were used for exorcism. In ancient times coins were also 209 placed in tombs for use by ancestors in the next life. Whenever this practice was condemned, imitation money 226 was used instead. Millions and millions of imitation paper dol- 231–4 lars are still burnt at celebra-tions of Chinese New Year across the world.

229 Gold presentation piece of the Heaven and Earth Society, nineteenth or twentieth century. This coin-like piece, issued by a Chinese secret society, is full of codes and symbols and many of the characters have hidden meanings. Two of the characters on the reverse were designed to be unintelligible to non-members. The character at the top is made up of abbreviations of the society's motto 'Obey Heaven and Follow the Way': 川大丁首 expands to read 順天行道. The character at the bottom expands to read 忠心義氣 ('faithful in heart, loyal in spirit'). (× 3)

230 Coin sword, made with brass coins of the eighteenth century tied to an iron rod. Coin swords were used to drive away evil spirits and illness. Coins issued by the Kangxi emperor (1662–1722) were thought to be most effective, as the reign name Kangxi implies good health and the Kangxi emperor himself reigned for a full sixty years. The Qianlong tongbao coins on this sword were issued by his grandson, the Qianlong emperor (1736–95), who also reigned for sixty years. (× ⅓)

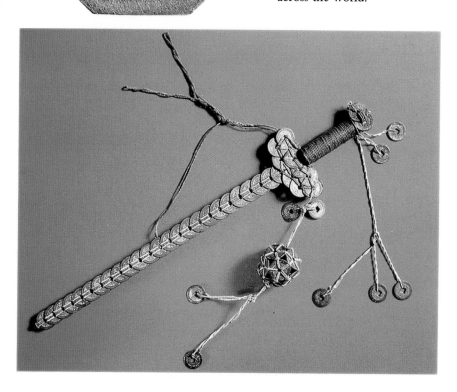

HELL BANK NOTE

No.A15917248 冥通銀行 No.A15917248

伍仟萬

萬仟佰拾元

DOLLARS

50000000

FIFTY MILLION DOLLARS

50000000

地府銀充

HELL BANK CHEQUE

BANK OF HADES

冥天總充

HEAVEN MAIN OFFICE

日期
DATE:

收款人
PAYEE

前存 Last Bal	$	
存入 Deposit		
合計 Total		
支取 Drawing		
餘額 Balance		

支票號碼
Cheque No. 0550001

BANK OF HADES

冥天總充

HEAVEN MAIN OFFICE

19

STAMP DUTY PAID

新交
PAY

幣
DOLLARS

或持票人
OR BEARER

$

戶號
A/C No.

0550001

231–4 Money for the dead, 1970s–1990s. Every year millions of imitation paper dollars are burnt as offerings to the ancestors. Since the nineteenth century the paper dollars have taken the form of notes printed in the name of the Bank of Hell. To keep up with modern advances in the world of finance and banking, deposit accounts, cheque cards and cheque books are also offered. In the 1970s a Hong Kong printer of Hell notes added a satirical element to his products, replacing the portrait of the King of Hell with those of British, American, Russian and Chinese statesmen. (**231–3** × ½)

The discourse of money

Money is a spiritual thing. It has no rank yet is revered; it has no status yet is welcomed. Where there is money, danger will turn to peace and death will give life. Where money slips away, honour will turn to baseness and life will give death. They say 'Money holds power over the spirits' – if that is true, just think of its power over men!

LU BAO, *The Money God* (c. AD 300)

The discourse of money in Chinese monetary history has centred on two topics: first, the advantages and disadvantages of coins, whether they should be entirely replaced by useful commodities such as cloth and grain; and second, who should be allowed to issue coins, government or private enterprise. The debate is practical as well as ethical. Many Chinese scholars and officials wrote about their concerns over money, recognising that the circulation of money had the power to change human relationships and that money thereby had the potential to destroy the order existing in society. Those writers who opposed the use of coins and money tended to favour trade exchange in grain and cloth. Gong Yu (c. 45 BC) advocated the abolition of coins in favour of these:

Since the appearance of the *wuzhu* coins over seventy years ago, many people have been found guilty of illicit coining. The rich hoard housefuls of coins, and yet are never satisfied. The people are restless. The merchants seek profit. Though you give land to the poor people, they must still sell cheaply to the merchant. They become poorer and poorer, then become bandits. The reason? It is the deepening of the secondary occupations and the coveting of money. That is why evil cannot be banned. It arises entirely from money.

However, when coins were banned as a consequence of such moral concerns, problems arose from the use of grain and silk as money. The silk was woven so fine that it was of no use, and grain was sold wet, making it heavier and therefore more expensive, yet, like the fine silk, useless.

For Confucianists money itself represented neither good nor evil, and they believed that coins could, or even should, be cast by people other than the state. The Legalists, by contrast, being sceptical of human nature, believed that all issuing of money should be carried out by the state. The Legalist Jia Shan of the Han dynasty said in 175 BC: 'Coins are useless things, yet we can exchange them for wealth and honour. Wealth and honour are the staff of the Emperor, and if the people had them they would be equal with the Emperor. This should not be encouraged.'

Much later, during the nineteenth century, following two important wars against foreign powers (the Opium War and Sino-Japanese War), Chinese intellectuals were forced to consider Western economic thought and practice. In 1901 Yan Fu (1853–1921) translated Adam Smith's *Wealth of Nations* into Chinese. Yan disagreed with many of Smith's views, such as his labour theory of value. He believed rather that the value of goods was determined solely by the relationship between supply and demand, and he added notes to his translation to make clear his dissent from Smith's ideas: 'Value is a straightforward matter. Two nominally similar things are matched and numbered. If it is only a matter of the labour they contain, then things stand in isolation, and their value would not vary over time.' In 1892 Zheng Guanying (1841–1918) wrote his *Words of Warning to a Flourishing Generation*, in which he complained about the unfair practices of the foreign banks in China and encouraged the establishment of Chinese banks: 'As of now, the silver bills used by foreign merchants do not have their backing verified by either Chinese or foreign officials. They are made solely at the whim of their issuers, without regard to quantity.'

Modern money

In the nineteenth century, as the Chinese government struggled to maintain its hold on the monetary situation, issuing 1,000-cash token coins and paying its official salaries in non-convertible paper money, it is not surprising that more valuable foreign silver dollars were much sought after. By the mid-nineteenth century the Chinese were beginning to make their own dollars, albeit unofficially:

In the district of Shunteh, south of Canton, there is said to be a very large establishment, in which as many as a hundred workmen are frequently employed. Dollars are there manufactured of all grades of value. . . . These false coiners are said to possess European stamps, procured at great expense, but sometimes they attempt imitations, in which the omission or disfiguring of some letter betrays the deception to a European eye. So common, however, are their dollars in circulation, that men from this district are most usually selected as shroffs [moneychangers].

J. P. MORRISON, *Chinese Commercial Currency* (1844)

By the 1880s small silver 10- and 5-cent coins issued in the British colony of Hong Kong were flooding into south China. The Hong Kong government had been trying to encourage China to adopt the Hong Kong dollar as its national coin since the 1860s, proposing several different designs and denominations. Eventually, the Governor-General of Guangdong and Guangxi sought imperial permission to mint silver dollars on Western machinery. The new Western-style mint (with machinery and personnel imported from Birmingham) opened

235 Silver dollar of the Republic of China, struck at the Guizhou Provincial Mint in 1928. The design of the motor car commemorates the completion of the Guizhou provincial highway in that year. By the 1920s silver dollars were in use in most parts of China, but they were often produced locally. (× 2)

in Canton in 1889 to strike 5-, 10- and 20-cent pieces, half dollars and dollars – foreign denominations that brought yet more kinds of coin into the marketplace. The silver coins were treated as bullion, and the copper cents (10-cash pieces) as cash coins according to the current silver–copper price. An unexpected turn of events was that by the 1900s the Chinese authorities in Canton were selling their small silver coins at a discount, making it profitable to ship them into Hong Kong. The Hong Kong mint in the meantime had sold its machinery to the Japanese Osaka mint, and in the 1870s Japan issued its own silver dollars.

The influence of imported monetary systems in China increased as the nineteenth century progressed, particularly in the south, revealing the inability of the

China's first silver dollar notes

The Hu-peh (Hubei) Government Mint was established in 1893 by the brilliant Chinese statesman Zhang Zhidong (1837–1909). Zhang had opened China's first Western-style mint in Canton (Guangzhou) in 1889, with machinery and personnel supplied from Birmingham. That same year he was transferred from Canton to the city of Wuchang as Governor-General for Hubei and Hunan provinces, a position he held for eighteen years. On the strength of his successes with the Canton Mint and the profits its silver coins had brought to Guangdong province, Zhang submitted a proposal to the Qing court in 1893 requesting permission to open a new mint, the Hu-peh Government Mint, to make silver dollars. Permission was granted almost immediately, and the new mint was built on the site of the former Three Buddha Pavilion in Wuchang.

The Hu-peh Government Mint issued silver dollars, silver taels (Chinese ounces), standard cash and paper money. Its first paper money was in denominations of silver taels and strings of standard cash, but by 1899 there was an extreme shortage of standard cash in Hubei, and Zhang requested permission from the Qing court for the mint to issue notes denominated in silver dollars. Wang Bing'en, a former supervisor at the Canton Official Monetary Bureau who had come to work in Hubei in 1896, suggested that the mint should issue paper money dollars, and that they should be printed by the printing office of Japan's Department of Finance (Okura-sho). Zhang authorised the mint to order dollar notes from Japan to a face amount of 1 million dollars. This was his first attempt to create a circulation of dollar banknotes. Before placing the order in Japan, he gave Chinese engravers a chance to show him what they could accomplish, but their work failed to satisfy him. (Previously, as director of education in Sichuan in the 1870s, Zhang had set up a printing office for issuing the classics and dynastic histories.)

The dollar notes were successful. This was in part due to the mandate from the imperial court (printed on the reverse of the notes) which stated that the notes could be used in all official payments, including all taxes to the government, and that the notes would be redeemed for the silver dollars on demand at the Wuhan Government Monetary Office. Zhang's influence was far-reaching: his financial reforms more than doubled the annual income of Hubei from about 7 million taels in 1899 to 15 million taels when he left Wuchang in 1907. He was also a keen industrialist, opening an iron foundry and mine in Hubei as well as cotton mills, silk factories and tanneries, and it is largely due to his initiative that the Wu-Han cities of Hubei came to be known as the 'Chicago' of China.

236 Silver dollar note issued by the Hu-peh Government Mint, 1899–1909. The two dragons (symbol of the emperor) each hold the Hu-peh dollar, showing both front and back of the coin. The English and Chinese inscriptions are the same. On the Chinese side, the dragon is replaced with the inscription *Guangxu yuanbao* in both Chinese and Manchu. The five lines of inscription on the front of this note read:

A. (horizontal across top, right to left) *Guang xu yuan bao*, in Chinese, then repeated in Manchu script ('Guangxu period [1875–1908] original treasure')

B. (vertical, down right) *Hu bei yin yuan ju* ('Hu-peh Government Mint', literally, Hubei silver dollar office)

C. (vertical, down centre) *Pin piao qu yin yuan yi da yuan* ('With this note collect one large silver dollar')

D. (vertical, down left) *Lü zi di jiu bai wu shi hao* ('Serial no: Lü 950')

E. (horizontal across bottom, right to left) *Zhong ku ping qi qian er fen* ('Weight: seven mace and two candareens on the Treasury Scale')

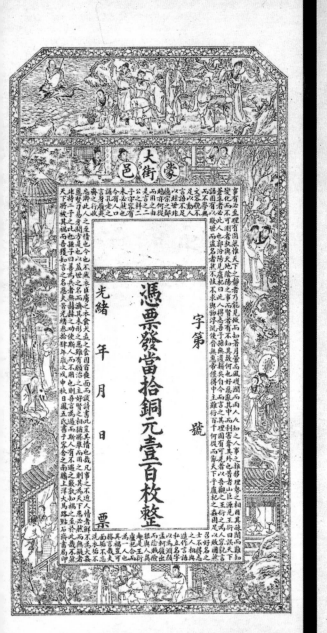

大街 蒙邑

憑票發當拾銅元壹百枚整

字第　　號

光緒　年　月　日

票

237 Trial printing of note for 100 copper cents, prepared for a private bank, probably in Shanghai, 1908. From the late nineteenth century many large and small private banks in China issued their own paper money, often with elaborate designs. This unissued note was designed at the famous Dianshizhai Studio, Shanghai, in 1908 by the little-known artist Wu Songqing. Surrounding the central panel, on which the name, serial number and date could later be completed, is a border of text taken from a famous piece of classical prose. Around the text is a 12 mm border containing miniature scenes from a traditional story. On the reverse Wu presents the story of a young scholar seeking romance in the temple grounds, presenting ten scenes in a space only 60 × 132 mm. (× ¾)

imperial government to counter foreign domination. It is perhaps no coincidence that the south was also the stronghold of the nationalist republicans who overthrew the empire in 1911.

After the First Opium War (1840–42) foreign commercial banks were established in Chinese cities, and many issued banknotes for use in China. Some, such as the Hongkong & Shanghai Banking Corporation, issued silver dollar and silver ounce banknotes; others, such as the Imperial Bank of Russia, issued notes in foreign units. Eventually the Chinese government saw the need to issue their own silver ounce and silver dollar denominated exchange notes and established the *Zhongguo tongshang yinhang* (the Imperial Bank of China) in 1897. Provincial official silver and coin offices also began to issue new-style silver dollar bills. In 236 addition to these notes, paper money was also issued privately by the old-style credit institutions, such as money shops and pawn shops, which had been issu- 237 ing paper money for centuries, and by larger mercantile establishments as well as governmental institutions such as the railway offices.

It is no wonder, given the sheer number of paper money issuers, combined with the silver–copper exchange systems that differed from region to region, that foreigners trying to work within China despaired of ever understanding how the money system operated. In the words of J. R. Michael, a speaker in a debate held by the Hong Kong Chamber of Commerce in 1903: 'I would ask what is the currency of China? Can anyone enlighten us?'

The Early Modern Period

The cause of the ruin of Spain is that riches ride on the wind, and have always so ridden in the form of contract deeds, of bills of exchange, of silver and gold, instead of goods that bear fruit and which, because of their greater worth, attract to themselves riches from foreign parts and so ruin our inhabitants. We therefore see that the reason for the lack of gold and silver money in Spain is that there is too much of it and Spain is poor because she is rich.

GONSALEZ DE CELLORIGO, *Memorial de la Política necesaria y útil a la República de España* (1600)

238 Silver testone of Galeazzo Maria Sforza, Duke of Milan (1468–76), showing the duke's portrait. Renaissance-inspired realistic portraiture, introduced to gold ducats of Milan in the 1460s, became the particular hallmark of the new large silver coins in 1474 with its use on this testone, the first Milanese lira. This coin set the pattern for the denomination as it spread through Italy and beyond. (× 1½)

In the later fifteenth century European money began a period of transformation stimulated by a trio of influences. First, the appearance of coin changed under the impact of artistic developments during the Renaissance. Second, new sources of bullion allowed the money supply to grow, with a range of consequences for prices, denominational systems and monetary use. Third, the European Age of Discovery (from which arose some of the new bullion supplies) opened up almost limitless scope for exploration, investment and exploitation and laid the groundwork for a worldwide economy.

Perhaps one should also add to these the impact of the Protestant Reformation, breaking the Catholic world-view and permitting, as it were, a new 'theology' of money to develop. Not that Protestantism was necessarily more of a friend to old-fashioned 'usury' than the Catholic Church. 'I want no shares! This is speculative money and I will not make this kind of money multiply' was Martin Luther's retort to an offer of shares in a silver mine. But around 1545 Calvin was to be more accommodating, though usury should still not offend against charity: 'God did not forbid all profits so that a man can gain nothing. For what would be the result? We should have to abandon all trade in goods.' Yet in many respects this argument had in practice long been won, and Catholic Genoa was to be as important as Protestant Geneva or Amsterdam in monetary and banking development, while on the other side the Dutch Calvinists inveighed against the evils of money-lending just as vigorously as did their Catholic counterparts.

New bullion, new worlds

From the 1460s Europe's silver production again took wing, with the Schwaz mine in Tyrol earning its ruler Duke Sigismund the nickname 'the Wealthy' (whereas his father had been surnamed 'the Penniless'), the mines of the dukes of Saxony at Schneeberg and later Annaberg enabling their owners to dine off solid silver tables, and St Joachimsthal (Jachymov) in Bohemia, discovered in 1512, outperforming them all (see fig. 109). The flood of silver stimulated new

239 Silver testoon of Henry VII, King of England (1485–1509). The testone's English equivalent was the testoon, the first shilling coin with the first realistic portrait on English coins. (× 1½)

240 Silver guldiner of Sigismund, Archduke of Tyrol, dated 1486, showing him flanked by a heraldic shield and a helmet. The rich veins of the Schwaz silver mines near Innsbruck first came to light in the 1470s; in 1482 Sigismund introduced his testone-like pfundner; in 1484 he added a half guldiner, worth half a goldgulden, and finally the guldiner of 1486. (× 1½)

241 Silver guldiner of Friedrich the Wise, Duke of Saxony (1500–1508), Annaberg mint. New silver mines in the Erzgebirge Mountains (at Schneeberg, Annaberg and Freiberg) allowed guldiners to appear in north Germany in about 1500, also bringing portraiture to the coinage there. The output of Annaberg quickly eclipsed that of Schwaz. (× 1½)

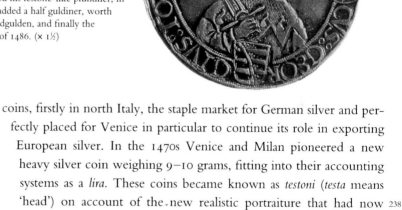

242 Silver thaler of Stephen, Count of Schlick (1505–26), St Joachimsthal mint. The Saxony mines were outproduced by St Joachimsthal, discovered in 1512, and the output of Joachimsthalers, introduced in 1519, was enormous. (× 1½)

coins, firstly in north Italy, the staple market for German silver and perfectly placed for Venice in particular to continue its role in exporting European silver. In the 1470s Venice and Milan pioneered a new heavy silver coin weighing 9–10 grams, fitting into their accounting systems as a *lira*. These coins became known as *testoni* (*testa* means 'head') on account of the new realistic portraiture that had now 238 entered coin design, and the type spread into Switzerland, south Germany, France and England. 239

Soon the silver issuers themselves made direct use of their resource, replacing small gold coins (florin or ducat equivalents) with large silver coins 240–41 of the same face value, usually around 30 grams in weight. One of these, the *Joachimsthaler guldengroschen* of the St Joachimsthal mine and mint, gave a generic 242 name to the new coin type: *thaler* (from which 'dollar' is derived). As the sixteenth century advanced, this development spread, increasing the range of silver coins to higher denominations, on top of which were added completely new and higher levels of gold denominations. Supplies of gold for this expansion came from West 245 Africa, as they had done for centuries, but in the later fifteenth century the Portuguese had established direct access through their explorations in the region.

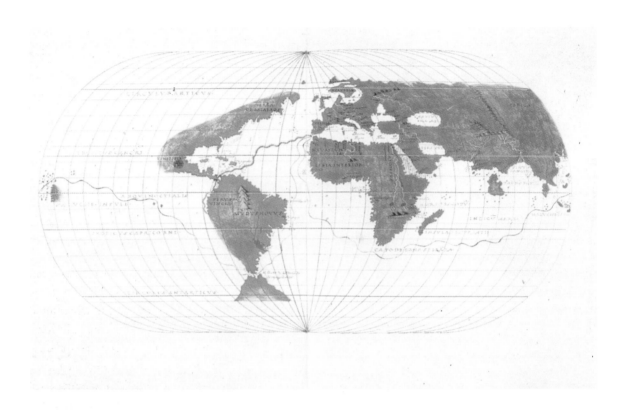

245 Gold cruzado of Joao II, King of Portugal (1481–95), showing a cross with the royal titles: King of Portugal, Algarve and Guinea. Joao II adopted the title King of Guinea in acknowledgement of one of the sources of his country's wealth – West African gold (× 1½)

243 (*left*) The world chart of Battista Agnese, 1536. This map, completed in Venice on 13 October 1536, shows the world as then known. The blue line tracks Magellan's circumnavigation of the globe, 1519–22, and the gold line illustrates the route by which the Spanish transferred gold from Inca Peru to Spain. This was to become the route used for transporting silver from Potosi (British Library).

244 (*left*) Detail of an elephant from a 5-guinea coin of Charles II, England, 1675. The guinea coin took its name from the Guinea of Africa, from where large quantities of gold were brought to England by the Royal Africa Company. The elephant on this gold coin indicates that West Africa was the source of the gold it contains.

246 Gold double excelente of Ferdinand and Isabella, monarchs of Spain (1474–1507). The coinage system introduced in 1497 provided the first national coinage for Spain, dominated in the sixteenth century by the ducat-sized gold excelente and its multiples. (× 3)

Thus they bypassed Italian and North African intermediaries and were able to produce their own plentiful ducat-equivalent *cruzados*. To this was added in the 243 same period the first fruits of the booty of the Americas, as the long-accumulated gold treasures of the civilisations of Central and South America were looted and shipped home to fuel the extensive gold coinage of early sixteenth-century Spain. 246

The real wealth of the New World, however, would be not in gold, but in silver. Just as output from Joachimsthal and Schwaz was flagging in the 1540s, silver deposits were discovered first in Mexico and then, greatest of all, at Potosi, the Silver Mountain itself, in Bolivia: 'Rich Potosi, the treasure of the world, the King of Mountains, and the envy of kings', as the motto on its coat of arms proclaimed. By 1600, this mining town in the mountains already had 150,000 inhabitants. The silver ingots were taken overland to the coastal port of Arica, where they were loaded onto the galleons of the Armada del Sur (Armada of the South) and shipped up the west coast of South America to the Caribbean via Panama, and from there to Spain. A flood of silver entered the currency systems of Europe, and indeed the whole world. Silver ingots and newly minted coin (mostly 8-*real* pieces, or pieces of eight, the Spanish thaler equivalent) 247 flowed into Spain in the later sixteenth and early seventeenth centuries, and almost as quickly flowed out again. In the last decade of the sixteenth century 2,700 tonnes of silver were imported into Spain. One important consequence of the new source of bullion was to undermine the prosperity of Germany, as its locally mined silver fell dramatically in price in the face of the rival source.

247 Silver 8 reales, dated 1653, of Philip IV, King of Spain, Potosi mint, showing the Pillars of Hercules and the motto *Plus ultra* ('There is more beyond'), symbols of Spain's empire. The 8 reales (piece of eight) was revived in the 1530s and came into its own as the first world trade coin in the late sixteenth century. Mints near the silver mines of Mexico and Peru produced huge quantities of these coins for export both to Europe and to the Far East. (× 1½)

A good portion of the American silver went to pay for the Habsburgs' ruinously expensive wars, directly to the armies or (more usually) to service loans from their bankers and creditors in Genoa, Antwerp, Augsburg and Portugal. Much also went to buy the goods the Spanish wanted which, ironically, were largely procured through the agency of their rebellious subjects the Dutch, who were then dominating the carrying trade of Europe and indeed much of the world. Nevertheless, it proved a resource that underpinned rock-solid credit for Spain through a succession of defaulted loans, technical bankruptcies, devalued currency and horrendous expenditure well into the seventeenth century.

American silver also went much further afield, passing through traditional channels into the Middle East, along with silver from the mines of Saxony,

248 Silver franc of Henry III, King of France (1574–89). The first silver franc was deliberately designed to absorb silver flooding into France from Spain's Flemish provinces. It was intentionally made of silver of the same standard as Philip II's daalders, for ease of reminting. (× 1½)

249 Silver piastra, dated 1579, of Francesco I de' Medici, Grand Duke of Tuscany (1574–85), showing St John the Baptist, patron of Florence. The quantity of silver in the later sixteenth century saw the eclipse of many gold coinages, including that of Florence. (× 2)

250 Silver thaler, dated 1649, of the Holy Roman Emperor Ferdinand III as king of Hungary, countermarked for Russia under Tsar Alexis I with the date 1655. Russian trade with the West brought in large silver coins, which were countermarked for local use until Russia began its own Western-style coinage. (× 1½)

Bohemia and Tyrol, and from 1565 across the Pacific on Spain's 'Manila Galleons' or 'China Ships' to the Spanish Philippines, where it was traded for goods from China and South-east Asia. In the seventeenth century, however, the supplies from the Americas to Spain gradually diminished, as mine output declined and more was retained for colonial use. But American silver remained significant right through the eighteenth century, when new discoveries and improved techniques revived its productivity.

Within Europe itself monetary boundaries were by no means fixed, any more than they had been in the Middle Ages. Foreign coin could often be an important element in the local currency, particularly when there was little local coinage produced or when a small-scale issuer bordered a more prolific and important neighbour. In sixteenth- and seventeenth-century Ireland, for instance, currency was usually a mixture of English, Scottish and other foreign (mostly Spanish) issues; in lesser Italian states such as Mantua, Modena or Lucca, 249 local coinage would be subordinated to Venetian, Florentine or papal issues; Venetian coinage dominated the Dalmatian coastline and its Balkan hinterland; in Russia Western coinage became increasingly familiar, with German thalers countermarked for use alongside the tiny local silver *dengi*; and Swedish and 250 Saxon coin dominated swathes of late seventeenth-century Poland.

Despite the overlapping circulation patterns of many individual coinages within Europe, confusion may have been more apparent than real. For instance, in the Holy Roman Empire, with its scores of autonomous coin issuers, the standards of the thaler were generally followed, apart from in parts of southern Germany which preferred the slightly smaller silver *gulden*. Thus coins of many issuers had the same standards of weight and fineness despite their different appearance.

States, coins and inflation

The growth in bullion supplies appears to be intimately entangled with the sixteenth century's most striking economic circumstance, the so-called 'Price Revolution', which saw inflation raise prices sixfold between about 1540 and 1640, little enough nowadays but bewildering to contemporaries. To put this in context, prices in 1500 were little different from those in 1300, while the century from 1650 to 1750 was also one of relative price stability. The precise role of bullion supplies in this has been contested, but the coincidence in time between inflation and the arrival of silver seems too great to ignore. The impact of these price rises was exacerbated by the failure of wage levels to keep up: in England, for instance, real wages may have been effectively halved between the late fifteenth and mid-seventeenth centuries. Furthermore, taxation undoubtedly increased in the course of the sixteenth century, becoming established as the prime means of providing for the running of the state, though in practice

the money it produced was spread among the political and financial elite rather than being spent on extensive state services.

The new bullion supplies had certain consequences for the coinage itself, in its denominational structure and its usage, two factors that were probably related. Firstly, there was a general expansion in the range of large and small denominations. In the later sixteenth century new, larger, silver and gold coins were introduced. Gold ducats and *scudi* in the Italian states gave way to silver *ducatoni*, scudi and *piastras*, with *doppie* (double ducats) increasingly the standard gold piece. Gold half-crowns and crowns in England were replaced by silver ones, with gold one-pound and thirty-shilling sovereigns at the top of the scale; the Spanish piece of eight and gold double *escudo* (doubloon) became internationally familiar coins, as did *daalders* and double ducats of the Dutch Republic in the seventeenth century. However, many states still produced gold coins equivalent to the Venetian ducat (from this time often called the *zecchino*, or *sequin*) for use in international dealings: these included the Dutch, the Swedes, the Danes and the Poles, the Holy Roman Emperor in Bohemia, Hungary and Austria, and many lesser German princes.

251 Triple unite, dated 1644, of Charles I, King of Great Britain, made at the Oxford mint during the Civil War and showing the king holding sword and laurel branch, offering war or peace. In the late sixteenth and early seventeenth century very large gold and silver coins were struck for many rulers, often intended for presentation purposes. (× 2)

252 Silver daalder, struck by the Dutch in Leiden when under siege from the Spanish in 1574, showing the city's shield with the legend 'God Preserve Leyden'. The production of special coinages in cities under siege was a particular feature of the sixteenth and seventeenth centuries.

The range of intermediate denominations within monetary systems also increased from the late medieval level of around six or eight to ten, twelve or more in most states. This development improved the flexibility of denominational systems in the market-place, indicating perhaps a serious growth in the level of daily transactions and immediate payments. In addition, older coins would sometimes remain in the currency, officially revalued or accepted on the basis of weight and fineness: in Stuart England, Second Coinage *unites* of James I, originally worth one pound (20 shillings), later circulated at 22 shillings, alongside the lighter unites of Charles I, which were worth a pound, while, during the rampant debasement and overissue of Spanish low denominations under Philip III and Philip IV in the 1620s and 1630s, older issues of 4 *maravedis* were revalued and countermarked to first 8, then 12 maravedis.

Despite the effects of inflation in the sixteenth and seventeenth centuries, the lower denominations in

253 Mining 4 thalers, dated 1662, of Christian Ludwig, Duke of Brunswick-Lüneburg, showing the white horse of Westphalia crowned by the Hand of God and hovering over a silver-mining scene in the Harz Mountains. The conical buildings housed horse-powered draining, lifting and ventilating systems. (× 2)

general survived and in fact became much more prevalent, suggesting that coin was being used more frequently in small-scale transactions by individuals. They were given a boost by the revival of coinage in copper, begun by Portugal, Venice and Naples in the late fifteenth century, then spreading throughout Italy, France, Spain, the Low Countries, Scotland and England by the early seventeenth century. Token coinage within a precious-metal system was difficult to manage, and it did sometimes lurch out of control through overissue and the effects of counterfeiting (considerable in both England and France in the early seventeenth century), which tended to drive out good money. Governments often struggled to contain it by demonetisation, by restricting circulation, by withholding status as legal tender (i.e. its acceptance in payment being voluntary not compulsory) and by crying it down (i.e. reducing the face value). But token coinage proved too useful to be abandoned. When England ceased to

255
256–7

The manufacture of coined money

The early modern period witnessed probably the most dramatic change in methods of coin production. In early sixteenth-century Europe the hand-striking techniques familiar since ancient times were still universal. By 1700 they had all but vanished, with the advent of a range of mechanised methods of manufacture.

Although early mechanised presses scored high in producing aesthetically pleasing coin, traditional methods, refined over centuries and well co-ordinated in factory-like mints, were often swifter and more accurate in providing coin to the correct standards. However, problems were gradually overcome, and the potential advantages of mechanised techniques could be demonstrated.

The preparation of blanks was aided by roller-mills which produced uniformly thick strips from which the blanks could be cut with metal punches. There were a number of ways in which the actual coin-striking process itself could be mechanised. One involved the use of dies with curved faces, either striking individual blanks (the rocker press), or striking onto strips of metal passed between paired rollers each engraved with several dies (the rotary press).

However, victory went instead to the screw press, which simply added motor force to the traditional way of striking between two dies. The power behind the new presses could be human, animal or water. The provision of power was the main remaining limit on mechanised productivity, and this was to be answered by the harnessing of steam power in the late eighteenth century.

254a Mint workshop, from the *Spiez Chronicle* of Diebold Schilling, Bern, Switzerland, 1486. At the back the correct alloy is smelted and cast into bars, which are hammered flat (left) so that blanks can be cut out with shears, stacked and hammered into a circular shape (centre foreground). The blanks are struck between two iron dies, impressing both sides of the coin simultaneously (centre left). On the right mint officials examine finished coins (Burgerbiliothek Bern, Mss. h.h.I.16, p.222)

254c Unfinished strip of English copper farthing tokens of Charles I (1625–49). The main early rival to the screw press was the rotary press. It could strike coin continuously in large numbers, cylinder dies impressing long strips of metal at a time, from which the finished coin would be clipped or stamped. Some of the greatest European mints employed this method, notably Hall in Tyrol and Segovia in Spain. In England the technique was used for the farthing tokens of the early seventeenth century.

254b Scenes from a stained-glass window depicting the Konstanz mint, south Germany, about 1624. The working of the Konstanz mint after mechanisation is depicted in a sequence of nine panels. The last three, illustrated here, show the screw presses being manually operated, the finished coin being tested for weight and fineness, and finally its issue from the mint (Konstanz, Rosgarten Museum).

254d A Boulton coining press in the Royal Mint, London, from the *Saturday Magazine*, 23 April 1836. In the late eighteenth century the engineer James Watt and the manufacturer Matthew Boulton applied steam power to coin production at their Soho mint in Birmingham. Their techniques and machinery were exported widely, and were applied at the Royal Mint in 1810. These first steam-powered presses simply added steam to the screw process. During the nineteenth century, lever presses would displace screw presses and steam eventually gave way to electricity.

255 Copper cavallo of Ferdinand I, King of Naples (1458–94). In the fifteenth century a few issuers replaced base-silver low-denomination coin with purely token copper pieces. Ferdinand I was one of the first, introducing the cavallo in 1472.

256 Copper double tournois, dated 1584, of Henry III, King of France. Henry III introduced copper coinage in 1575, combining the innovation with the use of new mechanised coining techniques patronised by his father, Henry II.

257 Base 4 maravedis, dated 1624, of Philip IV, King of Spain, countermarked to 12 maravedis. Despite the wealth of silver coming to Spain from the Americas, her expenses were equally huge. The government attempted to manipulate the currency, reducing the quality of the base-silver coinage and making it pure copper. This policy escalated, with even the older copper coin recalled and revalued upwards, flooding Spain with worthless money.

258 Copper private farthing token dated 1660, issued by John Morse of Watford (Hertfordshire) and showing the figure of Death (*mors*). Token small change was added to English currency under James I and Charles I, but huge overproduction and forgery caused these royal farthing tokens to be abandoned in 1644. Instead, for the next three decades small change was provided by tokens issued by thousands of private traders. (× 4)

produce royal farthings in the 1640s, thousands of private, local issues took their 258 place.

In any case, maintaining precious metal for lesser denominations did not of itself guarantee automatic stability. While ducat and thaler equivalents throughout Europe were generally maintained to standard, the temptation for rulers to overvalue and overissue lesser coins for profit or convenience was always there, regardless of whether these were base silver or copper. This occurred in Germany in the 1620s, the *Kipper- und Wippezeit* (literally 'clipper and see-saw time'), as princes debased for profit in the early years of the Thirty Years War (1618–48); and in Poland in the 1630s and 1640s, where local debasement was compounded by counterfeits produced at the Swedish-held towns of Ebling and Riga on the Baltic.

Despite all its problems, perhaps for the first time since the Roman period, low-denomination money was playing the role of small change in a way that would be recognisable today, making the daily use of coin for small-scale transactions feasible and gradually eroding the old systems of barter, offsetting of debts, payment in kind and petty credit. Wage labour was certainly continuing to increase, while rises in the urban population and growing population mobility also underpinned the enhanced internal monetisation of large areas of Europe. Furthermore, particularly in western Europe, industrial activity was beginning to create something approaching a mass consumer market. Physical coin was thus becoming an absolute essential for the day-to-day existence of an ever larger part of the population of Europe.

The source of most European copper was Sweden, especially the great Falun mine. Demand for copper, particularly for coinage, enhanced the Swedish royal revenues, contributing to the country's prominent political and military role in seventeenth-century Europe. To maintain copper prices at reasonable levels by absorbing enough of its own output, Sweden introduced a non-token copper currency, the famous plate money: sheets of copper were stamped with dies to 259 indicate their value in terms of silver *dalers*, with denominations ranging from 1 to 10 dalers. To cope with the practicalities of such a cumbersome coinage, Sweden made precocious use of paper money in the mid-seventeenth century. We shall read more of this important development later.

State expenditure was as affected as all other expenditure by the Price Revolution. State income, whether from direct or indirect taxes or other dues, could not be automatically raised: while taxation certainly became more regular, this trend could easily provoke constitutional crisis and rebellion. We may recall the important role played by the thorny question of taxation in the outbreak of the German Peasants' Revolt in 1525 and the English Civil War in 1642. Yet government was becoming more sophisticated (and hence expensive), and government service more wage-oriented. Above all, the costs of

259 Copper 8 dalers, dated 1658, of Carl x Gustav, King of Sweden. For the Swedish kings of the seventeenth and eighteenth centuries, utilising their rich copper supplies in a non-token coinage had the advantage of retaining stocks of metal in the country and thereby maintaining its international value. Enormous plates like this 8 dalers (28 × 65 cm, 14 kg) were inconvenient to use and encouraged the local popularity of early paper money. (× ¼)

261 Silver leeuwendaalder, dated 1604, of Holland, United Provinces, showing the lion of Holland. In the seventeenth century the mints of the Dutch Republic produced a number of different thaler-sized coins. Some were intended for foreign trade, including the leeuwendaalder, which became a popular trade coin in the Levant and Asia.

262 Gold ducat, dated 1675, of the city of Hamburg, showing the Virgin and Child. The production of gold coins to the standard of the ducat was widespread throughout the cities and states of the Holy Roman Empire from the mid-seventeenth century. The ducats were intended to facilitate regional and international trade in an area with a multiplicity of coin issuers.

260 (left) The Gold Weigher, Dutch, circle of Matthias Stomer, 1642. At first glance this appears to be simply a portrait of an old woman testing a gold coin, using a balance and weights. In fact, the picture is an allegory of avarice, personified by the old woman, in thrall to money, on her way to Hell, as indicated by the mocking young servant with his devil's horns (Kassel, Staatliche Kunstsammlungen).

warfare grew: wages, provisions and equipment all cost more, particularly with developments in artillery, while the scope of war also expanded, reflecting the European and worldwide interests of the Habsburg dynasty. To function, states needed credit as never before, and stable, long-term public debts were the answer, becoming almost universal by the end of the seventeenth century.

The resulting state loan stocks were traded as the objects of speculation in the Amsterdam stock market, which emerged in the early seventeenth century for trading in such government stocks and in shares in the Dutch East India Company. This was the most important of the bourses and exchanges which arose in the early modern period, the Dutch Republic in the mid-seventeenth century holding as much capital as the rest of Europe together, though by the end of the century London was to be its great rival. However, as the history of paper money was to show, it was not easy to disengage the money supply from the tight grip of bullion supplies, and the preference for hard money long survived.

The range of European currency systems expanded in line with commercial and colonial expansion. Capital was multiplied through investment in such ventures, and international coinages, not intended for domestic use, fuelled this trade. The Spanish piece of eight was joined by the trade coins of the Dutch Republic in the seventeenth century, its *leeuwendaalders* preferred in Asia and the Levant, its *rijksdaalders* in the Baltic, its gold ducats in Russia and its silver ducats in India and China. Exporting precious metal was an essential part of trade, particularly for the Dutch, despite the reputation of the seventeenth century as the great age of state bullionism. In the eighteenth century a third great silver coin joined the 8-reales piece and leeuwendaalder as international trade coins: this was the Austrian thaler, fossilised in appearance from 1780 as the Maria Theresa thaler, but in wide use in the Levant, Ethiopia and Arabia from the middle of the century onwards.

Meanwhile, European money and monetary systems began to be exported across the world. In Asia the Portuguese, the Dutch, the French, the English and the Danes all established stations and settlements to advance and safeguard their trade routes, and with these came Western-style money, mingling with and influencing local traditions. In the New World the exploding trans-Atlantic trade was mostly with European settlers exploiting directly the resources of a new continent. In Central and South America the Spanish set up mints near the principal mines, to turn some of the silver into coin for ease of shipment, and later opened other mints to serve the growing immigrant communities there. In North America and the West Indies the English and French colonies were less

263 Silver conventionsthaler, dated 1768, of the city of Nuremberg, showing a panorama of the city. Within the Holy Roman Empire coinages were usually aligned on thalers of common standards, one for northern principalities and another for Austria and the southern states. In 1753 the latter agreed a conventionsthaler standard based on the Cologne mark. (× 3)

264 Gold dobra, dated 1739, of Joao v, King of Portugal, Rio de Janeiro mint, Brazil. The Minas Gerais gold mines of Brazil were discovered in 1692–4. Two series of coins were struck in Brazil, one for internal currency and the other, based on the dobra, for international use. The dobra circulated widely in Europe in the early to mid-eighteenth century.

well served in the seventeenth and eighteenth centuries. With little local bullion to be converted into coin, they had to make do with a range of expedients – often Spanish coin, sometimes cut up, stamped, plugged or pierced – as the home governments were reluctant to send precious-metal coin out of the home country.

As American silver production waned in the mid-seventeenth century, the balance between gold and silver in currency gradually shifted back in favour of gold, particularly from the 1690s, when gold from Portuguese Brazil began to make a significant impression alongside silver from Spanish Mexico, which, however, remained plentiful (more silver was apparently recovered from Guanajuato in the eighteenth century than from Potosi in the sixteenth).

Local circumstances affected the ways in which different countries attracted and used bullion: in England for instance, due to its historical and maritime links with Portugal, gold dominated the currency and Portuguese gold coins themselves were in wide circulation, while silver from Spanish America came more plentifully to France. Overall there was much more bullion of whatever sort

265 Silver 'Lima' crown of George II, England, 1746. In July 1745 English privateers captured two French treasure ships returning from Peru. More than 78 tons of gold and silver bullion from the two ships was landed at Bristol and transported to the Tower of London, where it was used to produce coinage. The word 'Lima', added beneath the king's portrait, celebrates this exploit.

available in Europe in the late seventeenth and early eighteenth centuries than there had been in the sixteenth, but there was no equivalent shock in terms of price increases. Instead trade was becoming truly global and precious metals had a high purchasing power worldwide.

In the eighteenth and nineteenth centuries coin would be increasingly joined by paper in the provision of currency. However, for most people coin remained the normal medium for daily business, except under compulsion, and in any emergency would be the preferred option for hoarding and saving. The failed experiments in government-backed paper money in the early eighteenth century, which we shall move on to later, helped ensure that the official provision of money was usually focused on coin, dogged though this continued to be by problems of bullion supply, bimetallic tensions and the difficulty of ensuring adequate and trustworthy small change.

Paper money has already been mentioned as a new element in early modern Europe. It is now time to look in greater detail at the history of the introduction and spread of banknotes – generally unsuccessful at first, but soon, like copper small change in the seventeenth century, becoming a vital part of currency systems throughout Europe, and changing the way people in Europe used and thought about money.

Banknotes and paper money

The expedient, therefore, of symbolical money, which is no more than a species of what is called credit, is principally useful to encourage consumption and to increase the demand for the produce of industry.

JAMES STEWART, *An Inquiry into the Principles of Political Economy* (1767)

In 1690 the economist Nicholas Barbon reported that, for want of a public bank, 'The Merchants of London . . . have been forced to carry their cash to Goldsmiths, and have thereby raised such a credit upon Goldsmiths' Notes that they pass in Payments from one to another like Notes upon the Bank.' His words predated the foundation of the Bank of England by four years, but in fact neither paper currency nor banking was a new invention. Circulating paper money was introduced in China as early as the eleventh century AD and later government issues enjoyed prolonged popularity during the Yuan dynasty (1206–1367), while banking emerged as a specialised profession in Italy in the later thirteenth century, encouraging the use of bills of exchange and written instructions as means of payment. However, it 266 was not until the end of the seventeenth century that circulating notes and centralised banking, sometimes but not always in association, began to lay the foundation of the currency systems we take for granted today. Barbon was witnessing, and approving, the beginning of a revolution.

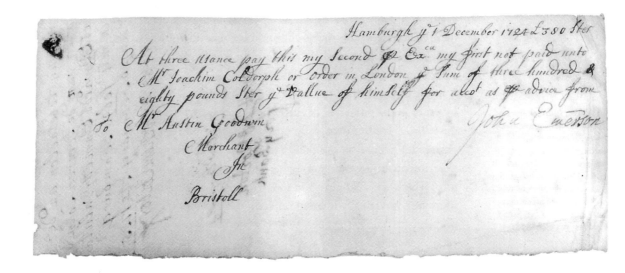

266 Bill of exchange, 1724, drawn by John Emerson in Hamburg on Austin Goodwin, a Bristol merchant, to pay £380 to Joachim Coldorph in three months' time. Initially developed by fourteenth-century Italian banking houses, bills of exchange have endured as a means of providing credit and of making payments across a distance. Written instructions to an agent authorise payment to a particular person at a specified future date. (× ⅔)

267 Request to pay £25 15s from an account held with Morris and Clayton, 'Scriveners in Cornhill', 1665. This handwritten document is a forerunner of the modern cheque. Sir Robert Clayton was one of the most eminent and successful scrivener bankers: he became Lord Mayor of London in 1679 and was a director of the Bank of England from 1702 until his death in 1707. (× ½)

Not everyone shared his enthusiasm, however; as with all revolutions, change came fitfully and often painfully. In Britain a variety of financial services were available from Elizabethan times, provided by merchants and scriveners who accepted valuables and money on deposit, giving notes in receipt. Scriveners 267 acted as legal and clerical middlemen, writing out bonds and contracts for trade; for them, as for merchants and goldsmiths, taking on more of the financial work was a logical extension of their business. By the second half of the seventeenth century goldsmiths and scrivener-bankers offered a wide range of banking services, including loans, interest-bearing deposits, foreign coin exchange, cheques and promissory notes. Clearly there was a demand for such facilities, but there were also dissenting voices. In 1676 an anonymous pamphlet was published on the *Mystery of the New Fashioned Goldsmiths or Bankers*. The writer deplored the goldsmiths' move into the 'unlawful practices' of lending money at high rates of interest, claiming that they would charge double or treble interest for discounting bills of exchange, according to whether 'they found The Merchant more or less pinched'. Such men surely could not be trusted, and the writer hoped that 'people will suddenly come to their wits, and begin to examine why a Goldsmith-banker should be better Security than another man, or fitter to be trusted for ten times more than he is worth: They give only personal security

268 English Exchequer Bill for £100, 1720. Interest-bearing Exchequer Bills were introduced in 1696; a form of public borrowing, they were issued in return for money advanced to the government. From the early eighteenth century the bills were accepted in payment of taxes, and could be redeemed at the Bank of England. Many carry several endorsements on the back, showing that they circulated among the public. This bill was part of an issue to lend money to the infamous South Sea Company. (× ⅔)

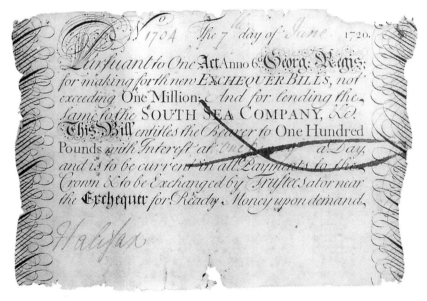

and many times their Notes for £500, £1,000 or more, when they owe before they give that Note, twenty times the value of their own Estates. . . .' No doubt embittered by personal experience, this observer nonetheless perceptively identified the basic prerequisites for successful banking and paper currency: people must have faith in the banker and his notes, and these must be issued on the basis of sound financial backing.

The honour of creating Europe's first freely circulating banknotes goes to the 269 Livonian Johan Palmstruch, who founded the Stockholm Banco in Sweden in 1656. His story is interesting for both his initial success and the circumstances of his failure, which with the hindsight of history could have been a pertinent warning to subsequent ventures elsewhere. The Stockholm Banco was a private

269 One hundred-daler note of the Stockholm Banco, Sweden, 1666. There are no known surviving examples of the Stockholm Banco's first note issues. Notes of this series are valued in silver coinage, and the signature of Johan Palmstruch, the bank's founder, can be seen centre left; indeed, the notes were colloquially known as *Palmstruchers*. Printed on watermarked paper, the notes carried eight signatures, several impressions of personal seals and the seal of the bank. (× ¾)

concern, but in practice it had close links with the state: it was set up under a royal privilege; half of its net profits were payable to the Crown; its chief inspector was the chancellor of the exchequer. Furthermore, Palmstruch took care to consult the government over the nature of the note issue, introduced in 1661. Sweden's copper-plate money was an ingenious response to the problem of maintaining the price of Swedish copper, but it was huge, heavy, inconvenient and depreciating in value. 'Credit notes' were thus issued as transitional alternative currency. At first the project was a success, but within a few years, the bank had lent too much and issued too many notes, which it could no longer redeem. In 1667 a government commission found Palmstruch guilty of mismanagement and ordered him to repay monies owed to the Crown. In contrast to the favour he had earlier been granted, Palmstruch was now faced with the death penalty, though it was later commuted to a prison sentence.

There are certain parallels between this episode and the first incidence of banknotes in France, some fifty years later. These were the initiative of John 270 Law, a Scot who, like Palmstruch, had travelled and been unsuccessfully involved with various financial schemes before finding powerful support. Law's

270 Portrait of John Law,
c. 1715–20, attributed to Alexis
Simon Belle (London, National
Portrait Gallery).

271 Note for 50 livres tournois, issued by John Law's Banque Royale in France and dated 2 September 1720. Despite the bank's promise to pay the bearer on demand in silver coin, public confidence in Law's notes was shattered by an edict of May 1720 devaluing the paper currency by 50 per cent. In October a further edict decreed that the notes were damaging to trade, and that future commercial transactions were to be conducted with gold and silver. Before the end of the year, Law had fled from France. (× ¾)

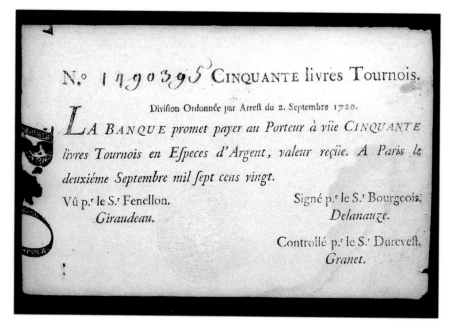

mentor was the Duc d'Orléans, the Regent of France, under whose guidance he established the Banque Générale in 1716. In January 1719 it was effectively nationalised, becoming the Banque Royale and issuing notes guaranteed by the Crown. However, Law's ambitions went far beyond a bank directorship and personal wealth. In January of 1720 he was made Controller-General of France, aiming to bring prosperity to the nation and its people through his bank, a company set up to colonise the Mississippi, and his control of state finance. Law was imaginative, clever and idealistic. His policies were based not on short-term expediency, but on a long-cherished theory of promoting domestic industry through the provision of credit in the form of paper money backed by the value of land. But he relied too much on speculation in every sense, and perhaps underestimated the power of political enmity: later he observed, 'If I had the work to do over again, I would proceed more slowly but more surely and I would not expose the country to the dangers which must necessarily accompany the sudden disturbance of generally accepted financial practice.' By December 1720 he had long since lost the backing of the Regent, and the bank and his Mississippi Company had both collapsed, shattering public confidence and earning him international and lasting notoriety. Law's great 'system' was ruined, and his only refuge lay in exile.

Quite apart from the element of personal drama, the experiences of Law and Palmstruch are similar in several respects: both were genuinely attempting to promote economic activity by creating a new medium of currency, issued through banks that, whatever their legal status, were highly centralised and

272 Dutch satirical print of the Rue Quincampoix, site of the Paris Stock Exchange, recalling the collapse in 1720 of John Law's Mississippi Company. The poem beneath this image recounts the mixed fortunes of investors, and warns of dire fates in store for stockbrokers making boastful promises based on nothing more than wind, smoke and deceit.

enjoyed a considerable measure of powerful patronage. But these circumstances, apparently propitious, were not enough to guarantee stability and public confidence.

The limitations of state power and the mixed blessings of early paper currency are also evident in the note issues of the British colonies in North America, the first government issues in the West. Chronically short of coin and relying heavily on bills of exchange for trade, the colonies needed some form of locally circulating currency. In 1690 the Massachusetts Bay Colony produced 273 the first issue of paper bills to finance a military expedition to Canada. Military expenditure prompted early issues in several other colonies, but bills were also used to fund more peaceful purposes such as municipal building works or discharging public debts. Despite their official status and incentives – in

Massachusetts a 5 per cent premium was offered when taxes were paid in bills – public reaction was ambivalent. The exchange value within and between colonies changed constantly; furthermore, in many colonies the value fell, through overissue and depreciation. In Massachusetts, as early as 1691, a writer

273 Note for 1 dollar, issued by the State of Massachusetts Bay, 1780. The bills of credit issued by the British colony of Massachusetts in 1690 may be considered the first government issue of paper money in the West. Notes issued here and in other provinces were often valued in Spanish dollars, reflecting the importance of foreign specie and the lack of British coinage.

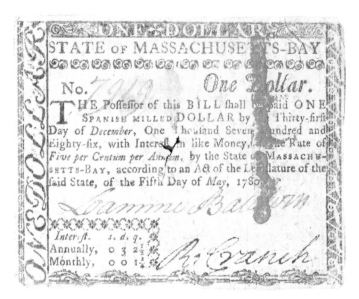

in favour of paper money regretted that it was already losing value against silver, but he saw that confidence and consensus could solve the problems: 'If but a competent number of men, who *Deal much*, would but give your selves the trouble of Meeting, to Debate, Agree, Conclude, and Engage upon giving a *just Reputation* to our *Bills*, the whole Country must and will joyn with them in it.' Later, in Britain, this very policy was often adopted to rescue banks facing a run of anxious customers, but for the moment not everyone was prepared to be so easily persuaded. In 1719 another anonymous commentator looked at the growing number of notes and rising prices and drew his own conclusion:

> Tho the Law allows five per Cent. advance to Bills in Publick payments . . . I say, notwithstanding these Acts in favour of the Bills, yet men don't esteem them as Money, but will give (as I am told), Twelve Shillings in Bills for an Ounce of Silver, which ounce by our Law is but a small matter above Seven shillings; A Law indeed might lay restraints and threaten Penalties, but it can't change Men's minds, to make them think a piece of paper is a piece of Money.

He had a point. In the eighteenth century and much of the nineteenth – indeed, some might argue until the collapse of the gold standard – there was a prevailing belief that paper money could only function effectively if it was convertible on demand into gold or silver coin. Even Adam Smith, a strong defender of banking and banknotes, stipulated this as an essential condition. Yet it was often precisely a lack of coins, or of stability in their value, that stimulated the issue of paper money. Thus, in the British colonies of North America bills of credit met a need so badly felt that colonial assemblies would withhold the salaries of governors refusing to sanction their issue. This continued even after the Revolution (1776-81) provided the imperative for what was in effect the first federal issue, sanctioned by the new Continental Congress on behalf of the United Colonies. Such a duality of opinion was the typical response to the introduction of paper money everywhere: indeed, the public's view was often as fickle as the paper itself was perceived to be. Some of the problems were due simply to prejudice against an unfamiliar and intrinsically worthless form of currency, but much depended too on the available alternatives and on the reputation and financial stability of the issuer.

Given that many of the first attempts to issue paper money were experiments conducted under conditions of political or economic turmoil, it is perhaps hardly surprising that they were prone to failure. But adverse circumstances could be accommodated, as is demonstrated by the first enduringly successful note issuers in the West, the Bank of England and the Bank of Scotland, founded

274 Bank of England 'running cash note' for £635, issued in 1699. Such notes were given as receipts for money deposited at the Bank, and customers could cash them in part, leaving a balance in their accounts - see the annotations in the lower left-hand corner. Because the notes were made payable to the depositor or bearer, they could circulate: whoever presented the note at the Bank could draw on the account held there (Bank of England). (× ½)

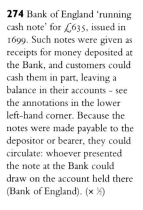

in 1694 and 1695 respectively. The Bank of England was established at a time 274 of crisis in the currency and a war with France; indeed, a major role of the bank was to lend money to the hard-pressed government, as a 'Fund for Perpetual Interest'. A year later, the Bank of Scotland was created by an Act of the Scots 275 Parliament in recognition of 'how useful a publick Bank may be in this kingdom', which was suffering from an inadequate coinage supply, few credit facilities and failed harvests. There were significant differences between the two

275 Note for £12 Scots (£1 sterling) of the Bank of Scotland, 1723. The Bank of Scotland began issuing notes on its foundation in 1695, and is one of three Scottish banks still issuing their own notes in the 1990s. This note was worth £1 sterling but gives the value in Scots currency, a common practice long after the Act of Union of 1707 created an integrated monetary system. (× ½)

276 Twenty-pound note issued by Dawson Coates and Lawless in Dublin, 1770. Many merchants and small traders issued notes in Ireland in the eighteenth century. Coates and Sir Nicholas Lawless (son of the original partner) were both original stockholders in the Bank of Ireland in 1783, and Lawless was one of its first directors. Their own bank failed in 1793, but their creditors were ultimately paid in full (M. O'Grady). (× ¾)

institutions, especially in their relationship to the state – the Bank of England handled much government business, while the Bank of Scotland was expressly forbidden to lend to the state – but there were also important similarities. Each grew from the long-considered plans and ambitions of individual projectors acting with the support of influential business groups, and, crucially, they operated on the joint-stock principle of a broad capital base subscribed by a large number of shareholders. Soon after opening, both banks began issuing their own notes, a key function which, despite challenges, each has continued without a break for three hundred years.

In the course of the eighteenth century banks issuing their own notes opened 276–8 in towns across Britain, often run by merchants, businessmen and landowners keen to promote local trade and industry. The pace of growth was slower in

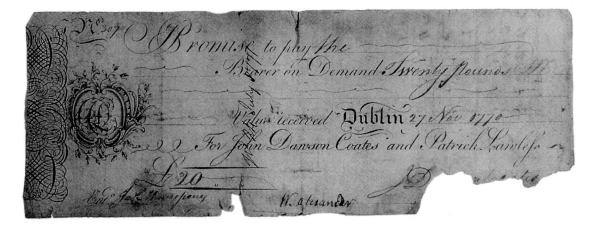

277 Ten-guinea note of the Great Yarmouth Bank, 1783. In Britain in the early eighteenth century there were only a handful of note-issuing local banks outside London; by the early 1800s there were several hundred, much expansion occurring with the growth of industrialisation from the 1760s. The success of the banks and the popularity of their notes depended on the local reputation of the partners, whose names were printed on the note - here, 'Sam.[l] Mason, Rob.[t] Woods & Comp.[y]' (× ¾)

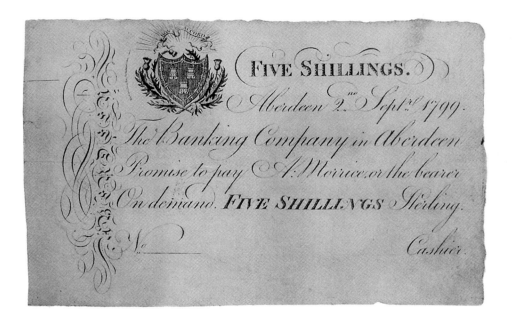

278 Five-shilling note of the Banking Company in Aberdeen, 1799. This bank was established in 1767, at a time when the region was suffering from an acute shortage of coin. One of the aims of the bank was to provide local notes to replace those 'issued and signed by people unknown in the part of this country'. The partners actively supported local industry and improvements, and the bank operated successfully until the commercial crisis of the late 1840s, when it was taken over by the Union Bank of Scotland. (× ¾)

Colonial American currency

In the seventeenth century the area now known as the United States was anything but. Several European countries controlled areas of the Eastern seaboard, including Britain, the Netherlands, France and Sweden. For trade, and to finance the wars between the colonial powers, the colonies issued and used a wide variety of currencies, including (but not restricted to) coins and paper money.

279a English tobacco paper, eighteenth century. Tobacco, being a valuable export commodity, was used as currency alongside coins and paper money in some areas of North America. A 1740 pamphlet published by Hugh Vance in Boston, *An Inquiry into the Nature and Uses of Money*, explained the situation: 'The Word, *Currency*, is in common Use in the Plantations . . . and signifies *Silver* passing current by Weight or Tale. The same Name is also applicable as well to Tobacco in *Virginia*, sugars in the *West Indies* &c. . . . And according to that Rule *Paper-Currency* must signify certain Pieces of Paper, passing current in the Market as *Money*.'

279b Silver 'pine-tree' shilling, Massachusetts, 1667–74. In 1652 the colony of Massachusetts Bay started producing coins of a very simple design, stamped with 'NE' and Roman numerals indicating the denomination, and made from melted-down Spanish pieces of eight. But these coins were easily clipped and counterfeited, so minting was stopped after only a few months and the following year a new design was introduced, with a tree on the obverse. This silver 'pine-tree' shilling was issued from 1667 to 1674 but still bearing the date 1652.

279c Tin token made for the British American colonies, 1688. These tokens were made at the Royal Mint at the Tower of London and shipped out to America. The inscription on the reverse gives these coins a value of ¼ of a real, showing the extent to which American colonies were linked to the Spanish currency system as well as the British one.

A TABLE of the Value and Weight of COINS, as they now pass in ENGLAND, NEW-YORK, CONNECTICUT, PHILADELPHIA, AND QUEBEC.						
Sterl. l. s. d.	N. York, l. s. d.	Least Weight dwt.gr.	connectic. l. s. d.	Philad. l. s. d.	Quebec, l. s. d.	Least Weight dwt.gr.
ENGLISH Shilling, 0 01 0	0 01 9	dwt.gr.	0 01 4	0 01 6	0 01 4	dwt.gr.
crown, 0 5 0	8 9		6 8	7 6	6 8	
Guinea, 1 1 0	1 17	5 3	1 8	1 14	1 8	5 5
Spanish Piftereen, -	1 7		1 2 1-2	1 4	1 2	
Dollars, -	8	17 6	6	7 6	6	17 12
Piftole, 0 16 6	1 9	4 8	1 2	1 7	1 1	4 4
Portugal Moidore, 1 7 0	2 8	6 18	1 16	2 3 6	1 16	6 18
* Half-Johannes, 1 16 0	3 4	9 0	2 8	3 0 0	2 8	
French Ninepence,	-			-	1	
crown, 0 5 0	8 6	-	6 8	7 6	6 8	17 12
Piftole, 0 16 0	1 8	4 5	-	1 6 6	1 1	4 4
Louis D'or or Guinea, 1 1 0	1 16	5 4	-	1 13	1 8	5 3
German caroline.	1 18	6 8	-	1 14	1 10	5 17

    * At a Meeting of the Chamber of Commerce, the 7th of August 1770, it was Resolved, That the Members of that Corporation would, in future, pay and receive all H A L F   J O E S, that weigh 9 Penny Weight, at £. 3 : 4 : 0, and for every Grain they weigh more, allow three Pence per Grain; and every Grain they weigh less, deduct 4d.

279d Coin conversion table, from a 1771 New York almanac. The money of the American colonies varied in value: a New York shilling was not necessarily equivalent to a Philadelphia shilling. This, combined with the variety of currencies in circulation, meant that tables like this one were printed to show the relative values and weights of coins compared with the currencies of account of different states.

279e English gold guinea, 1772, countermarked 'EB' by the New York goldsmith Ephraim Brasher. Estimates of the total amount of cash in circulation in the American colonies in the 1770s vary considerably, from 30 million to 10 million dollars, with anywhere from 25 to 75 per cent of the total estimated as being precious-metal coinage. Because of a shortage of precious metals on the East coast of America, silver and gold coins were imported from countries including Britain, Portugal and Spain (or Spanish America) and used to supplement the locally issued base-metal and paper currencies.

279f Tin pattern for a silver dollar, made for the American Continental Congress, 1776. In the 1760s new taxes imposed on the British Colonies led to calls for independence, and the freedom of the thirteen United States was declared on 4 July 1776. This trial coin design, prepared in the same year, was not issued at that time, but a very similar design was used on the first coins issued by the United States, the so-called 'fugio' cents of 1787.

280 Note for 74 scudi issued by the Banco di Santo Spirito di Roma, 1786. The bank was founded in 1605 by Pope Paul V. Part of its function was to provide funds for charity by working with the *monti di pietà*, institutions which helped the poor by lending small sums of money at very low interest rates. The Banco di Santo Spirito issued its first notes as receipts for deposits of coin; circulating notes payable to bearer were issued from 1724 until 1796. (× ¾)

England, but the rapid expansion of banking and note issue in Scotland demonstrated well the rewards and risks they could bring, also experienced in England in the nineteenth century. In a poor country short of coin but with relatively high levels of literacy, people were willing recipients of notes both from reputable sources such as the Royal Bank of Scotland or the Banking Company 278 in Aberdeen, and from such feckless concerns as the notoriously improvident Ayr Bank. But even after the calamitous failure of the latter, note-holders got their money back through the support of the Bank of Scotland and the Royal Bank, and sales of landed estates. For many of the shareholders it was a disaster; for Scottish banking generally it was a merely a warning and an affirmation that strength lay in sound management and sufficient reserves of capital. Throughout Britain the number of banks continued to grow, meeting and creating a demand for paper money. Many were small private concerns, especially in England where until 1826 the Bank of England had a monopoly of joint-stock banking, but time and experience showed the advantages of large-scale banks, often with branch networks, a trend that was in due course acknowledged and encouraged by banking legislation in the nineteenth century. Contrary to the belief of the disenchanted pamphleteer in rural Massachusetts, it was indeed the

consolidation of good practice by the law that allowed men to trust money in the form of paper.

Early issues of paper money in the West were all essentially speculative. With no established procedure to draw on, there was little alternative but to learn from experience, costly though that could be for banker and customer. It is easy to concentrate on the spectacle of failure, but even the abortive schemes of Palmstruch and Law enjoyed some success and closely foreshadowed the future form of note issues by central banks. Moreover, whereas early types of paper credit, such as bills of exchange, were used predominantly by merchants and financial agents, the seventeenth and eighteenth centuries saw the spread of paper money as a form of circulating currency used throughout society.

The dangers of unchecked note issues were far from over, as imminent revolutions were soon to prove, but as the end of the eighteenth century approached, paper money was used in 280–82 some twenty countries around the world, produced by state banks, private issuers and even by European powers for use in remote colonies. The next two centuries witnessed a progressive change in the circumstances of issue, from experiment and expediency to centralisation and control, fulfilling

282 Note for 6 livres tournois for the Isles de France et de Bourbon (now Mauritius and Réunion), c. 1780s. These were at this time administered by France as a single colony with a common currency system. Paper money appears to have been issued from the 1760s, at a date when France itself was not using notes.

281 Twenty-five-gulden note of the Wiener Stadt-Banco, Austria, 1762. This is an example of Austria's earliest paper money, although the bank had been founded in 1706. The notes were issued in exchange for deposits of cash, in an attempt to offset state debts. Initially, notes to the value of 12 million gulden were authorised, but by 1801 this figure had risen to over 1,000 million, as more notes were printed to pay for wars. (× ¼)

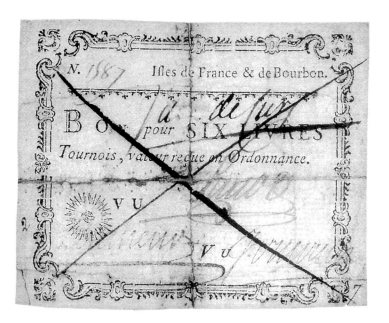

Adam Smith's recommendation of the 'substitution of paper in the room of gold and silver money'.

Conclusion

From the bullion flood of the sixteenth century to the emergence of token coinage, centralised banking and banknotes in the next two centuries, money underwent significant changes: there was more of it in circulation in an increasing variety of forms, and it was beginning to fulfil more functions for more people. At the beginning of the period people's thoughts about money were primarily religious and moral in tone. They were still inseparable from deep-seated Christian anxieties about excessive wealth and God's judgement on the unjust rich. By the end of the period, however, man-made law and the temporal state formed the conceptual frame of reference within which the various aspects of money were discussed. People began to theorise rationally about the nature of money and the part it played in society. This was both caused by and stimulated the possibility of monetary innovation and experiment. Current understanding usually lagged behind the complexities of monetary reality – as in the faltering early stages of banknote issue – but there had been an irrevocable change of mind and of practice. The profound implications of this intellectual shift would be worked out in practice in the next two centuries.

Africa and Oceania

Of all the forms of money . . this is certainly the most curious.

W. COOTE, *Western Pacific* (1883)

283 Silver dollar issued in 1791 by the British Sierra Leone Company for use in the West African settlement established for freed slaves. The issue was not successful and was withdrawn by 1805. This was the first ever coin to be issued with the specific denomination 'dollar', three years before the first US silver dollars in 1794. Like the US coin, it was intended as a substitute for the ubiquitous Spanish 'piece of eight'. The Sierra Leone dollar also had a value of 10 macutas in terms of the African unit of value. (× 4)

Coins and paper money are now found in every country of the world. Yet in some countries, particularly in Africa and Oceania, their use is still confined to a minority of the population, the rich and city-dwellers. Cheque books, credit cards, telephone banking and the other apparatus of money use in the developed world are still unknown in many areas, while coins and paper money are often employed in ways that would

Modern money in Africa

The introduction of European-style coins and paper money in sub-Saharan Africa began in the late eighteenth century, but only became distinctively African during the consolidation of European rule in the late nineteenth century. The imagery of the coins and notes of the colonial period reflects European interests, but since the achievement of independence African states have retained the European forms of money but asserted their own identities in their choice of designs. The introduction of European-style money to the independent kingdom of Ethiopia was accompanied by a similar desire to project an African national identity. The new monetary systems did not serve all the economic and social needs of their users, so in many contexts the local forms of 'money' continued to be used.

284b Cupro-nickel 10 shilingi of Tanzania, issued in 1988. The front of the coin depicts Julius Nyerere, the President of Tanzania and the architect of its independence in 1961. The back of the coin shows the arms of the new state supported by a man and woman in African dress, holding elephant tusks. The inscription is in Swahili, the official language of Tanzania.

284c Cupro-nickel 10 cents of British East Africa and Uganda, issued in the name of King Edward VII, 1910, for circulation in Kenya, Somaliland and Uganda. This coin circulated as a tenth of a British India rupee, the standard unit of currency in East Africa. The design, featuring elephant tusks, represents the wealth accruing to the colonial power from the natural resources of the region. Britain began to supply local currency for this area from 1897.

284a Bank of West Africa note for 1,000 francs, specimen of an issue for French West Africa, printed about 1945. The front of the note shows an African mother and child embraced by Marianne, the personification of France, wearing a laurel crown. This note is typical of French colonial issues, combining depictions of the peoples under their rule with allegorical images of the French state as a 'parental' guardian of its subjects. (× ¼)

284e Silver thaler, a later restrike of the 1780 thaler of Maria Theresa, Empress of Austria, made for trade in Ethiopia and Arabia. This coin was so popular in the countries bordering on the Red Sea that Austria, Britain, France, Italy and Germany made copies of it for export to Ethiopia and Arabia.

284f Silver thaler (*birr*) of Menelik, King of Abyssinia, struck at the Paris Mint and dated 1892 in the Ethiopian Era (AD 1900). The front of the coin shows the king's portrait; the back shows the Lion of Judah, the emblem of the kingdom of Abyssinia. The popularity of the Maria Theresa thaler in Ethiopia prompted Menelik to have his own version struck. Although the French mint produced a handsome coin for him, it was not a success, because his subjects preferred to use the familiar Austrian coin.

284d Note of the Central Bank of the States of West Africa for 5,000 francs, issued in 1984 for use in the former French colonies of West Africa (detail). The imagery refers both to the long history of West African culture, through a fourteenth-century brass head from Nigeria, and to the region's modern fishing industry.

284g (*below*) Bank of Ethiopia note for 2 thalers (*birr*), issued in 1933, with the portrait of Emperor Haile Selassie (1930–36, 1941–74). Western-style money only became widely used in Ethiopia during Haile Selassie's reign, even though the Maria Theresa thaler continued to circulate in some regions until the 1960s.

285 Silver ackey of the British settlement of Gold Coast (now Ghana), struck in the name of George III in 1818. The ackey was a weighed amount of gold used by the local people in trade with European settlers. The coin is struck to the weight of a British half-crown. Its issue was not a success. The inscription records the establishment of the British right to trade in Africa by Act of Parliament in 1750.

seem rather alien to a Western observer. In this chapter we continue the history of the European expansion into newly discovered worlds and the introduction of European monetary practices to these regions, and also look at 283–5 the multiplicity of indigenous money systems that preceded the worldwide intrusion of coin-based money from Europe and which still exist in parts of the world today.

Salt and the culture of coinage

As European travellers began to encounter peoples without coinage, they brought back to Europe accounts of various items that they thought were being used as quasi-coinage. Salt was among the most prevalent of these. An early Portuguese traveller, the missionary Francis Alvarez who was sent as a royal emissary to Ethiopia (Abyssinia) from 1520 to 1526, mentioned in his account of his journey the local practice of using salt to make payments: 'Salt is current instead of money from the Red Sea to Congo on the West Sea. It is said to be cut out of mountains and cut into blocks a hand and a half in length, four fingers broad and three fingers thick.'

The British merchant Alexander Hamilton, who visited Ethiopia in the early eighteenth century, also encountered the use of salt there: 'The current small money of Ethiopia is salt, which is dug out of the mountains as we do Stones from our quarries. . . .' By the end of the century European traders had brought silver dollars and gold ducats into use in the Red Sea ports in modern Eritrea which served the Ethiopian kingdom, and some of these had penetrated the hinterland to circulate alongside salt. 'There are no coins minted in Abyssinia, but those of other countries circulate here, particularly Venetian sequins, and Imperial or Austrian Dollars. . . . Large payments are generally made in Ingots of Gold, which are weighed by the *Wakea* or Abyssinian Ounce; and for small payments Salt Bricks dug out of the mines are adopted, about 80 of which are valued at a Wakea of Gold.'

These authors thought that the Ethiopians used salt as a primitive form of 286 coinage, and that salt fulfilled the function that coinage performed in European

286 Salt bar of the kind used in payments in Ethiopia (Abyssinia) during the nineteenth century. It was made from rock salt, cut by hand to a specific size and wrapped in reed to protect it during use. (× ⅓)

287 Bronze penny of British West Africa, issued in 1958 in the name of Elizabeth II. The British West African coinage began in 1907 and was issued for circulation in Gold Coast, Nigeria, Gambia and Sierra Leone. It was the first successful attempt by the British to issue coins for its colonies in West Africa.

society. They were also generally of the opinion that the use of a natural product such as salt instead of precious-metal coinage was itself a mark of the primitiveness of the societies they encountered. Yet the kingdom of Ethiopia had once had its own coinage. Under Roman influence, a gold, silver and bronze coinage had been issued by the Ethiopian kings of Aksum from the third to seventh centuries AD, and Islamic and European coinage did occasionally make its way into the area from the coastal regions.

In a similar way, the coin-using Chinese thought that the inhabitants of their more remote provinces, whom they regarded as less civilised than themselves, used materials such as salt or cowrie shells as a primitive substitute for coins. Chinese historians also thought that cowries were used as money in China itself before the introduction of coinage, and Chinese writers observed the use of salt to make payments in distant provinces of the Chinese Empire. The ninth-century Chinese writer Fan Chuo described monetary practice in southern Sichuan Province in western China: 'Whenever business is transacted, they reckon in the lump of salt.' Marco Polo wrote about trading conditions in the same province at the end of the thirteenth century:

> Let me tell you next about their money. They have gold in bars and weigh it out by saggi; and it is valued according to its weight. But they have no coined money bearing a stamp. For small change they do as follows. They have salt water from which they make salt by boiling it for an hour. They let it solidify in moulds, forming blocks of the size of a two penny loaf, flat below and rounded on top. When the blocks are ready they are laid on heated stones beside the fire to dry and harden. On these blocks they set the Great Khan's stamp and currency of this sort is made only by his agents. Eighty of these blocks are worth a saggio of gold. But traders come with these blocks to the people who live among the mountains in wild and out of the way places and receive a saggio of gold for sixty, fifty or forty blocks according as the place is more isolated. . . . These traders travel all over the highlands of Tibet where the salt money is also current. They make an immense profit, because these people use this salt in food as well as for buying the necessities of life; but in the cities they almost invariably use fragments of the blocks for food and spend the unbroken blocks.
>
> *The Travels of Marco Polo*, trans. R. E. Latham (1958)

There is also evidence of the use of salt in payments in Saharan Africa. The fourteenth-century Arab traveller Ibn Battuta reported that he had found a salt-mine at Taghaza (in modern Mali) on the way to Timbuktu, where blocks of rock salt were extracted for trade southwards into the Kingdom of Mali. He writes: 'The negroes use salt as a medium of exchange as gold and silver is used elsewhere. They cut it up into pieces and buy and sell with it.'

Copper in Africa

Copper and its alloys, bronze and brass, have been called the 'red gold of Africa'. Although West Africa was one of the world's richest sources of gold before the nineteenth century, the local people had a high regard for copper and brass for ornamental objects and for use in payments. As Africa's gold was exported to Europe to be made into coin, European copper and brass flowed into West Africa. The copper mines of Central Africa were also an important source. By the nineteenth century copper was widely used in a variety of forms as a means of payment.

288a Copper alloy bracelet (manilla), Nigeria, fourteenth century. Examples of manillas excavated from archaeological sites in Nigeria suggest that heavy copper alloy bracelets, often so large or unusually shaped that they could not have been worn, were in use by the thirteenth century. From the second half of the fifteenth century Portuguese traders used copper and brass manillas to purchase slaves from the kingdom of Benin (in present-day Nigeria). (× ½)

288b Brass manilla made in Britain for export to Nigeria, late nineteenth century. The recognition of the importance of manillas in the economy of several regions in West Africa prompted Portuguese and other European traders to make them specifically for trade with the native peoples of the region. Small manillas of this type were still being used as money in eastern Nigeria until the 1940s.

288c Brass decorative plaque, originally mounted on a pillar of the royal palace in the kingdom of Benin, Nigeria, fifteenth to sixteenth centuries. The small figure to the right above the central figure represents a Portuguese trader holding a manilla. In several Benin plaques there is a clear association between manillas and the Portuguese, suggesting that they were an important source of these bracelets.

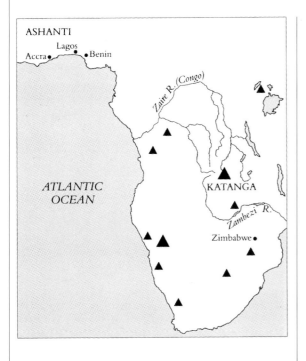

288d Copper sources in Africa.

288e Copper 1-macuta coin of Jose I, King of Portugal (1750–77), made for use in Portugal's West and Central African colonies. The macuta denomination is based on an African unit of value.

288f Copper cross-shaped ingot from Central Africa. Ingots of this type were made of locally mined metal from the copper belt (in the Democratic Republic of Congo and Zambia). Archaeological finds suggest that cross-shaped copper ingots were being made as early as the thirteenth century in this area. This example is probably of the nineteenth century, when such ingots were widely used for payments in the Katanga province of the Belgian Congo. (× 1⅓)

288g Bronze ewer made in England, 1377–99, found in the royal palace of Ashanti, Gold Coast (Ghana) in 1895. This massive ewer, decorated with royal arms and motifs of the English king Richard II and a moralising verse, appears to have travelled to Ashanti as part of the flow of copper into West Africa.

288h Gold proof of bronze 5-franc piece of Katanga, a province of the Democratic Republic of Congo, which achieved independence briefly from Congo in 1961. The design depicts a copper ingot of the type produced in the copper mining regions of Central Africa since the thirteenth century.

'Curious money'

Besides salt and metals, European travellers and merchants described a wide range of objects as money when they encountered peoples who did not use coins in Africa, America, Asia, Australasia and the Pacific. They came across some very unexpected things which they interpreted as money, such as massive stones, pieces of wood, feathers and even human skulls.

Some of the earliest sources are the Portuguese navigators and traders who in the late fifteenth century opened up direct contacts with Africa, and their

289 Simbos, olive shells used for payments by the Mbuun and Pende people in the Belgian Congo (now the Democratic Republic of Congo), together with a basket for carrying the shells, collected in 1909. Simbos were also recorded as being used at an earlier date by the native people of Portuguese Angola, where they were known as *lumache*. (× ⅓)

accounts mention copper rings, cloth, shells and pieces of wood in use in 288, 300 western Africa. Duarte Lopez described the use of shell money in Angola 289 during the sixteenth century:

> An island called Loanda . . . furnishes the money used by the King of Congo and the neighbouring people; for along its shores . . . they sift out certain small shell-fish called Lumache. . . . It must be remembered that gold, silver, and other metals are not used as money in these countries; and so it happens that with gold and silver in abundance, either in mass or in coin, yet nothing can be bought except with Lumache.
>
> FILIPPO PIGAFETTA, *Report* of the Kingdom of Congo (1591)

Shell money was also described in many parts of North America. In 1705 the English historian Robert Beverley wrote about the native peoples of Virginia: 'The Indians had nothing which they reckoned riches before the English went among them, except *Peak*, *Roenoke* and suchlike trifles made 290 out of *Cunk* shell. These past with them instead of Gold and Silver and served them both for Money and Ornament.' These ornaments, made from clam shell, were called *wampum* by European settlers. In Central America early Spanish settlers mentioned the use of small copper axes and cocoa 291 beans by the local people in Mexico soon after its conquest by Spain.

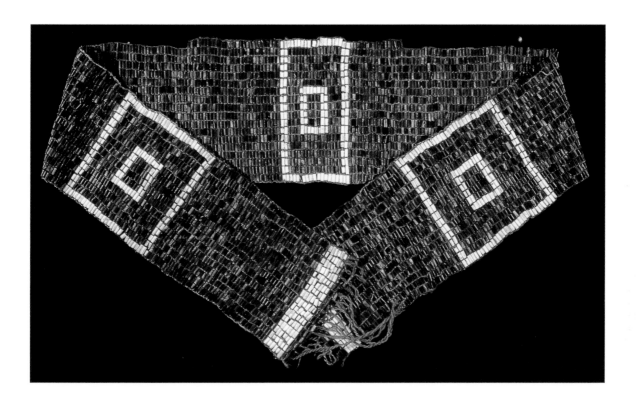

290 Wampum, a belt of beads cut from clam shells, of the type used in the early colonial period by the native peoples of the north-east woodland region of North America. The purple beads were made from the rim, the white from the body of the shells. European settlers also manufactured wampum for trade with the native Americans. (× ¼)

Although coinage had had almost as long a history in South Asia as in Europe, early European travellers found cowrie shells being used there as a means of payment: 'Their other small money are the little shells which they call *cori*' (J. B. Tavernier, *Collections of Travels through Turkey into Persia and the East Indies*, 1684). The export of cowries to Africa from Gujarat in western India had led to a shortage of small change, and almonds were used in their place: 'For small Money they make no use of these shells, but of little Almonds' (Tavernier).

Coins had also been used in South-east Asia from the seventh to the twelfth centuries, but foreign travellers and traders encountered many other means of payment. An eleventh-century Arab text, *'Aja'ib al-Hind*, records that among the native peoples of the Nias island off Sumatra ingots of copper were used in the same way as gold was used by the Arabs, while

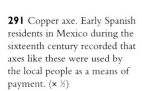

291 Copper axe. Early Spanish residents in Mexico during the sixteenth century recorded that axes like these were used by the local people as a means of payment. (× ½)

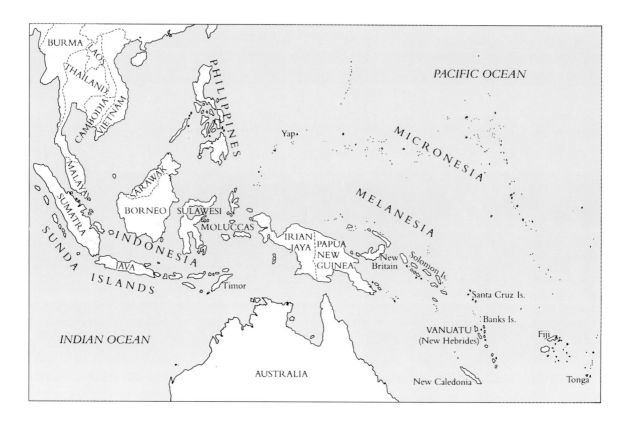

292 Oceania.

on other islands human heads were used as articles of exchange. Chinese reports of trade in the region describe the use of chopped pieces of silver in payments in thirteenth-century Java because 'they have no stringed copper coins' (i.e. coins like the Chinese). Chinese accounts also mention the production of monetary tin ingots in fifteenth-century Malacca: 'In all their trading transactions they use the pieces of tin instead of money.' As in India and China, cowrie shells were also reported in use as money in mainland Southeast Asia. The fourteenth-century Chinese writer Wang Dayuan records their use in Lop Buri in Thailand: 'It is the rule to conduct their trade with cowries instead of coins.' European travellers and traders entering the region also found unfamiliar means of payment. A fifteenth-century Venetian traveller, Nicolo de' Conti, described the currency of human heads in Sumatra: 'In one part of the island called Battech [Batak] the inhabitants eat human flesh. . . . They keep human heads as valuable property, . . . store up the skull and use it as money. When they desire to purchase any article, they give one or more heads in exchange for it according to its value. . . .' Other European accounts describe the use in payments of rice, beeswax, tobacco, brass cannons, iron bars, etc.

The last region of the world to be explored by coin-using traders and

293 Tambu shells from New Britain, in Papua New Guinea, nineteenth to twentieth century. The shells are holed and threaded onto lengths of rattan. Since the nineteenth century, visitors to the island have described their use in payments such as bride-wealth, adultery fines and blood-money. (× ½)

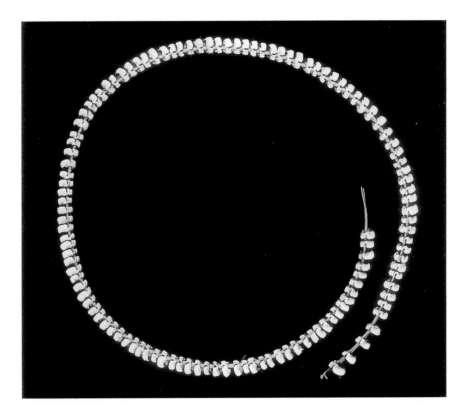

294 'Feather money' roll of Santa Cruz Islands, part of the Solomon Islands, nineteenth to twentieth century. The feathers were glued to a long fibre belt, shells and beads tied to the end of the belt and the whole wrapped in palm-leaves. They were used in ceremonial payments. (× ⅓)

295 Yap islanders with examples of their stone 'money'. Stone disks were being used in payments on Yap Island in the Pacific (now in the Federated States of Micronesia), when Europeans first visited the island in the nineteenth century. The stones, some as large as 4 metres across, were cut by the Yap islanders from limestone quarries on the Pelew islands, about 400 miles from Yap.

travellers was Australasia and the Pacific. In many islands no particular means of payment were encountered, but in others, particularly in Micronesia and Melanesia, early European visitors found a perplexing array of objects which they identified as money, including shell, cloth, feathers, teeth and stone. 294–5

The people of New Britain, an island to the north-east of New Guinea, for example, were reported to use shell money called *tambu* in the late nineteenth 293 century. It was made from small humped shells threaded onto a stiff rattan cord. '*Tambu* or *diwarra* was the national currency just as much as the coinage of any civilised country' (G. Brown, *Melanesians and Polynesians*, 1910). The means of payment most surprising to Westerners was the various forms of feather money used in the Santa Cruz and Banks Islands, further out in the Pacific. 'In Santa Maria and Meralava [in the Banks Islands, Vanuatu], . . . feather money of a special kind is in use. The little feathers near the eye of fowls are bound on strings and generally dyed a fine crimson. They are used as necklaces or anklets, by way of ornament and distinction, but also pass very much in the way of money' (R. H. Codrington, *The Melanesians*, 1891).

This selection of travellers' and traders' responses to unfamiliar forms of money in Africa, America, Asia and Australasia all reflect the monetary precon-ceptions of the writers themselves, and of the societies from which they came. Coinage (and later paper money) was the normal form of money and means of payment for all of them – European, Chinese and Muslim Arab alike. These coin-using people encountered peoples using salt, shells, cloth, feathers, pigs, etc. in contexts where they thought they would have used coins or paper money. As a consequence, they identified these objects as primitive forms of money, used instead of coinage. Their response was often one of wonder, like that, for example, of a traveller in the Pacific who remarked of the cloth money on the Island of Maewo (in Vanuatu): 'Of all the forms of money which I have seen this is certainly the most curious, for it cannot be carried about, and is never moved, even when it passes from one owner to another' (W. Coote, *Western Pacific*, 1883). For the local peoples themselves, of course, these means of payment were far from unfamiliar or unusual.

In identifying these unfamiliar objects as money, the various writers we have encountered were trying to make sense of the strange societies they met and to communicate them to their readership by drawing analogies with the customs of their homelands and by pointing to obvious cultural differences. For travellers this was a matter of curiosity, whereas for missionaries it was a route to understanding the mentality of potential converts. For traders it represented a commercial necessity, as they sought ways to open up negotiations with local peoples who did not use coinage in transactions.

But were salt, shells and human heads really used in the same ways as

296 Bride-wealth banner, Papua New Guinea Highlands, 1980s. In the Highlands of New Guinea, a man is expected to make a bride-wealth payment to his wife's kin. In the 1950s and 1960s such payments took the form of pearlshells (*kina*), which were presented on impressive banners. Cash, in the form of paper money, has now displaced pearlshells in the local economy, but is presented on banners topped with bird of paradise plumes, in exactly the same way as the pearlshells used to be.

297 *Kina* pearlshell from Papua New Guinea. Used in the 1950s and 1960s to make payments in the Papua New Guinea Highlands, this type of shell has given its name to the standard currency unit adopted when Papua New Guinea became independent in 1975. (× ⅓)

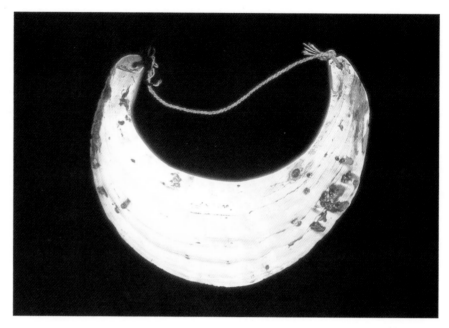

298 Five-kina note of the Bank of Papua New Guinea, first issued in 1981. The note depicts a bird of paradise on the front and a *kina* shell on the back. Notes of this issue were used on the bride-wealth banner depicted in **296**. (× ¾)

299 Cupro-nickel 1-kina coin of Papua New Guinea, dated 1975, with a stylised bird of paradise emblem on the front and crocodiles on the back. The coin is holed for carrying on a string, for the convenience of rural people.

Europeans used coins and banknotes? The evolutionary view of human history was typical of a period in which Europeans tended to take their own cultural standpoint as the measure to judge all others, and understood their own culture as the pinnacle of human development. We have already seen that Chinese and Arab writers were not so very different in this respect, and specifically when they looked at indigenous money systems in the world around their own. Such ethnocentric ideas are still common in twentieth-century Western society, and they continue to affect our understanding of non-coin monetary systems. Many modern scholars of the history of money have tended to describe them as 'primitive money', with the implication that such forms of money are in a general sense less developed than coinage.

To the extent that this widely accepted view has been rejected and modified, it has been mainly through the work of ethnographers and anthropologists in the twentieth century. Their investigations have revealed a new understanding of the wide variety of human cultures and monetary systems, and questioned the twin ideas of human evolutionary development from simple to complex, and the assumption that West (or East, or wherever) is best.

Money and ethnography

Already in the 1920s the anthropologist Bronislaw Malinowski was criticising 'primitivist' conceptions of indigenous societies and their economics: 'Another error more or less explicitly expressed in all writings on primitive economics, is that the natives possess only rudimentary forms of trade and exchange.' Since then the work of anthropologists has continued to explore local payment and exchange systems and the societies within which they operate, and now they can be seen as anything but rudimentary. Most importantly, it is now recognised that tribal societies have integral forms of social development in their own right, and that we should not assume that Western concepts of money also underlie apparently analogous phenomena in other parts of the world. Thus it would be wrong to assume that salt money or feather money were used in the same ways and for the same reasons that the Western tradition, say, has tended to use coins and paper money. One of the main differences between tribal and Western systems is the extent to which commercial considerations determine the reasons for making payments of various sorts. By no means all societies are so centred on trade and exchange as are those of the West. Indeed, it is arguable that Western culture and its money systems, far from being 'normal', are actually an historical anomaly in their fixation on the commercial. If this is right, it would be an even greater mistake for Westerners to interpret other monetary systems as a more primitive version of their own.

So how are we to approach indigenous money systems? Perhaps we can see something of the profound differences between 'traditional' and Western,

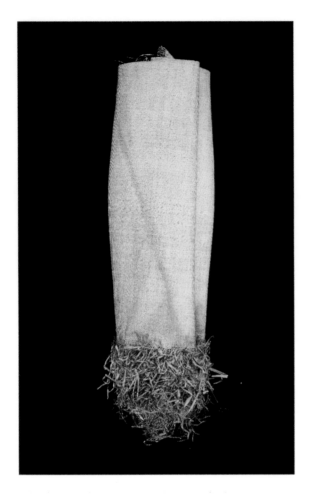

coin-based, monetary systems by examining a particular case of interaction between them. From 1949 to 1953 the British anthropologist Mary Douglas spent time living among the Lele people in the Kasia District of Belgian Congo (now the Democratic Republic of Congo), and in 1958 she published an account of their use of cloth money in a country dominated by the coin-using Belgian 300 colonial authorities. Cloth money had a long history in the Congo. Its use was mentioned in the seventeenth century by Jean Barbot, a French government agent in Africa. In the twentieth century Mary Douglas observed that the cloth was woven from raffia by Lele men, who could weave about two or three cloths in a day. They were sewn together when worn or used in payments, often in multiples of ten. Barbot's account from more than 350 years earlier contains similar details.

By the time of Douglas's visit the Lele were familiar with a currency based on coins and paper money, denominated in Belgian Congo francs and 301 centimes. They were also expected to pay their taxes and fines to the Native Tribunal in this currency. In reality they often made payments to the tribunal in cloth at an official exchange rate of

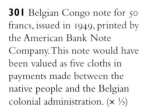

300 Piece of raffia cloth from Angola, acquired in 1866. Cloth mats like this were used to make payments by many of the peoples of Angola and the Democratic Republic of Congo. (× ⅓)

301 Belgian Congo note for 50 francs, issued in 1949, printed by the American Bank Note Company. This note would have been valued as five cloths in payments made between the native people and the Belgian colonial administration. (× ⅓)

302 Piece of camwood, a native tree of Central Africa, used as a pigment for personal decoration. Collected from the Kuba people in Belgian Congo, nineteenth or twentieth century. For large-scale payments, camwood could be used as a substitute for raffia cloth. (× ⅓)

10 francs per cloth. The Lele also had contact with European money and coins through the wages of their young men who worked for colonial employers. Within the Lele community, however, the colonial francs did not have a direct role except when acting as a substitute for payments in cloth, and then their value had to be translated into cloths in order to be usable.

In high-value 'payments' within their community the Lele often used camwood (a wood used 302 to make pigment), salt, copper bars, goats and, before the 1930s, slaves, but they were all still valued in terms of cloths. This was a traditional practice in the region, described three hundred years previously by the Dutch writer Olfert Dapper, who mentioned slaves and camwood being used in the kingdom of Kongo alongside 'little pieces of cloth and such bagatelles, which they esteem as much in their country as gold and silver in Europe' (O.M. Dapper, *Description de l'Afrique*, 1686). Among the Lele, Douglas observed that the functions of cloths and camwood in the Congo were not the same as those of European money. The Lele did not have a market-based economy, for, according to Douglas: 'goods are distributed mostly on the basis of status, and not by purchase'. They only exceptionally exchanged goods by barter or by exchange, whether for cloths or francs, and then normally only for high-value goods and with other communities. The only sales for cloth within the Lele community that she observed were for the work of carvers and other skilled craftsmen, but these exchanges were only possible provided the buyer had no kinship ties with the seller.

Clearly, then, Lele cloth 'money' was not employed in the same way as European money, as its use for commercial purposes was restricted by social conventions. But there was a wide variety of non-commercial 'payments' required in Lele society for which cloth 'money' was mandatory. Their main function was to reinforce social relationships among the Lele, thus cloths were used as entrance fees to religious cult groups, fees to ritual healers and as marriage dues; as rewards to Lele wives for giving birth and for reporting would-be seducers; and as fines for adultery, compensation for fighting within the village, fulfilment of blood debts, and tribute to chiefs. They were also given as ritual

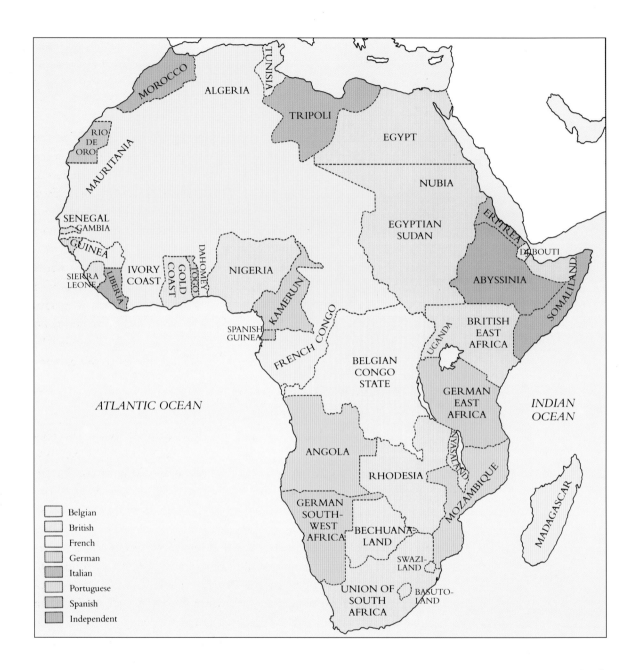

303 Africa, *c.* 1910.

Belgian
British
French
German
Italian
Portuguese
Spanish
Independent

gifts to mark rites of passage and to resolve occasions of tension. If an individual did not have enough cloths to make a payment expected of him, he could call on his kinsmen to make contributions or loans.

The Lele valued cloth in the same way as the Europeans valued gold and silver, but because Lele society was very different, payments in cloth were made in response to a very different set of circumstances which were, for the most part, not commercial but social in character. Moreover, when coins and paper

304 Steel 20-cedis coin of Ghana, dated 1991, depicting a cowrie shell of the type formerly used as money in the region. The cedi denomination, derived from the Ghanaian word meaning cowrie shell, was adopted in 1965. (× 1½)

money began to penetrate Lele society, they were used in the same way as cloth money within the community, and were only exchanged commercially in dealings with the colonial administration. Thus the Lele attempted to preserve the integrity of their own 'money' system in the face of social changes caused by colonial domination.

Change did come to the Lele, however, and it was largely brought about by the disruption of the traditional cloth money system through contact with the monetary economy of the Belgian colony. Traditionally, the older members of Lele society owned more cloths than the young, and effectively used these cloths as a means of control over younger men who had to borrow from them in order to marry and join the required cult groups. But Mary Douglas observed young Lele men working for foreigners and earning colonial francs, which they then transferred into the cloth system at the official exchange rate. Their wages provided them with an alternative means of acquiring cloths without resorting to their elders. The traditional structures of social control across the generations were severely weakened as a consequence. The use by the Lele of coins and paper money in recent decades has continued to increase, but this should be seen as a reflection of social change among the Lele rather than a result of a linear development from primitive to sophisticated money.

Money in transformation

The political and economic domination of large areas of the world by coin-using societies has certainly had a profound effect on indigenous money systems everywhere. But intruding merchants and colonial powers also had to adapt themselves to local systems in order to do business with the societies that they wanted to exploit.

Perhaps the most remarkable example of this phenomenon also comes from Africa. In the fourteenth century Ibn Battuta reported that Arab merchants were trading cowries into the kingdom of Mali in West Africa, where cowries were used as the local money. The earliest Portuguese accounts also mention the trade in cowries in the Songhay kingdom, which ruled a large part of western Africa following the collapse of Mali in the late fifteenth century. It is not clear exactly in what ways Africans were using cowries, but European traders began to exploit the local taste for cowrie shells and imported them in huge quantities from the Indian Ocean and the Maldive Islands to trade for slaves and other

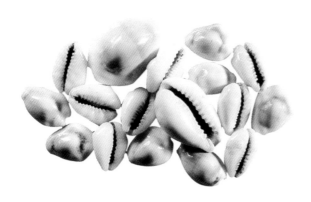

305 Cowrie shells of the variety collected by European traders in the Maldive Islands, for export to South Asia and Africa as a form of money.

goods. By the late seventeenth century Portuguese, British, Dutch and French traders had created such a demand for cowries in West Africa that they began to drain out of India, where they were also in use as money, in order to supply the African market.

Cowries seem to have been more successful than coinage in penetrating traditional African payment systems because they had a distinct role as personal ornaments, and European traders took advantage of their widespread acceptability to establish a regular means of commercial payment with African peoples. Such immense quantities of cowries were imported into western Africa that they became widely used in many regions in place of traditional currencies. Traditional practices were severely disrupted by the imported cowries in the same way as Belgian colonial currency affected Lele customs. Europeans used cowries primarily as a means of executing commercial transactions, whereas

306 Cut French coins and iron weights from central Madagascar, collected in the 1890s. The coins are cut from French 5-franc pieces. The larger example was made in 1848/9 at the Paris Mint; the smaller pieces are earlier issues made between 1832 and 1848. The iron weights were made locally for weighing the coin fragments in payments. French coins were imported until 1943, when a Western-style coinage was made for the island at the Pretoria Mint in South Africa.

307 Necklace made from silver 8-reals coins of Spanish Mexico, seventeenth to eighteenth century. This necklace of whole coins was used as a ceremonial gift to solicit blessings in the Merina kingdom of central Madagascar. (× ⅓)

308 Aluminium bronze 20-franc piece of French Madagascar, struck in Paris in 1953. The design is based on a map of the island flanked by plants and two sculptured standards resting on cattle horns. Among the Mahafaly people of southern Madagascar, tombs of noble families are decorated with standards and cattle horns. The coin design refers to the importance of the symbols of the ancestors in Malagasy culture. (× 1½)

309 One thousand-ariary note of the Malagasy Republic (the title of Madagascar as a state since 1958), issued in 1966. The ariary was worth 5 colonial francs. (× ¾)

Africans desired their acquisition for different reasons. Europeans also controlled the supply, and their dominant position in the cowrie system inevitably tended to undermine local monetary customs.

Nevertheless, the transformations brought about by the introduction of European means of payment and monetary attitudes do not always work to the detriment of indigenous systems. In Madagascar, for example, export and import trade conducted by Arab and European traders brought European silver coins into the island. By 1895, when Madagascar came under French colonial rule, they had become an important means of payment on the island, particularly in the Merina kingdom. But the coins reaching the island were generally

too large for local day-to-day needs. They were therefore cut up in order to 306 make them usable, with the value being determined in part by weight, but the fact that the silver came from a coin was important, as it was regarded as guaranteeing the purity of the metal. In addition to their use in trade and exchange, coins also took on a role within local ancestor worship. Whole coins were kept 307 and given as an offering to the king in expectation of blessings from the ancestral spirits, which he was supremely qualified to bestow. In present-day Madagascar, too, before an animal sacrifice takes place among the Betsimisakara, amusing speeches are made by orators, who receive coins from their audience, both as a reward in recognition of their eloquence and as a means of associating with the blessing of the ancestors, which is the object of the sacrifice itself. In this context, then, the monetary and religious uses of coins operate simultaneously, both as a payment to an individual and as a religious offering, because of the wider ritual associations which coins have in Malagasy society.

Money as a social phenomenon

The functions of Western money are historically linked with a particularly European concern for material productivity and profit, especially evident in the

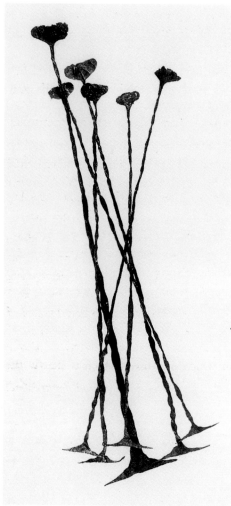

modern period. But this is far from a universal human characteristic. It can be argued that modern Western society is historically anomalous in its concentration on these areas of human endeavour.

There is an obvious danger of creating an unreal dichotomy between developed and non-industrial, indigenous socio-economic systems, but we might attempt the following generalisation about the differences between their money systems. Modern Western money has increasingly tended to allow the calculation of price and value equivalents between all sorts of goods and services. This is a concomitant feature of the rise of the importance of the market economy in industrialised countries, in which buying and selling are the primary ways of acquiring and distributing commodities, and labour is paid for with money. Outside this type of market economy, the use of monetary media of whatever form tends to be restricted in scope to particular social contexts and, in the realm of exchange, to transactions involving specific types of commodity. The creation and maintenance of social relationships, through gift-giving and

310 Iron Kissi pennies of Liberia, collected in the 1950s. These iron rods were used as currency in Liberia until the 1950s. The shape is thought to indicate the quality of the iron used; half the rod is hammered, half is twisted; one end is drawn to points, the other is sharpened to a blade. If the iron can be worked in these four ways it is shown to be of good quality. (× ⅓)

311 Copper cent of Liberia, 1833. This token was issued for the newly settled colony of Liberia, created in 1822 on the west coast of Africa by the American Colonization Society (founded in 1816) as a new home for freed African slaves returning from the USA. In 1848 Liberia became Africa's first republic, founded on the model of the USA and using the US dollar as its standard unit of currency, but with small change issued in the name of Liberia. (× 3)

ritually conditioned exchanges and payments, have frequently been much more important than market-oriented exchange as factors determining the ways in which local monetary systems have operated.

Because of the political and economic power of industrial societies, the forms and functions of their money have been particularly influential in many parts of the non-industrial world. But it is not always the case that local systems are simply transformed through contact. Indeed, as in the case of the Lele, local systems can be flexible and active in accommodating coins and banknotes for their own purposes, transforming their function in the process from a general-purpose medium of payment and exchange into something assimilable to social practices familiar to the society in question.

Given these profound differences between the modern, Western concept of money and the practices considered in this chapter, it is legitimate to ask whether we are at all justified in using the word 'money', even in inverted commas, in these contexts. There is clearly some danger of perpetuating the ethnocentric misconceptions that have already been discussed. The use of the word 'money' perhaps also encourages us to concentrate too much on the material object – the medium itself – rather than on the social processes in which it is used, which is exactly the mistake made by the travellers cited above. What is needed, then, is a somewhat

312 Iron hoe made for use in bride-wealth payments in Sudan, nineteenth to twentieth centuries. The small finial atttached to the leading edge of the blade shows that it was not intended to be used as a tool. (× ⅓)

313 Gold 15-rupee coin of German East Africa, struck in 1916 at an emergency mint at Tabora. Like many other territories on Africa's eastern coast, the German colony, later called Tanganyika (now part of Tanzania), used British Indian silver rupees as its standard unit of currency. The Tabora Mint was set up to make coins for the German colony during the First World War, when coins could not be supplied from Europe. (× 4)

314 Silver rupee of British India, struck at Bombay in 1891, countermarked with a crowned PM for circulation in the Portuguese colony of Mozambique.

315 Bronze penny of the British colonies of Rhodesia (Southern and Northern) and Nyasaland, struck in the name of Elizabeth II, 1955. These three territories were the last British colonies in Africa to be given their own currencies. Before 1932 South African or British coins were used by the British settlers. Southern Rhodesia (now Zimbabwe) then had its own coins, but Northern Rhodesia (now Zambia) and Nyasaland (now Malawi) only had coins from the beginning of the Rhodesia and Nyasaland issue in 1955.

modified concept of money, which is able to account for both modern and pre-modern money systems.

Most general definitions begin with the idea of money as a 'medium of exchange'. The disadvantage of this formulation for our purposes is that it would exclude, for instance, the Lele cloth system, in which the cloths were only rarely used as a means of exchange for commodities. Rather than 'exchange', perhaps 'means of making payments' is a more appropriate starting-point, as this would allow us to account for systems in which commodity exchange was not the focus of attention. As a 'means of making payments', then, money, be it coins or cloths, should operate within a conventionally recognised payment system which requires the use of specific objects of generally accepted, though not necessarily denominated, value. In order to allow for the full range of possibilities, we must allow that the nature of the payments may vary radically, from the purely commercial discharging of a debt, for a commodity or service, to socially binding and socially conditioned distribution and ownership-transfer from man to man, or from man to god. So, too, the particular objects and materials chosen as the medium of payment may differ greatly from culture to culture. But underlying the diversity, the materials selected do generally seem to belong to the group of available materials regarded as valuable or prestigious by the societies concerned. The Western world has a money system which has developed out of a preference for precious metal, while Pacific islanders had a preference for shells of various types, and it is no coincidence that these materials were in each case highly prized and extensively used for decorative purposes in both secular and religious contexts.

Defining the concept of money is clearly a problematic area, precisely because it is so familiar and yet so varied in its behaviour and appearance between different societies, and because it has changed so much in history. Perhaps the last word on this difficult subject should go to an inhabitant of one of the regions that have been considered in this chapter:

If money were made from iron and one could make knives, axes and chisels with it, then there could be some point in giving a value to it, but as it is I see no value in it. If a man has at his disposal more yams than he has need for, then he can exchange them for pigs or bark cloth. Of course money is easy to handle and is practical, but, as it does not rot, if it is preserved, people put it aside instead of sharing it with others (as a chief should do) and they become selfish. On the other hand if food is the most precious possession a man has (as it should be the case because it is the most useful and necessary thing) he cannot save it and one will be obliged either to

exchange it for another useful object or share it with his neighbours, lower chiefs and all the people in his care, and that for nothing without any exchange. I know very well now what makes Europeans so selfish – it is money.

FINOW, CHIEF OF THE TONGA ISLANDS

Curiously, perhaps, these observations on the destructive effects of Western money on social relationships echo in some respects the words of Karl Marx, whose ideas have been so important in the history of money in the modern world, the subject of our final chapter.

316 Cupro-nickel-zinc 10-ngwee coin of the Republic of Zambia, 1987. The front shows a portrait of President Kenneth Kaunda, the back a crowned hornbill. Each denomination of Zambia's coinage was decorated with typical examples of its fauna and flora. (× 1½)

317 Silver sixpence of Fiji, issued in the name of George VI and dated 1941. Fiji was the first of the Pacific island countries to have its own coinage, struck at the Royal Mint, London, from 1934. (× 4)

The Modern Period

The value of the yellow metal, originally chosen as money because it tickled the fancy of savages, is clearly a chancy and irrelevant thing on which to base the value of our money and the stability of our industrial system.

D. H. ROBERTSON, *Money* (1928)

The provocative language of this remark brings into sharp focus the issue which dominated the nature of money in the industrialised world in the nineteenth and twentieth centuries. Should money be based on a physical substance and derive its value from the rarity and desirability of that substance, or should it, in a world where man has achieved a self-conscious mastery of nature, be a creation of government, subject to and responsive to rational manipulation and control?

These two themes – the material of which money should most appropriately consist, and the extent to which the management of money should, and could, be regulated by government action – will accompany us through the history of money in these centuries. Since the late eighteenth century the changes in the former have been considerable. The monetary systems of Europe and America in that period were still primarily based on precious metal, both in terms of the material out of which coins were made and the standard of value for all banknotes. At the end of the twentieth century, by contrast, physical currency was no longer required for many monetary transactions, which could be carried out purely by means of accounting procedures using cheques, credit and debit cards, or electronic and computer technology. Some of these, of course, have existed in previous centuries. Bills of exchange, for example, have been mentioned at various points in the course of this book. But such developments in the pre-modern period generally involved the expectation that, *in extremis*, debts could always be called in as hard cash – gold and silver – for which bills were only a convenient and occasional substitute.

In the pre-modern period of Western history, then, money as a concept remained firmly rooted in the material of gold and silver. Writing in the early twenty-first century, we can affirm that this is largely no longer the case. Gold and silver are no longer the prime symbols of money or exchange value, and neither cash nor credit cards are conceived of as substitutes for specific amounts of precious metal. British banknotes still bear the words 'I promise to pay the bearer on demand the sum of [. . .] pounds' (i.e. 318 in gold) but this legend is a mere antiquarian survival, the historical significance of which is mostly lost on the British themselves. The source of the

Bank of England

Promise to pay the Bearer
on Demand the sum of

One Pound

A 19L

318 Detail of the promissory clause from a Bank of England £1 note of 1955–60. This wording dates back to goldsmiths' notes of the seventeenth century assigning a specific sum to a named individual. On banknotes the clause originally meant that they could be exchanged for gold, although in practice this was not always possible. When Britain finally left the gold standard in 1931 the words ceased to have any practical significance, but they remain as a statement of confidence and authority.

perceived value of money, then, has changed radically over the last two hundred years. In the process, money has become much more flexible and, perhaps, manageable, but, as we shall see, this profound development has not occurred without considerable theoretical debate and a certain amount of catastrophe.

Fiduciary money and convertibility

In itself, the idea of using materials other than gold or silver in the Western monetary tradition is by no means new. In the fourth century BC the Greek philosopher Plato advocated the use of a base-metal coinage for his ideal city, the virtue of which would be established by law for domestic trade only (*Laws*, 313). In eighteenth-century Europe base-metal coinage began to be produced in large quantities as fiduciary money (money whose value depends on trust rather than on the value of the material from which it is made), and was subsequently complemented by the extensive use of paper money in Europe and America.

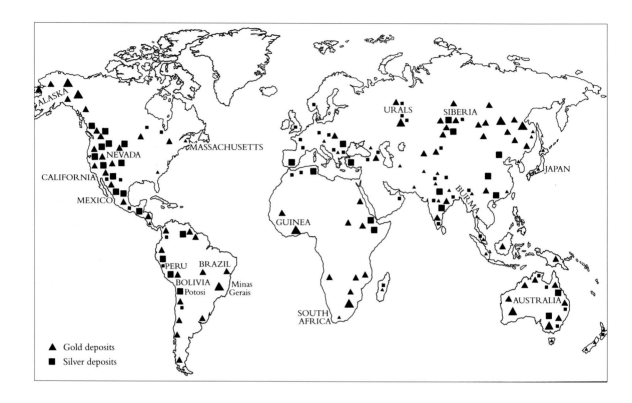

319 Major gold and silver sources.

Originally both these types of token money derived their value from an implicit or explicit undertaking that they could be exchanged or converted into precious-metal currency, whether gold or silver, which formed the basis of the gold standard. Such forms of currency, particularly banknotes, came to play such an important role that governments were simply unable, on an increasing number of occasions, to offer to convert it back to gold on demand. It was the combination of the pressure caused by a shortage of money coupled with the growing intellectual discipline of economic and monetary rationalism that eventually led to the end of the gold standard as the cornerstone of monetary policy in the Western world.

The use of paper money increased greatly in this period. For a long time previously bills of exchange had provided a means of payment and credit without the actual transfer of precious metal. But the advent of banknotes and other promissory notes created a situation in which this facility became available to a much wider public and on a much greater scale. Government and individuals realised their potential as a means of increasing the money supply, since they allowed more credit to be created by enabling a depositor to make a loan to a creditor without any increase in the amount of precious metal available. The total value of notes issued by a bank often exceeded the value of the amount of gold and silver it held in reserves, but this did not

320 *The Stoppage of the Bank* by Rolinda Sharples, 1822, showing anxious customers gathering outside the Bristol Bullion Bank which had temporarily suspended payment of its notes. Many country banks operated with inadequate gold reserves and were unable to meet the combined pressures of excessive note issue, over-generous lending and, indeed, customers wishing to exchange their notes for coin (Bristol City Museum and Art Gallery).

matter provided all the depositors and creditors of a particular bank did not try to convert their paper into precious metal at the same time. If they did, 320, 322 then the bank would either collapse or need to be protected by the temporary suspension of cash payments. This is what happened in Britain during the Napoleonic Wars; in 1797, to preserve the Bank of England's rapidly falling gold reserves, the Privy Council ordered the Bank Directors to 'forbear issuing any Cash in Payment until the Sense of Parliament can be taken', and the resulting 'Restriction Period' was to last until 1821. Despite 321 such real and potential problems, issues of paper effectively enabled a great increase to take place in the amount of credit in the economy. On the other hand, the difficulties of restricting such a growth of credit in the face of the temptation it offered to individuals and governments to overissue provoked a large number of financial crises.

New money could thus be put into circulation in two ways. One was by the discovery of new sources of precious metals, as happened in Africa and 319 the New World, the impact of which has been described in Chapter 7, or during the gold rushes of the nineteenth century. The second was through the increased credit supplied by banks, a development encouraged by the issue of circulating paper money from the seventeenth century onwards. The similarity in the consequences of an increase in supply in the two

The Restriction Period in Britain, 1797–1821

Britain's gold supplies were severely depleted in the late eighteenth century by wars with America and France. The situation was exacerbated by a commercial crisis which ruined many businesses and country banks, yet in such circumstances there was little choice but to rely increasingly on credit, token coinage and paper money. This practical reality was legally enforced in February 1797 when the Bank of England was ordered by the Privy Council to stop redeeming its notes in coin. The policy of cash suspension lasted until 1821.

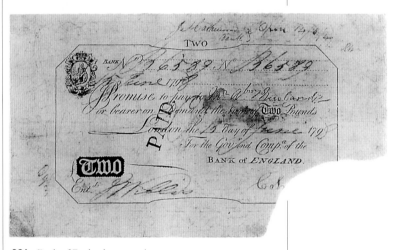

321b 'Bank Restriction Note', 1819, by the cartoonist George Cruikshank. Cruikshank saw a woman hanged for passing a counterfeit note and was prompted to portray public distress at such cruel punishments. He parodied the Bank of England's note design, signing it 'J. Ketch' – the common nickname for the hangman. (× ½)

321a Bank of England note for £2, 1798. The £1 and £2 notes issued by the Bank between 1797 and 1821 were easily imitated by a competent copperplate engraver: between 1797 and 1818, 313 people were hanged for offences relating to forgery. However, the notes were widely accepted as much-needed replacements for scarce coin (Bank of England). (× ½)

321c Cartoon of 1797 by James Gillray satirising the replacement of gold coins with low-denomination notes. William Pitt, the British Prime Minister, hides sacks of gold under the Bank counter and offers notes to a willing John Bull.

321d Silver token for 5 shillings, made from Spanish 'pieces of eight' and issued by the Bank of England in 1804. Boulton and Watt's new steam presses at the Soho Mint in Birmingham were able to obliterate the original designs, overstriking them with a new patriotic British design depicting Britannia.

321e Silver 8 reales of Spain, countermarked for use in Britain. Spanish 'pieces of eight' had been held in the Bank of England vaults for bullion value, but in 1797 and 1804 they were stamped with the head of George III, the British monarch, and circulated to alleviate the shortage of British silver coin. They were greeted with derision: 'The Bank to make their Spanish dollars pass, stamped the head of a fool on the neck of an ass.'

321f Five-shilling note issued by the British Linen Company, 1797. Shortage of coin and the Bank of England's suspension of cash payments for its notes had an impact throughout the entire country. Scottish banks also had only limited stocks of precious metal, and many issued notes for 5 shillings as an alternative to silver coin. (× ½)

321g Copper token 1 penny issued by the Birmingham Workhouse in 1814. In the absence of coinage, different forms of token currency became interchangeable. These tokens could be saved up and exchanged at the workhouse for £1 notes.

different forms of money, precious metal and paper, was not lost on contemporary commentators. The importation to Europe of enormous new quantities of gold and silver during the early modern period had led to an increase in prices, and contributed to a growing awareness of the quantity theory of money. This theory, whose importance to modern political thought can hardly be exaggerated, holds that as the quantity of money available for the purchase of goods increases, so the value and price of those goods will increase proportionately. This is the theory in its crudest form, and it has been subject to considerable modification and refinement by economists. But its general acceptance in some form or other was crucial to the transition away from a money based on gold and silver, since it was clear 322–4 that the quantity theory should apply to paper money as well as to precious metal. In his *Principles of Political Economy and Taxation* (1817) the economist David Ricardo (1772–1823) wrote:

> There is no point more important in issuing paper money than to be fully impressed with the effects that follow from the principle of limitation of quantity. It is not necessary that paper should be payable in specie [i.e. gold and silver coin] to secure its value, it is only necessary that its quantity should be regulated.

The similar behaviour of paper money and precious metal in this respect suggested that money could be understood and controlled as an instrument of economic and social well-being. A preference for paper money would, moreover, have the advantage that it would be fully controllable and would not be subject like gold and silver to the vagaries of increased supply or a chance discovery. Total control has of course never been achieved, for a variety of reasons. However desirable an end it may seem, it has suffered from the fact that those who would attempt to exercise control are easily influenced by other considerations. Issuing paper was an easier option for gov-

322 One-pound note of the Bristol Bullion Bank, 1825, with stamps bearing witness to the partners' bankruptcy and to dividends paid to the creditor holding the note. This bank grew out of a silversmith's business in 1811; it weathered the panic of 1822 (see **320**), but it could not withstand the severe commercial slump in the winter of 1825/6, when over sixty country banks in England went out of business. (× ½)

323 Australian gold coin of 1853 from Port Phillip, Victoria, privately produced by an English firm intending to strike coins for bullion and sell them from their Melbourne store, known as the Kangaroo Office. The back of this coin (not shown) states that it contains 'fine Australian Gold. Two ounces'. However, in 1855 their plans were superseded by the official issue of gold sovereigns from the British mint at Sydney.

324 Gold sovereign of George III, 1818, with a design of St George and the dragon by Benedetto Pistrucci. In 1816 there was a general reform of British currency, setting the pattern for the next century, with gold as the currency standard. Sovereigns valued at £1 sterling and half-sovereigns were minted from 1817, along with new silver and copper coins. (× 1½)

ernments, for example, than collecting or raising taxes. Ricardo again:

> Experience, however, shows that neither a State nor a Bank ever has had the unrestricted power of issuing paper money, without abusing that power; in all states, therefore, the issue of paper money ought to be under some check and control; and none seems so proper for that purpose as that of subjecting the issuers of paper money to the obligation of paying their notes, either in gold or in bullion.

This was precisely how the Bank of England, for example, applied informal control over the country banks in England; it returned their notes to those banks in return for payment in metal. In addition, legislation in the nineteenth century was introduced to control banking practice and to encourage centralised and responsible note issue.

Revolution and war in the modern world

Although paper money allowed an increase in the amount of money in circulation beyond what was possible in the age of precious-metal money, to the general advantage of government and trade, the economic risks involved were consequently greater. Yet the existence of this immediately accessible and highly manipulable form of money was itself a revolutionary change, and it was a factor of central importance in the other revolutions that have characterised the modern world – both political and social. The most important of these were, without doubt, the French and American Revolutions and the Industrial Revolution in Britain, which simultaneously transformed both politics and economics in the late eighteenth century and themselves provoked a greater use of circulating paper money. Three examples make clear the importance of paper money in modern political revolutions. Local paper money had been issued by Britain's American colonies during the eighteenth century, but the American Revolution against British rule was financed by vast issues of 'Continental' bills: some $240 million was issued in this way between 1775 and 1779. A few years later in France, a country well aware of the potential of paper money from the fiasco of John Law's experiments earlier in the century, the Revolutionary government began in 1789 to issue paper *assignats*. These were initially intended only to function as treasury bonds with 5 per cent interest, a means of financing the extraordinary military expenditure entailed by the Revolutionary Wars and supposedly backed by the proceeds from the confiscation of Church lands. But the assignats quickly began to function as currency and were produced in ever increasing numbers to meet the continuing financial crises of the new Republic. Well over four million 400-*livres* notes alone were issued in the 1790s, clear evidence of a chronic lack of financial control which led to

325 Copper halfpenny token of John Wilkinson, the Warwickshire ironmaster, 1788, showing a blacksmith at work in a forge. Private commercial issues of tokens flourished in Britain in the late eighteenth century when there was no official copper coinage. Industrialists often took various initiatives to create circulating capital: even before he began issuing tokens in 1787, John Wilkinson had used his own small-denomination notes to pay his workforce, and he later became involved with local banks in Shrewsbury and Birmingham. (× 1½)

326 Copper 'cartwheel' twopenny coin of 1797, produced at the Birmingham Soho mint of Matthew Boulton and James Watt with their new steam presses. After a long period when few low-denomination coins were produced in Britain, a revised and regularised copper coinage was issued from 1797, and the new twopenny and penny coins attempted to match copper content to value.

a reduction of the value of the assignats to about one three-hundredth of their face value. Over a century later the Russian Revolution saw a huge surge of issues of paper money by the Bolsheviks, White Russians and other 'authorities', such as the Ukrainian army.

Revolutionary, self-constituted governments such as these are, by their very nature, risky ventures, unattractive for investors and lacking access to foreign loans to pay for their wars. Paper money provided a ready, short-term solution to the problem, but there was always a price to pay. Both governments and individuals, like John Law in France, were frequently tempted to overissue notes, as we have already seen. Whether this was motivated by political aims or personal greed, the consequences were always similar, namely the collapse in the value of the paper money. The notes were theoretically backed up with gold (or sometimes land), but their overissue made their redemption impossible or at any rate undesirable on the part of the issuing authorities, and their convertibility into gold or silver might be suspended as a result. American 'Continentals' suffered rapid depreciation, and, despite legal attempts to enforce their acceptance the government only managed to avoid repudiating them altogether in 1780 by redeeming them at a rate of 40 paper dollars to one silver dollar, effectively a repudiation rate of 97.5 per cent. One observer, writing in 1778, remarked, 'The Congress paper dollars are now used for papering rooms, lighting pipes and other conveniences.' Similarly, French assignats became quite worthless within a few years. Despite the National Assembly's attempt to declare them legal tender, the Republic could not avoid official bankruptcy in 1797. Just as revolutionary governments took advantage of the seemingly infinite accessibility of paper money, so overissue could threaten revolution in a previously stable state.

Turning to the intense social and economic transformations that characterise the history of the modern world, the role of paper money here has perhaps even more long-term significance than in more strictly political revolutions. The Industrial Revolution which began in Britain in the mid-eighteenth century made new demands on financial organisations. It required the redistribution of capital from agricultural to industrialising areas, and from old to new industries, and encouraged an expansion of credit to finance new businesses. Banks were both a product of, and a stimulus to, this growing economic activity. They facilitated the circulation of capital and 325–6 made advances to promote industry, trade and public utilities, such as transport. But the banks themselves often emerged as useful corollaries to other businesses, especially in the textile, mining and iron industries, and their success – or, frequently, failure – owed much to the general commercial climate or even the fate of a single enterprise: one bankruptcy could bring many others in its wake. It was, however, through the country banks that circulating paper money and more complex manipulation of money came into the hands of ordinary people.

In 1854, in his novel of life in a northern industrial town, Charles Dickens portrayed the relationship between factory owner Mr Gradgrind and banker Mr Bounderby. The close relationship between the two men symbolises the close relationship between manufacture and local banking capital in the growth of industrialisation. However, to some it seemed that money was achieving a new self-importance, as more than merely a means to an end. Describing the fictional industrial town of Coketown, Dickens was critical of this new social and economic order:

> The relations between master and man were all fact, and everything was fact between the lying-in hospital and cemetery, and what you couldn't state in figures, or show to be purchaseable in the cheapest market and saleable in the dearest, was not, and never should be, world without end, Amen.

As Europe and America experienced political and industrial revolutions in the eighteenth and nineteenth centuries, these changes in the social and economic world brought with them new opportunities, but also new tensions and concerns. The rise of a wage-oriented, industrial, urban, society brought with it concerns for the proper ordering and provision of small change. As a result, satisfactory token money for small change came to be regularly provided by most industrialised countries during the nineteenth century, with the almost complete eclipse of base silver for this purpose by copper and bronze. A range of new metals and alloys also began to be employed for coinage: cupro-nickel, and later aluminium and stainless steel. Silver, gold, paper and base metal were effectively brought together into a more manageable system in the late nineteenth century, facilitating the production of money of all kinds on a hugely increased scale, to satisfy the demands of the complex, monetised world of the industrialised West.

These changes brought with them debates about the nature of money, and money in all its forms, including coins, was affected by the industrialisation of Europe. Governments became increasingly active in supervising denomination systems, and in some areas of Europe local monetary systems were rationalised, and unified coinages adopted, for example in Germany

327–31 Five silver coins of countries in the Latin Monetary Union: France, 1 franc, 1867; Belgium, 1 franc, 1867; Switzerland, 1 franc, 1875; Italy, 1 lira, 1867; Greece, 1 drachma, 1868. In the nineteenth century there were several attempts to promote trade by coordinating the currencies of different countries. Set up in 1865, the Latin Monetary Union set common standards of weight and precious-metal content for the gold and silver coins.

Money in revolution and war

Money issued in times of war or revolution may be both a product of economic disruption and a symbol of political change. Such turbulent circumstances have often provided an incentive for creating paper money as a substitute for coins, which are likely to be hoarded, and to raise funds for the warring factions.

Even groups challenging an existing regime will tend to choose broadly conventional imagery to inspire public confidence in the stability of the currency; however, money is also a useful vehicle for propaganda.

332b French copper token for 5 sols, issued in 1792 by the Monneron brothers, merchant bankers in Paris. In addition to paper money, private tokens helped to supplant scarce coin during the French Revolution; indeed, one side of this token declares that it is exchangeable for paper assignats. The oth er side carries the legend 'Live in freedom or die'.

333a Bill for one-sixth of a dollar, 1776, issued in Philadelphia by the Continental Congress. Consensus of opposition to Britain during the American Revolution is illustrated here by linked circles, representing each of thc thirteen original states. The legends in the centre state 'American Congress we are one'.

332c French assignat for 400 livres, issued in 1792, the first year of the Republic. This dramatic design, engraved on steel, tich in symbols of power and victory. (× ½)

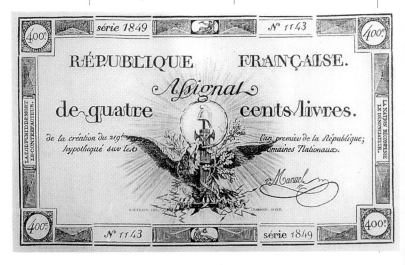

332e Confederate States of America $500 note of 1864, with patriotic images of the Confederate flag, the Great Seal of the Confederacy and a portrait of Thomas 'Stonewall' Jackson, the famous Confederate commander. The number of notes issued increased dramatically with the costs of the Civil War. (× ½)

332f United States note for 1 dollar, 1862. The first paper money issued under the Constitution of the United States was authorised in July 1861 to finance war with the Confederate States. The government suspended payments in specie to preserve the supply of gold and silver and coins, so the notes were inconvertible. (× ½)

332d Note for 5 zlotys, 1794, an example of Poland's first paper currency, issued by the insurgent Supreme National Council which was fighting against the foreign occupying forces. The note issue was devised by the revolutionary leader Tadeusz Kosciuszko, who had fought for the Americans in their War of Independence and been much influenced by the ideas of the French Revolution. (× ½)

332g South Russian note for 250 roubles with a portrait of a Cossack general, issued in 1918 by the anti-Soviet 'White Russian' High Command of the Armed Forces under General Deniken. The Russian Revolution and Civil War spawned a large number of note issues by separate states, regions and military forces. (× ½)

and Italy, replacing the multitude of currencies that had once circulated in the principalities and states of these countries. At the same time, there were international attempts to co-ordinate different monetary systems in the interests of facilitating free trade. Ambitious plans were proposed in 1867 to create a 'universal currency' based on the gold coins of Britain, France and America. This did not succeed, but another similar initiative did, and the Latin Monetary Union, in which France, Belgium, Italy, Switzerland and a number of other states combined in a coinage system with common standards of weight and fineness. Based on a bimetallic standard, the coins of each country were exchangeable with each other's at par and without limit, but the depreciation of silver in the second half of the nineteenth century put the arrangement under strain. Around the same time, the Scandinavian Monetary Union linked Denmark, Norway and Sweden in a system based on the gold standard. With the global financial turbulence caused by the First World War, however, both systems broke down, and the member countries went back to issuing their own currencies.

America in the nineteenth century

The tension between the issue of banknotes and the need to maintain a basis in gold was a common theme through most of the nineteenth century, and can be seen clearly in the mixed experiences of North America. In the early nineteenth century east coast cities including Boston, New York and Philadelphia led industrial expansion and the associated growth in banking. There was a huge increase in the number of banks and banknotes, with the attendant risks of inflation and depreciation of the value of paper money, linked to the specie in which it could be redeemed. However, on several occasions during the nineteenth century public confidence was lost, and if too many people tried to redeem their notes for gold and silver at the same time, there were bank runs and economic chaos. The short-lived Second Bank of the United States (1816–36) typified these problems: it held only a 20 per cent coin reserve against its liabilities; it initially lent widely and speculatively, then pulled in sharply, depressing economic activity; worst of all, three of its senior officers attempted to take over control by fraudulent means. Following the withdrawal of Federal funds, this bank – along with many others – foundered during the years following the so-called panic of 1837, which began on 10 May when payments in specie were suspended, and which led to great hardship and economic depression.

333 Silver 'Liberty' dollar of the United States, 1795. The first official coinage under the Constitution of the United States was authorised by an Act of Congress in 1792, which established a mint at Philadelphia. The silver dollar, worth 100 copper cents, was the standard unit in the decimal system, although there were many years when it was not minted and Spanish American silver continued to circulate widely. The newly independent nation chose emblems of liberty for all its early coins. (× 2)

334 Two-dollar note of the Planters Bank, Savannah, Georgia, 1860. In the first half of the nineteenth century the growing economy of the United States depended heavily on the vast numbers of notes issued by private chartered banks. The beautiful engravings on these notes presented a romanticised view of the country and its inhabitants – often shown at work, as in the idyllic farmyard scene on this example. (× ¾)

The discovery of gold near Sacramento in 1848 brought a flood of workers to California. Within four years more than 1 per cent of the population of the United States had moved to California, and gold production quickly became an important part of the American economy. This gold rush, combined with the increasing industrialisation of the east and midwest, contributed to the extraordinary economic development of the United States in the nineteenth century. This massive expansion once again encouraged the creation of banks, whose numbers had reached almost 3,000 by the early 1860s. But there was trouble coming, as the rift between the southern and northern states widened, and tensions increased. The issue was not just slavery, but also growing disagreements between the industrialising and urbanising north and the predominantly agricultural south on a number of issues. The ensuing Civil War (1861–5) was enormously expensive for both sides, forcing the country onto an inconvertible paper basis (as the government had no gold reserves left), where it remained for seventeen years. The era of the 'Greenback', as the inconvertible government bills were known, brought a re-establishment of central authority, the greater regulation of note issue by state banks and the elimination of their earlier excesses, but the problem of depreciation of paper remained. By the time the war had ended in 1865, a Greenback dollar was worth only 49 cents in gold, and there were discussions about whether the war debt paid in these notes should be repaid in coin. If so, there was likely to be a shrinkage of the money supply of the type that had previously caused such disruption; if not, there would be a 50 per cent repudiation of debts. The government tried to reduce the number of Greenbacks in circulation, but was forced to abandon this policy after only 10 per cent had been removed.

Although the United States returned to the gold standard in 1873 and the

336

334, 337

335 'Hard Times' token, America, 1837.
The shortage of precious metals during the economic depression of the late 1830s meant that tokens and other local and emergency issues became widely issued and used. Some were satirical, like this 'Hard Times' token commemorating the suspension of specie payments on 10 May 1837.

336 Gold coin for 50 dollars produced by Wass, Molitor & Co., San Francisco, 1855. The United States Mint Act of 1792 authorised a federal issue of gold coins, but their supply was erratic and often did not reach remote areas. As the law prohibited states, but not individuals, from coining money, exploitation of American gold mines encouraged a large variety of privately produced coins. During the American Civil War, the few gold coins that were issued were made at the San Francisco mint, from California gold, and sent to the east to support banking and the war effort.

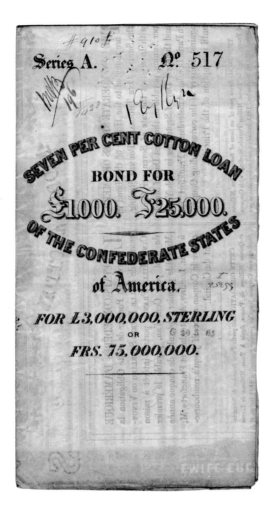

337 Confederate States of America 7 per cent cotton bond, 1863. As well as printing paper money, the Confederate states issued bonds in Europe. Funds raised by these loans were used to finance overseas activities, including the building of ships in Europe. They could, in theory, be redeemed for cotton on demand, but delivery of the cotton had to be taken in the Confederacy, making it all but impossible in practice.

Greenback returned to par in 1879, the question of whether or not the money supply should be reduced by the removal of the Greenbacks remained so important that in the elections of 1878 the Greenback Labor Party – which advocated the even greater issue of such notes rather then their reduction – polled over a million votes. Parallel to the problem of the Greenbacks, and arising from it, was a further debate about silver money. The silver dollar had disappeared from circulation during the Civil War and it was officially removed from the list of coins to be struck by the mint when the country returned to the gold standard in 1873. But the advocates of a larger supply of money, thwarted by the restriction of Greenbacks and a consequent depression of prices, saw the opportunity to increase the supply by establishing a 'free coinage' of silver that would take advantage of an increase in silver production in the western states, thanks to the discovery of silver in Colorado, and its decreasing value in the world market. This, it was hoped, would bolster commodity prices and return them to their earlier levels. However, by 1893 the country was in the grip of another economic depression, and the controversy came to a head in the election campaign of 1896. The 'silverites' of the Democratic Party advocated a bimetallic currency. This entailed unlimited coinage of silver and gold at a fixed ratio of 16 to 1 in order to allow prices to rise and thus alleviate the serious economic depression, which was also a worldwide phenomenon. They were opposed by the 'gold-bugs' of the Republican Party, who wanted to limit the issue of silver coin and control the money supply in favour of the industrial interests of the east. The debate was not resolved until the Gold Standard Act of 1900, which declared the gold dollar to be the standard unit of value. This move was made possible by an increase in world gold production and banking credit, which encouraged a rise in commodity prices and halted the deflation of the previous decades.

The banking boom and bust of the nineteenth century continued into the early twentieth century, until the crisis of 1907, which had begun as a credit crisis in New York, prompted the creation of the National Monetary Commission in order to reform the currency system. Even after the passage 338 of the Federal Reserve Act of 1913, the twelve banks of issue did not operate as a fully centralised banking institution until Roosevelt's economic reforms of the 1930s.

The American experience shows how debates about the nature of money, the control of the amount of money in circulation and the relationship between gold, silver and paper, had moved to the centre of the political stage in the nineteenth century. Millions of lives were affected by the different positions taken on these issues by the political leaders of the time. This was a new phenomenon in the history of money, caused by the extensive

338 United States Federal Reserve note for 20 dollars, 1914. The Federal Reserve system of centralised note issue was set up in 1913 and is still in operation today. The notes are issued by the Federal government, and put into circulation through the twelve Federal Reserve Banks. They were redeemable in gold until 1933. (× ¾)

development of paper money and the changed, and constantly changing, economic and political conditions of the modern world.

Intellectual changes

It is no surprise that the change in the role of money caused by the explosion of credit during the eighteenth century and the social changes brought about by the Industrial Revolution combined to produce new ideas about money and society and, of course, the relationship between them. This was the period that saw the birth of the study of that combination – what we now call the science of economics but in the eighteenth and early nineteenth centuries was called 'political economy'. The increasing volatility of money caused by its growing intangibility prompted the realisation that its manipulation could have enormous consequences on the very structure and nature of human society. It is not possible here to do more than touch on these issues, but the nature of the debate, which continues today, can be characterised by a contrast between two of its most important figures, Adam Smith and Karl Marx, whose radically different views constituted the intellectual bases of the two most significant economic and social systems of the modern world, capitalism and socialism.

339 Portrait of Adam Smith (1723–90), political economist and author of *The Wealth of Nations*, by James Kay, 1790.

Adam Smith (1723–90) published his *Inquiry into* 339 *the Nature and Causes of the Wealth of Nations* in 1776, at the very beginning of the Industrial Revolution, and it is widely regarded as the first work of modern economics. It covered many aspects of the nature of the economic system and the ways in which governments might influence it. Most important to the theme of this chapter is Smith's treatment of the concept of value. His view, known as the Labour Theory of Value, held that the value of any object is measured by the amount of labour for which it can be exchanged: 'labour therefore is the real measure of the exchangeable value of all commodities' (1, ch. 5). According to Smith, the wealth of a nation was not to be measured in terms of its stocks of gold and silver, but 'first, by the skill, dexterity, and judgment with which its labour is generally applied: and, secondly, by the proportion between the number of those who are employed in useful labour, and that

340 Equitable Labour Exchange note for one hour, 1832. The socialist reformer Robert Owen set up two exchanges, in London and Birmingham, where workers could exchange their products for notes to the value of the time needed to make the goods: as this note states, an hour's work was worth sixpence. The notes could be used to buy other goods, but the scheme failed when the exchanges became overstocked with less popular items. (× ¾)

of those who are not so employed.' The maximisation of wealth required that labour should work in the most efficient way possible. This demanded the abandonment of the restrictive trade practices of the past and the establishment of a free international trade, since the larger the market the labourer could reach, the greater the opportunity there was for him to work as productively as possible. Smith's theories also had a moral dimension, in that he believed that the furtherance of individual competition and 'natural liberty' in economic affairs would, through the guidance of an 'invisible hand', lead to social harmony more effectively than state action.

Smith's emphasis on the primacy of labour was to have far-reaching consequences for the question of how the value of a commodity should be distributed between the different parties who contributed to its production: the workers, whose subsistence provided the labour with which it was made in return for wages; the landlords, who provided the premises in return for rent; and the employers, whose capital provided the equipment and raw materials necessary for production in return for profit. The same questions arose for successive economic writers, who took forward Smith's vision of the equilibrium between the different parties in a way that assigned them differing rewards. The political economist Ricardo, for example, argued that wages should represent what was 'necessary to enable the labourers, one with another, to subsist and to perpetuate their race, without either increase or diminution'. Subsistence wages were thus justified in the interests of

MONEY: A HISTORY

profit and capital. If profits from manufacturing fell, as they inevitably did as a consequence of mass-production and fierce competition, wages had to fall as well.

During the late eighteenth and early nineteenth centuries there were critics of the all-pervasive role of money in the new industrial order of society. One such was the writer Thomas Carlyle (1795–1881), who in *Chartism* (1839) described the socio-economic change caused by the Industrial Revolution as follows: 'In one word, *Cash Payment* had not then grown to be the universal nexus of man to man. . . . With the supreme triumph of Cash, a changed time has entered.' But such critics did not manage to effect any fundamental change in the accepted vision of the classical theory of economics laid down by Smith and refined by followers like Ricardo. A more radical challenge was eventually proposed by the writings of Karl Marx (1818–83) and Friedrich Engels 341 (1820–95). Compare the above quotation from Carlyle with the following words from the *Communist Manifesto* of 1848:

> The bourgeoisie . . . has mercilessly torn apart the motley feudal bonds that connected man to his 'natural superiors', and has left no other nexus between man and man than callous 'cash payment'.

341 Portrait of Karl Marx (1818–83), political philosopher, from a 100-mark note of the German Democratic Republic, 1975 (M. O'Grady).

The similarities are obvious. Like Carlyle, Marx saw how the capitalists of the Industrial Revolution had caused the restructuring of the previous social order, but he went much further in his critique. He attacked the unequal distribution of wealth between worker, capitalist and landlord advocated by economists like Ricardo, arguing that it arose out of the capitalist system of production itself, which was the cause of an unjust distribution of political power between the various parties. The socialist revolution would correct these injustices and undo the disastrous social effects of the capitalists' obsession with money. The historical repercussions of Marx's political ideas are well-known, but their relevance for our purpose is to illustrate the rise of economic and monetary theory in the eighteenth and nineteenth centuries, as people became increasingly aware of the complex effects of money upon the structure of society in the context of the changed conditions brought about by the Industrial Revolution.

World wars and Keynesian economics

The material legacy of the nineteenth century to the twentieth was a system of money based on paper money and gold, into and from which paper 342-3 was normally convertible – the gold standard. The intellectual inheritance

342–3 Bronze medal of 1912 commemorating the fifteenth anniversary of Japan's adoption of the gold standard in 1897, and a gold 20-yen coin (× 2) of Emperor Mutsuhito issued in that year.

was an increased awareness of monetary theory and of the political and so-cial implications of money in history. Much had been learned from the ex-perience of the previous two hundred years, of the disasters that might arise both from the uncontrolled issue of paper money and the attempt to re-move it from circulation. A sort of practical equilibrium had been achieved between paper and gold, whereby the two forms of money were linked by a political and economic interdependence. Each element of this equilibrium, however, was as open to the same problems that had beset them for over a hundred years: the fluctuations in the price of gold due to chance or delib-erate manipulation, and the temptation for governments to resort to massive issues of paper to cover the costs of wars and other exceptional financial de-mands. Wars had previously caused the temporary breakdown of the gold standard and the suspension of convertibility – for example, in Britain from 1797 to 1821 and in America in the 1860s, as we have seen. But the final change from one element, gold, to the other, paper, came about when the First World War brought demands of an altogether different scale.

At the outbreak of the First World War (1914–18), the central banks of the great European powers had large reserves of gold whose principal function

344 One-pound note issued by the British Treasury in 1914. These notes were nicknamed 'Bradburys' after the Secretary of the Treasury whose signature appeared on them. Treasury notes for £1 and 10 shillings were produced as alternatives to gold sovereigns and half sovereigns, which the government wished to preserve for its own central resources during the war effort. Theoretically the Treasury notes were redeemable in coin; in practice the public was strongly discouraged from asking for gold. (× ½)

345–7 Currency from Austria illustrating political and economic turmoil during and after the First World War: gold 1-krone coin, 1864 (× 1½); 20-heller note, 1920; and 50,000-krone note, 1922 (× ¾). A currency system of gold and silver coins was set up in the 1850s and maintained after the reform in 1892. Local note issues for very low sums began during the war to provide small change; in contrast, during the 1920s massive inflation was reflected in notes of denominations up to 5 million kronen, but worth almost nothing.

was seen as a means of maintaining the international value of the currency against fluctuations which might arise due to trade deficits or surpluses. The operation of the gold standard meant that in the case of a trade deficit, gold would flow out to meet the deficit and so prices would fall; in turn the fall in prices would stimulate a rise in exports, leading to a trade surplus and in-flow of gold. Theoretically the cycle would continue indefinitely and act as an automatic regulator. But the outbreak of the First World War imposed such enormous strains that the system collapsed and the convertibility of notes into gold was suspended. The gold stocks which had been built up by France or Germany, for example, before the war were rapidly diminished by the need to pay for supplies with gold, since their own paper currencies

344

were not welcomed by parties not involved in the conflict. The victors at the end of the war were determined to recoup their loss of gold through the imposition of reparations on Germany. 'Hang the Kaiser and let Germany pay the cost of the war', was the slogan of the British prime minister David Lloyd George during 1918. When these reparations were finally assessed in 1921, the total was enormous: 132,000 million marks in gold. Unless 1,000 million gold marks were paid immediately the Allies threatened an invasion of the Ruhr, Germany's main industrial region. In order to meet this demand, Germany was forced into the paradoxical position of borrowing this sum in London. But continuing demands for further reparations, backed by military force, particularly from France, caused the collapse of the German currency as an inevitable consequence of the overissuing of paper money. The consequent failure on the part of the French to collect the gold they needed from Germany in turn caused the depreciation and collapse of the French currency.

The statistics associated with German inflation during the 1920s make astonishing reading. If 1913 is taken as a baseline, the effect on prices in Germany was as follows:

1913	100
1922	147,479
1923	75,570,000,000,000

The implications of monetary collapse for daily life were profound: 'I was amazed when I found today that one had to pay 24,000 marks for a ham sandwich, whereas yesterday in the same café a ham sandwich cost only 14,000' (*Daily Mail* correspondent, 22 July 1923). The sections of the population most affected by the monetary crisis were those who had their personal assets primarily in the form of cash (the value of savings was virtually wiped out within the space of a year) and those dependent on fixed incomes, whose wages suddenly became worthless (the idea of 'indexing' wages to inflation was not invented until after the Second World War). The 345-7 effect on the middle and lower-middle classes was catastrophic. A vivid evocation of this time can be found in the autobiography of the Austrian author Stefan Zweig (1881–1942), *The World of Yesterday*. He recalls the stability of nineteenth-century Austria, symbolised by its currency, the *krone*, circulating 'in pieces of shining gold, which seemed to guarantee its unchangeability. . . . Everything had its norm, its fixed measure and weight', whereas in Austria after the First World War 'an egg cost as much as a luxury automobile once had, and would in Germany later cost four billion marks – a sum roughly equivalent to the former value of all the houses in Greater Berlin'. When J. M. Keynes published his *Economic Consequences of the Peace* in 1919, with its indictment of contemporary political leaders and the principle of reparations in particular, he wrote prophetically: 'Mr. Lloyd George took the responsibility for a Treaty of Peace that was not wise, which was partly impossible, and which endangered the life of Europe.'

The political effects of the aftermath of the First World War cannot fail to impress themselves upon us even today. Its monetary effects were hardly any less significant. After the war, country after country went back to the gold standard – as Chancellor of the Exchequer Winston Churchill took Britain back in 1925 – and all European currencies had returned to it by 1928, although the United States, which had seen a huge influx of gold from Europe during the war, was the only one that managed to do so with any success. Britain's return, for instance, accentuated the uncompetitive prices of British goods on the world market, and the consequent cut in wage levels to compensate contributed to the General Strike of 1926. The return to the gold standard was desired not just as a form of conservative security, but also because it was regarded as a *sine qua non* for the establishment of stable international trade after the disruptions of the war. Before 1914 British gold reserves had provided the fulcrum of stability for world trade and currencies. But the war had shifted the balance towards New York, and London was no longer capable of covering foreign currencies with payments in gold as once had been the case. This was to prove an untenable position.

America had much of the world's money after the war, but large quantities returned to Europe in the 1920s in the form of loans to the bankrupt countries of Europe. There was also a post-war boom in trade, with American goods flowing freely into Europe. But the supply of these goods outstripped European demand for them, prices in America and Europe fell, and the brief respite from post-war instability came to an end in October 1929 with the Wall Street Stock Exchange crash. Industry was disrupted and 348 confidence in international trade and finance shattered. American money left Europe, and the Great Depression caused mass unemployment and poverty throughout the Western world. The weakness of the European economies and their dependence on American finance was made manifest when, in 1931, a financial crisis in Europe provoked a run on gold in London which Britain was unable to cover. Payment of gold was suspended, and by 1936 all Western currencies were off the gold standard again.

World events finally brought about the change that many economists had by now been advocating for a generation. J. M. Keynes (1883–1946) had fiercely attacked not only Lloyd George's policy of the imposition of war reparations on Germany but also Churchill's return to the gold standard in 1925. The American economist Irving Fisher (1867–1947) had for a long time criticised the unreliability of the gold standard as a basis for the world

348 Crowds outside the Brooklyn branch of the Bank of the United States as it closes its doors, 11 December 1930. The now infamous Wall Street Crash of 1929 was the turning point from post-war boom to the depression of the 1930s. Caused by a complicated mix of factors, not least the fears of investors that stocks were overvalued, the crash triggered losses across the world, bringing chaos and distress to many countries, institutions and individuals.

financial system because of the danger of unpredictable disruption by outside factors, such as the discovery of a new source of gold which would reduce its value and plunge the world into monetary chaos. Their criticisms were apt.

The gold standard had ultimately failed, but so long as it had been successful it had at least provided an element of predictability and discipline in international finance. The different currencies pegged to the standard were exchangeable with one another at a fixed rate, and had thus facilitated free trade. But free trade and economic liberalism were no longer seen as desirable ends in themselves, and the gold standard was thoroughly discredited. The currency problems were an obvious symptom of the world's protracted economic problems, and the system based on gold was clearly not equal to the new economic context of the inter-war years. A new approach was needed, and economists such as Keynes offered increasing government control over the whole economy as the answer. What Keynes, Fisher and others proposed was a new vision, in which gold and paper money were dissociated and gold was relegated to the role of a strategic reserve. They also promised a new sophistication in the management of monetary and economic affairs to overcome the financial and economic chaos which had seemed to characterise the first decades of the twentieth century. In the 1930s and 1940s governments first began to produce figures for the product and income of their national economies – a comprehensive digest of information over which government authority was meant to exercise beneficial regulation through the application of economic theory.

It was in this historical and intellectual context that Keynes laid the foundation of modern economic thought and monetary management. His most important work, *The General Theory of Employment, Interest and Money*, was published in 1936. It arose from his experience of the Great Depression and the inability of contemporary politicians and economists to provide a means of escape from its consequences. The greatest change envisaged was the assertion of political control over economic processes and money. No longer would states have to wait for economic changes to take place – for unemployment to bring about a reduction in wages, for instance – as a means of achieving recovery from a recession. By increasing demand through a deliberate but controlled government budget deficit, it would be possible to stimulate the economy into growth, to provide employment or to enable a nation to establish a welfare state. Roosevelt's New Deal in 1930s America, partially influenced by Keynes's ideas, introduced deficit spending, but it was only the growth of the American economy during the Second World War (1939–45) that finally brought the Great Depression to an end, both in the United States and in the other industrialised nations of the world. Industrial production increased and unemployment fell, ushering in a quarter-century of unparalleled economic growth in America, Europe and Japan.

The immediate reaction to Keynes's views and proposals was predictably unenthusiastic and his name was in some circles held in much the same opprobrium as that of Marx. The irony of this was that he had in fact provided a solution to one of Marx's main criticisms against the capitalist system, namely its inability to cope with the seemingly inevitable series of slumps and depressions, by restricting the potential of money and markets to cause social and economic disaster. But his views soon gained acceptance and the immediate post-war decades showed how effectively he and his successors enabled the capitalist system not only to survive but to come to dominate the world, paradoxically through curbing the excesses of money's liberty through government manipulation.

The post-war world and monetarism

Towards the end of the Second World War, it was increasingly believed that something needed to be done to guarantee economic stability by regulating the international financial markets and encouraging the flow of money

349 John Maynard Keynes addressing the Bretton Woods conference in 1944. The economist was called upon to advise representatives of the Allied nations on how best to build the post-war economy.

around the world. In July 1944 representatives of the forty-four Allied nations met at Bretton Woods, New Hampshire, for the United Nations Monetary and Financial Conference, which resulted in agreements to 349 maintain the value of currencies and the establishment of institutions including the International Monetary Fund. Countries that signed up agreed to keep their currency within one percent of fixed amount in terms of gold, or, as it worked in practice, in terms of the US dollar. The agreements in effect set up a triangular trade system, with the United States making profit from its trade with developing nations, using these profits to help finance the reconstruction of European economies, which would then provide markets for American products.

For some twenty years after the Second World War the Keynsian system worked, and the Bretton Woods agreements kept capital flowing. Britain and other Western countries enjoyed prosperity and full employment, and their economies grew. But during the 1960s spiralling inflation, with rising prices and severe deficits in the balance of payments, was seen to be a consequence of maintaining full employment. Despite deflationary measures, falling employment and the devaluation of sterling in 1967, the problem of inflation persisted. As accelerating inflation was unsustainable and politically unacceptable, it met a response in a new economic doctrine, that of 'monetarism', which sought to control inflation and maintain the value of the currency by restricting the amount of money in the economy. Like earlier theories of economic cycles or the automatic regulating mechanism of the gold standard, monetarism sought to create equilibrium through a self-stabilising process, and once again the effects were felt in their impact on employment levels and social welfare.

In the late 1960s the US dollar, and with it the Bretton Woods system, came under increasing strain from a combination of economic and political factors, fuelled by an oil crisis, until in 1971 the United States faced a huge balance of trade deficit and the Bretton Woods system collapsed. The consequent retreat by governments from active management of their economies and, indeed, the limits of their ability to exercise effective economic control were increasingly revealed in the 1970s and 1980s. Through the incessant progress of technology and international communications, money began to circulate in ways that were quite beyond the power of governments to regulate. Speculation on the international currency markets and the growth of international corporations and banks based in America and East Asia, with a huge stake in the world economy, rendered government sovereignty over national economies more and more difficult in Western countries.

Keynes was out. The 1970s and 1980s saw the return of a neo-liberalism in certain countries in the West – America and Britain above all. There was no return to anything like a gold standard, but governments in these countries attempted to withdraw from the management of money in the international market and left its operations to supposedly self-regulating global market forces. Instead of a fixed parity underpinned by the gold standard, the value of individual currencies was estimated in relation to a small number of powerful currencies on the world money markets, particularly the American dollar, the Japanese yen and the German mark. This was a procedure that guaranteed the prosperity of the markets themselves but not necessarily that of the national governments concerned, because its operation was largely out of their control.

At the same time as the managed economic systems of the 1950s and 1960s began to wane, economists studied in more detail the benefits of monetary and economic union. If several smaller countries joined together, or a smaller country adopted a trading currency of a larger neighbour, theorists argued, they could benefit both from reduced trading costs, as well as being cushioned from shocks due to fluctuations in the international

350 International Monetary Fund meeting in September 1971, the month after the Bretton Woods agreement had come to an end when President Nixon abolished the gold standard. The institutions it had created, including the IMF and the World Bank, lived on, altering their roles to meet the changed needs of the world economy.

money markets. Of course, this was in a practical sense nothing new, 328–32 but what was new was the theoretical discussion of the stages of economic integration and its effects on national and international economies, and the investigation of optimum currency areas.

Despite the collapse of the Bretton Woods agreement, the US dollar remained an important international currency. Indeed, the use of the term 'dollarisation' for the use of a foreign currency in a country reflects this continued dominance, although other currencies are also adopted by dollarised economies – including the European currencies, the Russian ruble and the Australian and New Zealand dollars. In some areas of post-communist Eastern Europe two domestic economies developed, one catering for those who only had access to the inflationary domestic currencies, and the other for the few who managed to earn dollars or German marks, opening up a whole new world of Western imports. Towards the end of the twentieth century such *de facto* monetary unions became increasingly officially recognised, with some countries officially adopting the currencies of a

Modern note design

The designs on modern paper currency are not only intended to indicate clearly the issuing authority and the denomination of the note, but also to make the note as difficult as possible to forge. These practical requirements provide many opportunities for creativity, and notes can reflect contemporary ideas of aesthetic appeal and national identity, with results that may be blatantly propagandist or carefully neutral, emphasising either change or continuity.

351a This note for 5,000 rials of the Bank Markazi Iran, 1981, depicts a cheering crowd declaring loyalty to the Ayatollah Khomeini. Earlier banknotes carried a portrait of the Shah of Iran; after his deposition in 1979, these notes circulated with the portrait obliterated by an overprinted pattern, as a temporary expedient until new notes reflecting the new political order were issued.

351b In 2002, twelve member states of the European Union introduced a new currency: the euro. The notes are intended to show the unity between European nations, with a window or doorway on the front symbolising openness and cooperation, and a bridge on the back representing cooperation and communication between Europe and the World. Europe's history is also commemorated, each denomination featuring a different historical period, from the classical arches on the 5-euro note to the 20th-century architecture on the 500-euro note. (× ¾)

351c Since 1929 the American 100-dollar bill has had a portrait of Benjamin Franklin on the front, and Independence Hall on the back. In 1996, to protect this high-value note from counterfeiting, it was redesigned. Among the new security features are the words 'The United States of America' printed along the lapel of Franklin's coat.

351d Banknotes printed on polymer rather than paper were first introduced in Australia in 1988. Security features such as clear windows make them harder to counterfeit, and they are much more durable than paper notes. Zambia became the first African country to introduce polymer notes in 2003, for the most-used denominations of 500 and 1,000 kwacha. (× ¾)

larger neighbour. In parallel with this, by the end of the twentieth century a number of economic and monetary unions were forming – including the euro, the West African CFA franc, the Central African CFA franc. Each monetary union is set up differently – some areas may use a common currency without having an economic union. Other countries may set up full economic and monetary union, ceding control over some aspects of economic policy to a central institution, as is the case with the euro and the European Central Bank.

The introduction of the euro in the twelve countries of the Eurozone in 2002 was the culmination of a long process which had begun in the 1970s. The first stage, implemented after the collapse of the Bretton Woods system in 1971, was the 1972 agreement between countries of the EEC to stabilise exchange rates by implementing a system known as the 'snake' which restricted currencies to a band of 2.25 per cent. In the early 1990s the system came under strain, and Britain was forced to withdraw from what was by then known as the Exchange Rate Mechanism because of the impact of currency speculators. The Maastricht treaty of 1992 set out the timetable for adoption of a single currency and creation of an economic and monetary union, and ten years later the euro notes and coins were issued and the old 351b, 3 currencies began to be withdrawn. Fears that the changeover from the old national currencies to the euro would result in large price rises were in some areas justified, and governments in some countries struggled to control inflation, having lost control over interest rates. Three European Union countries – the United Kingdom, Denmark and Sweden – remain outside the system at the time of writing, due to a combination of political reluctance and public resistance. At the same time, countries joining the European Union are now required to adopt the euro, meaning that the Eurozone will expand substantially in the coming decade. Whether this expansion leads to an exacerbation or amelioration of the current concerns among Eurozone and non-Eurozone countries remains to be seen.

East and West, North and South

In the nineteenth century, writers like Marx and Engels had described an idealised state based on common ownership, production, and the ending of the exploitation of workers. In Russia, the October Revolution of 1917 brought a communist government to power, and the area under Soviet influence increased after the First World War, following the break-up of the Austro-Hungarian Empire, and again after the Second World War. In the decades that followed, communist states were established in Asia and Central America, and Soviet control over Eastern Europe strengthened. Following an accelerated programme of industrialisation and nationalisation begun in the 1930s, the Soviet Union became one of the two superpowers of the post-Second-World-War era. Its centrally controlled economy grew as relations with America and its allies deteriorated, leading to the hostile standoff between the two superpowers known as the Cold War. However, economic 352 decline from the 1950s to the 1980s, followed by political instability, and combined with a thawing of relations with the non-Communist world, prompted the introduction of a restricted market system, with individual enterprise once more permitted. With the break-up of the Soviet Union in the early 1990s, the establishment of a central bank and a currency was an important marker of political independence for the new nations of Eastern Europe and the former Soviet Union. Russia itself also introduced further 353 market reforms in order to stimulate economic growth. The countries of the former USSR tended, however, to suffer from high inflation and eco-

352 Note for 100 koruna of the State Bank of Czechoslovakia, 1961, showing a male labourer and a female farm-worker against a background of industrial factories. Irrespective of the political ideology of a country's rulers, the design of its national currency will suggest stability, wealth and well-being. On notes of Eastern European and communist countries these have traditionally been represented by images of strong and effective workers.

nomic instability as their economies adjusted to the lack of state control. In contrast, in China a communist government has remained in power with a state-managed economy and a currency, the *yuan*, which was not convertible (that is, it could not be bought and sold on the international markets). Now, both Russia and China are predicted to become two of the most powerful economies in the world.

The post-war period of prosperity in the industrialised world also had very different effects on countries in Latin America and in post-colonial Africa and Asia. The legacy of colonial rule and monetary systems has been significant in many of these countries over the past five decades, and has led to social and economic instability in some. As Europe was reconstructed, the access of many of the least developed countries to the financial know-how and technological sophistication required for economic success in the late twentieth century was so limited that in many cases they could hardly be

353 Five sum note of the State Bank of Uzbekistan, 1994. Following the break-up of the Soviet Union in the early 1990s many of its constituent states began issuing their own currency. First note issues were often simple in appearance and hurriedly produced. However, the ornamental Islamic design on this second issue of Uzbekistan symbolises a re-emerging national identity.

counted as players in the global money game at all. Exploited as a source of raw materials required by rich Western economies, they were forced to sell them at low prices in order to earn what money they could in the form of more dependable foreign currencies with which to repay their ever increasing debts to Western banks. As well as incurring financial costs, loans from institutions such as the International Monetary Fund and the World Bank often came with strings attached, with targets set for economic reform and increased free trade. Such policies have been criticised by opponents of this so-called 'globalisation', who argue that they strengthen the industrialised nations, rather than the countries they purport to support, and increase, rather than decrease, the economic gap between them. The anti-globalisation movement consists of a loose coalition of organisations and protest 354–5 groups joined together by common critical responses to the liberal capitalist policies of the Western powers during the 1980s and 1990s. Of particular concern for these protesters is the domination of world trade by Western governments and corporations, and many would like to see reform of institutions such as the International Monetary Fund, World Bank and World Trade Organisation. New technology has been effectively used to organise large protests and worldwide action, some of which made the news as violent clashes occurred between police and protesters, most notoriously in Seattle in 1999 when World Trade Organisation delegates were prevented from entering the meeting, forcing the cancellation of the opening ceremony.

Countries with large debts to the Western banks often suffered from the chronic instability of their currencies and faced periods of hyperinflation, or in a few cases the complete breakdown of political and economic systems.

353–4 Globalise Resistance badges, UK, 2001, designed by Noel Douglas.

356 One thousand-cruzado note of the Banco Central do Brazil, 1987, reissued in 1989 with a new value of 1 cruzado novo (new cruzado) overstamped on the existing design. During the 1980s and 1990s frequent reissues and new note issues reflected severe inflation in Brazil.

In the 1980s the massive lending of the International Monetary Fund and World Bank was followed by the threat of defaults on the loans, and criticism of the policies and lending of these international institutions dominated by America and Europe. Some countries struggled to pay their debts, or even just the interest on them, and for some countries the only solution was to arrange the writing-off of large amounts of foreign debt. There are, nonetheless, some success stories. One of the indebted countries, Brazil, had a huge foreign debt at the end of the 1970s, when the International Monetary Fund imposed an austerity programme. This meant that the country could pay the interest on its loans, but caused economic decline and inflation. Despite reforms during the 1980s, by 1993 annual inflation 356 was at almost 5000 per cent, and the 1994 'Real Plan' pegged the currency to the dollar in order to stabilise it. Coupled with constitutional reform, these economic reforms worked, and the economy continued to grow strongly. In 2003 it was named as one of the four members of the so-called BRIC group – Brazil, Russia, India and China – of countries predicted to become increasingly important in the global economy. If this group lives up to its potential it could change the face of the world's money, and perhaps the real, ruble, rupee and yuan will join the dollar, euro and yen as world currencies.

The money in your pocket

Moving from these global economic concerns to the money in people's pockets, the twentieth century saw significant changes to the everyday use of money. Most importantly, precious metal was finally abandoned for all 358 circulating currency in daily use. Bronze fiduciary money was already common in the nineteenth century, but the twentieth century saw the transformation of all circulating coins into fiduciary money. It is interesting to note, however, the continuing influence of precious metals on the appearance of

Paying with plastic

Credit and banking are older than coins themselves, but it was not until the twentieth century that plastic cards started to be used for everyday payments. Charge cards limited to a particular company developed first, followed by credit cards which could be used to pay for goods and services from a range of companies. The world's first cash machine was installed in London on 27 June 1967, and during the 1980s debit cards began to replace payment by cheque. More than 50 per cent of transactions in countries such as the UK and the USA are now made by plastic cards, although cash is still king in the world as a whole.

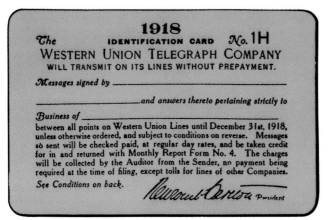

357b The development of credit cards began with an embarrassing evening in 1949 for businessman Frank McNamara who, discovering that he had not got enough cash to pay for dinner, resolved that this would never happen again. By 1951, 20,000 people were members of the Diners Club, and by 1967 the card was accepted in more countries than there were at that time members of the United Nations.

357a Western Union card, 1918, USA. In 1914 Western Union introduced a card which allowed customers to defer payments interest-free. The cards quickly got the nickname 'metal money', since they were made from a thin piece of metal.

357c As the use of debit and credit cards spread, companies developed status-symbol cards marketed to high-income customers. Cards might be gold or platinum in colour and name, or they might be designed by a famous designer: it's not just about how much you spend, but how good you look doing it.

357d When credit cards were introduced, both retailers and customers had to learn to use the new kinds of plastic money. Advertisements and leaflets were just some of the ways that Barclaycard was introduced as the UK's first credit card in 1966.

357e Sharia law-compliant card, issued by HSBC, 2005. The lending of money for interest is frowned on by many religions. Islamic Sharia law forbids making a profit by exchanging money, which means that interest cannot be received on savings, nor paid on borrowings. An increasing number of banks are working on ways to offer services such as credit and debit cards, mortgages and pensions to customers without involving the payment of interest.

358 Gold krugerrand of the Republic of South Africa, 1980, worth 1 troy ounce of fine gold. Although precious metals have all but disappeared from circulating currency, some countries still produce gold bullion pieces as a means of buying and selling gold as a commodity: unlike circulating coins they have no currency denomination, but state their weight and fineness of gold. (× 1½)

359 Copper-nickel crown, UK, 1977. The crown, originally a large silver coin, was made from copper-nickel from 1951. Equivalent to 5 shillings, crowns were still occasionally issued after the British currency was decimalised in 1971, like this design commemorating the silver jubilee of Queen Elizabeth II in 1977.

modern token money: middle-ranking denominations generally continued to be made out of a silver-coloured base metal, while the British £1 coin, 359 introduced in 1983 as the most valuable coin in circulation, is made of nickel-brass of a distinctly golden hue. Not only were coins changed in metal content and greatly reduced in intrinsic value, but as a consequence of this they also gave way before the increasing production and use of banknotes in an ever-larger proportion of retail transactions. The lowest-value banknote in circulation in England in 1900 was the £5 note, and it was worth more than sixty times its equivalent in 2000, which also happened to be the £5 note. Because the materials from which coins and paper money were now made, the choice of material for a particular denomination was determined by factors such as durability, production costs and security against forgery rather than by any more profound economic consideration. Coins in some countries replaced low-denomination notes; in others coins themselves dropped out of use, and only paper money is used.

In the twentieth century, large-scale commercial and financial transactions in many Western countries were increasingly no longer made in cash, and credit facilities, cheques and electronic money transfers were used instead. Gradually, these developments began to affect the use of money in everyday life, as bank accounts became more common for a larger proportion of the population and the accessibility of credit from banks and retail outlets became much more widespread. Technological developments produced such innovations as credit and debit cards which permitted the completion of most transactions without the use of cash. This change was carried further in some countries than in others, however, and the relative extent of its progress was by no means an indicator of economic sophistication or prosperity. In the mid-twentieth century people in the United States and Great Britain, for instance, quickly became accustomed to writing cheques for a wide variety of purchases and payments, whereas Germans and the peoples of other continental European countries remained largely wedded to cash in the post-war period for most day-to-day purposes.

Despite the globalisation of money, and perhaps also because of it, the maintenance of the national currency as a symbol of independent sovereignty remained important for both governments and their peoples. During the establishment of the euro as the common currency for the European Union, there were discussions about what symbols should appear on the new notes and coins. It was decided that the notes should have the same designs across Europe, to promote European unity and cooperation, but that the coins would have different reverse designs for each country. Some have chosen to retain an image of their monarch, while others feature artistic and

360 The reverse designs of euro coins are different for each country in the Eurozone. In preparation for the adoption of the euro by twelve European countries in 2002, around 52 billion coins, made from 250,000 tonnes of metal, were minted at sixteen mints across Europe.

historical symbols, but every country has retained its own identity on its coins. This has encouraged a new generation of coin collectors, who try to get one of every denomination from every country, confounding critics who had complained of the lack of numismatic diversity the euro would bring. Some countries, including Britain, continue to discuss whether they, too, should join the euro. Campaigners arguing against the adoption of the euro by Britain focus both on its economic implications and on the issue of national identity and sovereignty. In some ways, then, the modern world is very similar to the past, even though there have been so many and such significant changes in the way that money is issued and used.

Conclusion

The clearest characteristic of the modern period of world history is perhaps the rate at which change has taken place – particularly in relation to changes in technology and the sciences, in which the last 250 years have seen greater change than the preceding 2,500. The development of technology and technological expertise allowed man to become master of his environment and its natural resources, and the development of modern economic thought brought man to a similar position of apparent ascendancy over his economic life. In neither case was this ascendancy complete: just as the world became a place that submitted more to man's desires than he did to its whims, or so it was thought, so the stage was reached in the modern period where it seemed possible to make money into a pure instrument of social and economic benefit. But just as technology and its applications are difficult things to control, so it is with monetary affairs. The awakening of the separate 'personality' of money, as it was called by J. K. Galbraith (1908–2006), brought an increasing volatility to its character and behaviour. No longer subject to the processes of gradual change, money's ever versatile nature induced frequent and unmanageable crises on an unprecedented scale in the nineteenth and twentieth centuries. The process of change was accentuated by the enormous increase in the speed and volume of worldwide trade and communications, from the development of the telegraph in the mid-nineteenth century to the telephone and computer in the twentieth. This reached such a level that decision-makers in governments and central banks seemed sometimes to be incapable of coping with the pace of daily change in the world money markets, rendering weak currencies vulnerable and economic policies out of date overnight. By the end of the momentous twentieth century, with all its technological and intellectual advances, it was becoming less plausible than it had been in the immediate post-war period to imagine that economics alone could necessarily guarantee greater powers of prediction and control over money.

361 Still from the 'Man From Diner's Club' film, 1963. Despite the rise of plastic cards and electronic money transfers, cash is still the most important kind of money in the world.

And yet 'money' as a concept seemed to many to have become the main motivating factor behind Western culture: it became the prime focus of political debate and personal endeavour, both despite and because of its increasing elusiveness and power. This kind of attitude has been aptly termed 'fetishistic', in the sense that it attributes a quasi-supernatural quality to the object of its adulatory devotion, in this case money. After having read this book, the reader might well be justified in asking 'So what's new?'. If anything seems to be constant in the history of money, it is surely the complaints of the moralists against the apparently ruinous effects of money on human culture and society. This is fair comment. The motivation behind the complaint may not have changed for hundreds of years, especially if based on a sacred text such as we have met from the Gospels or the Qur'an. But the fundamental change in the theoretical concepts defining money, its release from the restraints imposed by precious metal, and the rapid development of the technology of banking and credit have qualitatively changed its modes of action.

Society itself has changed as well, of course. The Industrial Age closely associated the making of money and the making of things, particularly through cheap mass-production – 'where there's muck, there's brass!', as the saying goes. This was new in its day, but it was itself surpassed in the late twentieth century with the decline of heavy industry in many parts of the West and the onset of the 'post-industrial' society, in which the making of money seemed increasingly disconnected from industrial production. It seemed to be possible to make immense amounts of money on stock markets and money markets, although the operations of these were a mystery to the majority of the population. There was a general awareness of their importance for the national economy and monetary prosperity, but only very few understood how they actually worked. The picture must have looked very different from the emerging regions of the Pacific Rim, of course, where increasing national wealth was clearly connected with the successful industrialisation of those areas. But in the West, from whose perspective this book is written, money adopted an increasingly immaterial aspect as the end of the second millennium approached, both in the forms it took and in its means of acquisition. Hence the fundamental paradox of modern money: that something so intangible remains so very powerful.

Chronology

AFRICA

- **Pre 500 BC:** Monetary use of metal by weight in Egypt
- **500 BC–0:** Greek coins in Libya, c.500 BC; Carthaginian coins in North Africa, late 5th century BC; Greek coinage established in Egypt by Ptolemy, late 4th century BC
- **AD 1st–5th century:** North African kingdoms produce imitations of Roman coins, 1st century; Beginning of Aksumite coinage in Ethiopia, 3rd century; Vandal imitations of Roman coins in Carthage, 5th century
- **7th century:** Islamic coins issued in North Africa, 7th century

AMERICAS

- Although money of some sort probably existed, no record survives of what form it took, before c.1000
- **c.1000:** Silver penny [of] Olaf the Peace[...], Norway, 1067[...], earliest Euro[pean] coin found i[n] America[s]

ASIA

- **Pre 500 BC:** Grain and silver used for payments in Mesopotamia; Cowrie shells used as currency in China; Beginning of electrum coinage in Lydia (Asia Minor); China using bronze coins shaped like tools by c.600 BC
- **500 BC–0:** India adopts Greek-style coinage from Iran, 4th century BC; Adoption in China of round coins with square holes as standard currency, c.221 BC
- **AD 227–642:** Sasanian rulers in the Middle East produce large silver drachms, 227–642
- **7th century:** Standard bronze coinage introduced in China under Tang Dynasty, 627–49; First Islamic coins, 7th century; from 696 issues with inscription only
- **708:** Adoption of Chinese style coins in Japan, 708
- **10th century:** Introduction of paper money in China, 10th century

AUSTRALASIA

EUROPE

- **Pre 500 BC:** First silver coinage in Greece and Greek colonies, 6th century BC
- **500 BC–0:** Beginning of Roman silver coinage, c.300 BC; First British coinage, c.75 BC; Roman Imperial coinage begins under Augustus (31 BC–AD 14)
- **AD 3rd–6th century:** Civil wars cause crisis in Roman coinage, mid-late 3rd century. Diocletian restores stability c.290; Collapse of western Roman Empire. New 'barbarian' kingdoms imitate Roman gold coins, then develop their own types, 5th–6th centuries
- **8th–10th centuries:** Islamic coins used in Europe, 8th–10th centuries
- **late 8th century:** Revival of 'Roman Empire' by Charlemagne; silver pennies introduced across much of Europe, late 8th century
- **10th–11th centuries:** Kingdoms in Scandinavia and eas[tern] Europe adopt the silver penny, 10th–11th centuries

1200 1300 1400 1500 1600 1700 1800 1900 2000

AFRICA

...ili kingdom issues coins in East Africa; imported Chinese coins also circulate, 12th–15th centuries

...nic silver coins from North Africa ...ed in Europe, 11th–13th centuries

Portuguese report use of shells and copper rings as currency in West Africa, 15th century

Exploitation of African gold by Portuguese, 15th century

Introduction of European colonial currency in West Africa, late 18th–19th centuries

European travellers report use of iron hoes, shells, cloth, cattle etc., as currency in parts of Africa, 19th century

British Indian rupees in circulation in East Africa, 19th century

Production of gold coins from deposits in South Africa, 1883

Traditional forms of money in use in Ethiopia, Nigeria and Liberia until 1930s and 1940s, as well as banknotes and coins

AMERICAS

Shells and shell beads used as valuables in North and South America, copper axes and cacao beans in Central America before the Spanish introduce coinage, 16th century

Spain exploits silver resources and exports pieces of eight worldwide, 16th century

First North American coinage, made by British colonies, early 17th century

Coinage produced in Paris for French settlement of Quebec, 17th century

Brazilian gold rush. Portuguese gold coins exported to Europe, 18th century

Following the War of Independence, the USA adopts dollar coinage, 1794

End of Spanish Empire in the Americas, widespread use of pieces of eight, early 19th century

Discovery of Californian gold deposits in 1848 leads to the expansion of gold coinage

The Wall Street Crash. Collapse of America's Stock Market, 1929

First credit card, 1950

Nixon detaches value of US dollar from US gold reserves, 1971–3

ASIA

Chinese coinage adopted as currency in Indonesia, 12th–15th centuries

Introduction of European-style currency in India and the East Indies, 16th century

Silver rupee introduced in India by Mughal emperors, mid/late 16th century

Adoption of paper money in Japan, 17th century

English colonial coinage in India, 17th century

First mechanically produced coins in India, at Calcutta, 1790

European-style coinage based on the dollar adopted in China (yuan) and Japan (yen), 19th century

Mechanisation of coin production in China, 1890

Introduction of paper money in Iran and Turkey, late 19th century

End of silver standard in China, 1935

People's currency (Renminbi yuan) introduced in China, 1953

AUSTRALASIA

Shells and beads used in payments in Melanesia and Micronesia

Discovery of Australia and New Zealand by European explorers, 17th century

English settlement of New South Wales. Rum in use as money in the early years of the settlement, 1788

South American silver dollar used in New South Wales, 1815

First coinage in Pacific Islands, Hawaii 1840s

Gold deposits in Australia allow production of gold coins, 1851

Introduction of Australian Commonwealth coinage, 1910–11

Introduction of New Zealand coinage, 1933–40

Australia and New Zealand adopt decimal currency based on the dollar, 1966–7

EUROPE

Revival of gold coinage and introduction of large-denomination silver coins, 13th century

Introduction of copper coinage as small change, late 15th century

Mechanisation of coin production with the invention of the screw press, 16th century

Sweden produces first paper money in Europe, 1661

Foundation of the Bank of England, 1694

First European decimal coinage introduced in Russia by Peter the Great, c.1710

Mass production of coins made possible by the invention of the Boulton steam press, 1790s

Introduction of gold Napoleon in France, 1806, and gold sovereigns in England, 1817

Latin Monetary Union. Several European countries standardise their currencies to make them easier to exchange, 1865

Great War 1914–18 leads to increasing use of paper money and the collapse of the gold standard

First European credit cards, 1966, and cash machines, 1967

European single currency, the Euro, enters circulation, 2002

1200 1300 1400 1500 1600 1700 1800 1900 2000

Further Reading

GENERAL

A. Burnett's *Interpreting the Past: Coins* (London 1991) is an essential introduction to the world of numismatics, using examples from throughout history to demonstrate how to use the evidence that coins provide. *Coins in History* by J. Porteous (London 1968) examines the relationship of coinage to money, exploring some of the problems of economic history and how the study of coins can illuminate these, while *Numismatics* by P. Grierson (Oxford 1975) is another accessible guide to the history and technical background of coins and the issues they raise in historical research. More than simply a companion to the 1986 exhibition at the British Museum, J. Cribb (ed.), *Money: From Cowrie Shells to Credit Cards* (London 1986), an excellent introductory book, has wide-ranging chapters on the origin, development, production and use of different monetary systems. J. Casey and R. Reece's set of papers *Coins and the Archaeologist* (2nd edn, London 1988) focuses on the archaeological significance and interpretation of coin finds in England, with relevance for all eras.

D. R. Cooper, *The Art and Craft of Coin Making* (London 1988) follows the evolution of coin making from ancient to modern times and the changes in the manufacture of money. For a detailed survey of the world's money through the ages, see J. Cribb, B. Cook and I. Carradice, *The Coin Atlas* (London 1990), a comprehensive view of coins throughout history. It gives an account of coinage country by country, along with maps, historical information and plentiful illustration. Another useful survey of the history of coinage is the series of essays in M. Price (ed.), *Coins: An Illustrated Survey* (London 1980).

T. Crump's *The Phenomenon of Money* (London 1981) takes an anthropological approach to the questions raised within numismatic study. Other useful books concerned with monetary theory are *The Sociology of Money* by N. Dodd (London 1994) and *The Philosophy of Money* by G. Simmel (London 1978).

Two well-illustrated and captivating introductions for children are J. Cribb's *Eyewitness Guide: Money* (London 1990) and *The Story of Money* by J. Orna-Ornstein (London 1997), largely based on objects featured in the HSBC Money Gallery of the British Museum.

Periodicals
A Survey of Numismatic Research, published every five to six years, is a comprehensive review of numismatic literature published for the International Numismatic Commission on the occasion of the International Numismatic Congress. The Royal Numismatic Society, London, produces an annual journal, the *Numismatic Chronicle*; Spink and Son Ltd (London) publishes the *Numismatic Circular* monthly. The American Numismatic Society's *Numismatic Literature* is a twice-yearly review of numismatic publications.

Chapter 1
MESOPOTAMIA, GREECE AND EGYPT

C. Howgego's *Ancient History from Coins* (London 1995) is already a classic: this wonderful little volume provides an excellent introduction to coinage as evidence in a range of historical pursuits.

M. I. Finley, *The Ancient Economy* (London 1973) is a highly influential overview of the ancient economy by one of its greatest scholars. At the opposite end of the scale to Finley's approach is M. Rostovtzeff's *The Social and Economic History of the Hellenistic World* (Oxford 1941): Rostovtzeff assembled copious quantities of evidence for the economy of the Greek world after Alexander and organised it into a modernistic view of the ancient economy. P. Millett, *Lending and Borrowing in Ancient Athens* (Cambridge 1991) is a thought-provoking study of the role of credit in the social history of Athens, by one of the few ancient historians to thank his bank manager in the preface. Edited by I. Carradice, *Coinage and Administration in the Athenian and Persian Empires* (Oxford 1987) includes a number of important essays about the coinage of Athens and the Persian Empire in the fifth and fourth centuries BC.

Coinage in the Greek World by I. Carradice and M. Price (London 1988) remains the best one-volume introduction to the pre-imperial Greek coinages, with I. Carradice's *Greek Coins* (London 1995) the best illustrated short account of Greek coinage, conveniently arranged by century. Still the most detailed survey of Archaic and Classical Greek coinage is C. M. Kraay's *Archaic and Classical Greek Coins* (London 1976). G. K. Jenkins's *Ancient Greek Coins* (2nd edn, London 1990) is a more modern and better-illustrated account. For later coinage from Alexander the Great to 188 BC, see O. Morkholm, *Early Hellenistic Coinage* (Cambridge 1991).

Ancient Egypt: Anatomy of a Civilisation by B. J. Kemp (London 1989) is an accessible introduction to the debate about the nature of the ancient Egyptian economy. For a useful introduction to the pre-coinage economy of Mesopotamia, see also J. N. Postgate's *Early Mesopotamia: Society and Economy at the Dawn of History* (London 1992).

Chapter 2
THE ROMAN WORLD

A. M. Burnett, *Coinage in the Roman World* (London 1987) offers perhaps the best and most readable general summary of Roman coinage from early Republican Rome to the post-Roman period. Alongside monetary history are themed discussions on coinage and its role in Roman economy and society. *A Dictionary of Ancient Roman Coins* by J. Melville Jones (London 1990) is an essential companion for anyone wishing to decipher the basics of Roman coinage. Its useful dictionary format could have been improved by more illustrations, but nevertheless it offers accurate and detailed descriptions of the denominations, production technology and iconography.

J. Andreau's *Banking and Business in the Roman World* (Cambridge 1999) is a concise study of the historical and archaeological (e.g. from Pompeii) evidence for Roman financial life and the activities of the 'money men' of the Roman world from Republican times to the third century AD. *Coinage and Money under the Roman Republic* by M. H. Crawford (London 1985) provides a detailed monetary history of the Republican period, tracing the spread of coinage within the contexts of the Roman economy, society and expanding Empire. A good study into the financing of the Roman Empire (to the third century AD) is R. Duncan-Jones, *Money and Government in the Roman Empire* (Cambridge 1998). Part 1 explores the state's economic needs and problems, Part 2 surveys the evidence of coin hoards, and Part 3 examines the economic evidence obtainable from the coinage (e.g. production scale, supply and debasement). J. Banaji, *Agrarian Change in Late Antiquity: Gold, Labour and Aristocratic Dominance* (Oxford Classical Monographs, Oxford 2002) is a study of the late Roman economy drawing on its author's extensive knowledge of primary documentary sources. The work also examines in depth the peculiarities of the monetary economy and relationships of the new coin denominations of the late Roman Empire (from the late third century and overlapping with the early Byzantine period).

Although focused on Roman Britain, much of the content of the following volumes is equally applicable to the rest of the Roman world. *Roman Coinage in Britain* by P. J. Casey (Shire Archaeology 12, 3rd edn, Princes Risborough 1994) is an excellent short introduction to the subject of Roman imperial coinage and the currency system. R. A. Abdy's *Romano-British Coin Hoards* (Shire Archaeology 82, Princes Risborough 2002) introduces the subject of coin hoards, with an opening chapter that details the methodology and value of studying hoards

throughout the Empire. R. Reece's *The Coinage of Roman Britain* (Stroud 2002) provides a basic monetary history as well as discussion of the uses and methodology of studying coin hoards and site finds. It is more readable and less statistically orientated than his earlier *Coinage in Roman Britain* (London 1987). For an extremely handy short introduction to the extensive and varied coinage of the wider Empire, see K. Butcher's *Roman Provincial Coinage: An Introduction to Greek Imperials* (London 1988). It is impossible for a book of this size to provide comprehensive coverage of the local Roman coin types produced at city or province level but it includes tips for identification, a geographical survey, and covers topics such as their use, inscriptions and imagery.

See also:
Crawford, M. H., 'Money and exchange in the Roman world', *Journal of Roman Studies* 60 (London 1970), pp. 40–48
Hopkins, K., 'Taxes and trade in the Roman Empire, 200 BC–AD 400', *Journal of Roman Studies* 70 (London 1980), pp. 101–25
Howgego, C., 'The supply and use of money in the Roman world, 200 BC to AD 300', *Journal of Roman Studies* 82 (London 1992), pp. 1–32

Chapter 3
MEDIEVAL EUROPE

Those interested in the role of money in medieval Europe can benefit from a ground-breaking survey by Peter Spufford, *Money and its Uses in Medieval Europe* (Cambridge 1988; paperback reissue 2006). The same author's *Power and Profit: The Merchant in Medieval Europe* (London 2002) is a lavishly illustrated, informative companion. An older work that began to establish the modern study of medieval monetary history is C. M. Cipolla's *Money, Prices and Civilisation in the Mediterranean World* (Princeton 1956). Important collected papers by major scholars of the field include J. Day, *The Medieval Market Economy* (Oxford 1987), R. S. Lopez, *The Shape of Medieval Monetary History* (London 1986)

and H. A. Miskimin, *Cash, Credit and Crisis in Europe, 1300–1600* (London 1989). For the role of bullion flows, see the articles included in J. F. Richards (ed.), *Precious Metals in the Later Medieval and Early Modern Worlds* (Durham, North Carolina, 1983).

For an authoritative, clear and well-illustrated survey of the coins of medieval Europe, P. Grierson's *Coins of Medieval Europe* (London 1991) is unlikely to be superseded. Grierson's two volumes of collected articles *Dark Age Numismatics* (London 1979) and *Later Medieval Numismatics* (London 1979) offer wide-ranging insights into European money from the end of Rome to the Renaissance. Philip Grierson's own coin collection (now in the Fitzwilliam Museum, Cambridge) is the basis of an ongoing survey of the coinages of medieval Europe. Available to date are P. Grierson and M. A. S. Blackburn, *Medieval European Coinage 1: The Early Middle Ages (Fifth to Tenth Centuries)* (Cambridge 1986) and P. Grierson and L. Travaini, *Medieval European Coinage 14: Italy III (South Italy, Sicily, Sardinia)* (Cambridge 1998).

The best survey of Byzantine coinage is certainly Philip Grierson's *Byzantine Coins* (London 1982). For Byzantine monetary history, M. F. Hendy's *Studies in the Byzantine Monetary Economy* (Cambridge 1985) and *Coinage and Money in the Byzantine Empire, 1081–1261* (Dumbarton Oaks Studies XIII, Washington DC, 1969) offer a vast array of insight and learning. For a systematic listing of the issues of Byzantine coins, there is W. Hahn, *Moneta Imperii Byzantini* (3 vols, Vienna 1973–80).

Medieval Britain and England are well-served in the literature. There are recent, detailed, numismatic surveys in the Centenary Volume of the *British Numismatic Journal*, 73 (2003), edited by N. M. McQ. Holmes and G. Williams. Important collections of essays for early medieval Britain include M. A. S. Blackburn (ed.), *Anglo-Saxon Monetary History: Essays in Memory of Michael Dolley* (Leicester 1986) and B. Cook and G. Williams, *Coinage and History in the North Sea World c. 500–1250: Essays in Honour of Marion Archibald* (Leiden 2006). For later medieval Britain, a recent valuable introduction to the role of money is D. Wood (ed.), *Medieval Money Matters* (Oxford 2004). The *Sylloge of Coins of the British Isles* is an ongoing project with over fifty volumes already published: the contents of the *Sylloge* series and a useful *Corpus of Early Medieval Coin Finds* can be accessed through the website of the Fitzwilliam Museum at www.fitzmuseum.cam.ac.uk/dept/coins/emc.

In general, European coinages in this period are covered by country or region. France is served by N. J. Mayhew, *Coinage in France from the Dark Ages to Napoleon* (London 1988), and the later medieval period by H. A. Miskimin's *Money and Power in Fifteenth-Century France* (Yale 1984). In Italy, the role of money in Venice is exceptionally well covered, appropriately because of its importance in monetary history, by Alan Stahl's *Zecca: The Mint of Venice in the Middle Ages* (John Hopkins University 2000) and F. O. Lane and R. Mueller's *Money and Banking in Medieval and Renaissance Venice, 1: Coins and Money of Account* (Baltimore 1985). Three volumes to date of *Problems of Medieval Coinage in the Iberian Area* (vol. 1, ed. M. G. Marques, Santarem 1984; vol 2, ed. M. G. Marques and M. Crusafont i Sabatier, Aviles 1986; vol. 3, ed. M. G. Marques and D. M. Metcalf, Santarem 1989) cover Spain and its neighbours. The Netherlands have benefited from the work of Peter Spufford: *Monetary Problems and Policies in the Burgundian Netherlands* (Leiden 1978) and P. Spufford and N. J. Mayhew, *Coinage in the Low Countries* (Oxford 1979). For the Balkans and eastern Mediterranean, see the work of D. M. Metcalf, particularly *Coinage in South-East Europe* (London 1979), *Coinage of the Crusades and the Latin East in the Ashmolean Museum* (Oxford 2003) and, with P. Edbury (eds), *Coinage in the Latin East* (Oxford 1980). For Scandinavia, publication in English is strongest for the

Viking Age. J. Graham-Campbell and G. Williams (eds), *Silver Economy in the Viking Age* (London 2006) contains papers discussing the development and nature of monetary economy in Scandinavia during the Viking Age. A combination of history and corpus is provided for the earliest Swedish coinage by B. Malmer, *The Sigtuna Coinage, c. 995–1005* (Stockholm 1989) and *The Anglo-Scandinavian Coinage c. 995–1020* (Stockholm 1997), with a third volume due to be published shortly.

Chapter 4
THE ISLAMIC LANDS

S. Album's *A Checklist of Popular Islamic Coins* (Santa Rosa 1993) is an important source for Islamic numismatists, while an easy introduction to Islamic coins for both specialists and non-specialists is M. Broome's *A Handbook of Islamic Coins* (London 1985). For a good introduction to Islamic coins and their calligraphy, as well as Islamic history, see R. Plant, *Arabic Coins and How to Read Them* (London 1973). A catalogue of the Islamic coins in the British Museum collection, with detailed descriptions of legends in Arabic and Persian, can be found in the ten-volume *Catalogue of the Oriental Coins in the British Museum* by S. Lane Poole (London 1875–90).

C. E. Bosworth, in *The New Islamic Dynasties* (Edinburgh 1996), provides a detailed and user-friendly overview of all Islamic dynasties. For a catalogue of the early Islamic coins in the collection of the Ashmolean Museum in Oxford, see *Sylloge of Islamic Coins in the Ashmolean, 1. The Pre-Reform Coinage of the Early Islamic Period* by S. Album and T. Goodwin (Oxford 2002). J. Walker's catalogues record the British Museum's collections: *A Catalogue of the Arab-Byzantine and Post-Reform Umaiyad Coins* (London 1956) describes early Islamic coins imitating Byzantine coins and early Islamic coins with Qur'anic writing; *A Catalogue of the Arab-Sassanian Coins* (London 1941) details the British Museum's collection of Islamic coins of the early Arab

governors immediately after the Islamic conquest.

R. Gyselen, *Arab-Sasanian Copper Coinage* (Vienna 2000) is a specialist catalogue of early Islamic copper coins with figural representations of the Sasanian style and early Arabic inscriptions. H. M. Malek, *The Dabuyid Ispahbads and Early 'Abbasid Governors of Tabaristan: History and Numismatics* (London 2004) specialises in coins from northern Iran in the seventh and eighth centuries AD. For a catalogue of Buyid coins from south-west Iran during the tenth and eleventh centuries AD, see *Buyid Coinage: A Die Corpus (322–445 A.H.)* by L. Treadwell (Oxford 2001). See N. L. Lowick's *Islamic Coins and Trade in the Medieval World* (ed. J. Cribb, Aldershot 1990) for a collection of essays on coins and Islamic trade during the medieval period.

The two volumes of *Turkoman Figural Bronze Coins and their Iconography* by W. F. Spengler and W. G. Sayles (Lodi, Wisconsin 1992 and 1996) are informative and user-friendly publications about the twelfth-century Turkoman coins with figural and animal representation, from eastern Turkey, Syria and northern Iraq.

For an overview of the history of the Mongols in Iran, with reference to coinage, see J. Kolbas, *The Mongols in Iran. Chingiz Khan to Uljaitu 1220–1309* (London and New York 2006). The *Sylloge of Islamic Coins in the Ashmolean, 9. Iran after the Mongol Invasion* by S. Album (Oxford 2001) is a catalogue of Islamic coins from Iran from the late thirteenth to the nineteenth century AD.

See also:
Ali, Abdullah Yusuf, *The Meaning of the Glorious Qur'an* (London 1976)
Ashtor, E., *A Social and Economic History of the Near East in the Middle Ages* (London 1976)
Balog, P., *The Coinage of the Ayyubids* (London 1980)
Bates, M. L., 'Islamic numismatics', *Middle East Studies Association Bulletin,* in five

sections from vol. 12:2 (May 1978) to
vol. 13:2 (December 1979)
Ehrenkreutz, A. S., *Monetary Change and
Economic History in the Medieval Muslim
World* (Aldershot 1992)
Ibn Hanbal, Ahmad, *Musnad al-Imam
Ahmad ibn Hanbal*, ed. Samir Taha al-
Majzub (Beirut 1993)
Ibn Khaldun, *An Arab Philosophy of History:
Selections from the Prologema of Ibn Khaldun of
Tunis (1332–1406)*, translated and arranged
by C. Issawi (London 1950)
Lowick, N. L., *Coinage and History of the
Islamic World*, ed. J. Cribb (Aldershot 1990)
Mayer, L. A., *A Bibliography of Moslem
Numismatics* (London 1954)
Mitchiner, M., *Oriental Coins and their
Values: The World of Islam* (Sanderstead 1976)

Chapter 5
INDIA AND SOUTH-EAST ASIA

P. L. Gupta's *Coins* (New Delhi 1969,
numerous reprints and revisions) is a good
introduction to the different coinages of
India. Another useful guide to different
aspects of the coinages of several major
Indian dynasties is M. L. Carter (ed.), *A
Treasury of Indian Coins* (Bombay 1994).

The Kautilyan Arthashastra is translated into
English in three volumes by R. P. Kangle
(Bombay 1960–65). This manual of
statecraft is attributed to Kautilya, the chief
minister of Chandragupta Masurya (c. 310–
285 BC). For a history of the development
of monetary systems in South-East Asia to
AD 1400, see R. S. Wicks, *Money, Markets and
Trade in Early Southeast Asia* (Ithaca 1992).
J. Prinsep's *Essays on Indian Antiquities,
Historic, Numismatic, and Palaeographic* (ed.
E. Thomas, 2 vols, London 1858) is a series
of some of the earliest articles on Indian
coins, which chart the progress of research
between 1830 and 1858.

*The Indian Coinage Tradition: Origins,
Continuity and Change* by J. Cribb (Nasik
2005) is a comprehensive account of the
development of Indian coinage and of the
problems in creating a chronological
framework. The British Museum's

collection of the earliest Indian coins was
published in J. Allan's *Catalogue of the Coins
of Ancient India* (London 1936). Other early
Indian coins are covered in P. L. Gupta and
T. R. Hardaker, *Ancient Indian Silver
Punchmarked Coins of the Magadha-Maurya
Karshapana Series* (Nasik 1985), a primary
identification source book of all the
punchmark symbols and coin types known
in 1985. O. Bopearachchi and A. Rahman,
Pre-Kushana Coins in Pakistan (Islamabad
1995) provides a fully illustrated survey of
the coinage of Afghanistan and Pakistan
between the fifth century BC and first
century AD in a private collection. The
monetary history of early medieval north
India is explored in J. Deyell, *Living without
Silver* (Delhi 1990), while E. Errington and
J. Cribb (eds), *The Crossroads of Asia*
(Cambridge 1992) is a good introduction to
the pre-Islamic coinages of Afghanistan and
north-west Pakistan. The coinages of the
first Islamic dynasties of India are given a
comprehensive catalogue in *The Coins of the
Indian Sultanates* by S. Goron and J. P.
Goenka (New Delhi 2001). C. R. Bruce *et
al.*, *Standard Guide to South Asian Coins and
Paper Money since 1556 AD* (Iola 1981) is the
principal guide to coins of the Indian
subcontinent from 1556 to the twentieth
century. Later colonial coinages are
explored in *The Coins of the Dutch Overseas
Territories* by C. Scholten (Amsterdam 1953),
a general account of those of the Dutch
East India Company, and in *Coins of the
British Commonwealth of Nations* by F.
Pridmore (4 vols, London 1960–75), a
comprehensive history and catalogue of
British colonial coinages.

The three volumes of *The Jataka, or Stories
of the Buddha's Former Rebirths* (trans. E. B.
Cowell, London 1981) are an English
translation of Buddhist texts relating events
in the previous lives of the historical
Buddha. See also *Ardhakathanaka* (Haifa
Tale) by the Jain merchant Banarasi Das
(born 1586), translated into English,
introduced and annotated by Mukund Lath
(Jaipur 1981).

Chapter 6
CHINA AND THE EAST

A good introduction to the subject of
coinage in China and East Asia is F.
Thierry's *Monnaies de Chine* (Paris 1992).
Money and Credit in China: A Short History
by Yang Lien-Sheng (Cambridge,
Massachusetts, 1952) is also a very readable
introduction to the subject. Hu Jichuang's
*A Concise History of Chinese Economic
Thought* (Beijing 1988) is a translation of
one of the main Chinese reference works;
another main reference for Chinese
monetary history is Peng Xinwei, *A
Monetary History of China (Zhongguo Huobi
Shi)* (trans. E. H. Kaplan, 2 vols, Bellingham,
Washington, 1994). For an excellent
bibliography up to 1967, see A. R. Coole,
*An Encyclopaedia of Chinese Coins, 1: A
Bibliography on Far Eastern Numismatology
and a Coin Index* (Kansas 1967).

The Currencies of China (Shanghai 1926, rev.
edn 1927) is written by one of the leading
Western specialists on Chinese coins of the
twentieth century, E. Kann. Ting Fu-Pao
(Ding Fubao) has produced an illustrated
catalogue of rubbings of Chinese coins, *A
Catalog of Ancient Chinese Coins (including
Japan, Korea and Annan)* (Shanghai 1940,
many reprints; in Chinese). This has been
a standard reference for Chinese coins.
H. Wang brings an examination of the coin
and documentary evidence, together with a
catalogue of the coins collected by Sir Aurel
Stein, in *Money on the Silk Road: The
Evidence from Eastern Central Asia to c. AD 800*
(London 2004). Richard Von Glahn's
*Fountain of Fortune: Money and Monetary
Policy in China, 1000–1700* (Berkeley, Los
Angeles and London 1996) is an important
study of money in China during this
period, and also looks at the external
influences and effects. For a fully illustrated
catalogue of the British Museum ingot
collection (many from the Eduard Kann
collection), see J. Cribb's *A Catalogue of
Sycee in the British Museum: Chinese Silver
Currency Ingots c. 1750–1933* (London 1992),
which also has some useful background
information. For more about the money of

the Qing dynasty, see D. Hartill's comprehensive study of the 'cash' coins of the period, *Qing Cash* (London 2003) and H. Wang's 'Late Qing paper money from Dianshizhai and other printing houses in Shanghai, 1905–1912', in V. Hewitt (ed.), *The Banker's Art* (London 1995, pp. 94–117), a study of several notes in the British Museum collection.

N. G. Munro, in *Coins of Japan* (Yokohama 1904) provides a catalogue of Japanese money through the ages, with illustrations. Another readable account of Japanese monetary history is D. M. Brown, *Money Economy in Medieval Japan: A Sudy in the Use of Coins* (New Haven 1951). E. J. Mandel's *Cast Coinage of Korea* (Racine, Wisconsin, 1972) is a very useful guide to identifying Korean coins. F. Thierry's *Amulettes de Chine et du Vietnam: rites magiques et symboliques de la Chine ancienne* (Paris 1987) provides an illustrated catalogue of Chinese and Vietnamese coin-shaped amulets, with much useful background information. Futher information can be found in the same author's *Catalogue des monnaies vietnamiennes* (Paris 1987).

J. Cribb's *Money in the Bank: An Illustrated Introduction to the Money Collection of The Hongkong and Shanghai Banking Corporation* (London 1987) is a fully illustrated guide to an important collection, with excellent background information. For more specialist information relating to the metallurgy of the British Museum's collection, there is *Metallurgical Analysis of Chinese Coins at the British Museum* (London 2005) by H. Wang, M. Cowell, J. Cribb & S. Bowman. In addition, the *Review of Numismatic Literature* is published every five years by the International Numismatic Commission, and includes chapters on the various countries of East Asia. These reviews include the major publications in all languages.

Chapter 7
THE EARLY MODERN PERIOD

One of the major factors in the monetary history of the early modern world was the international movement of precious metal and the impact of this on money and prices. A valuable overall survey of this is P. Vilar's *A History of Gold and Money, 1450–1920* (London 1976; paperback reprint 1991), with a particular emphasis on the influence of Brazilian gold from the later seventeenth century. More detailed contributions in this area are A. Attman's *The Bullion Flow between Europe and the East 1000–1750* (Goteborg 1981) and *American Bullion in the European World Trade 1600–1800* (Goteborg 1986). Two volumes edited by E. H. G. van Cauwenberghe also focus on this topic as well as some other related aspects of international and regional coinage: *Precious Metals, Coinage and the Change of Monetary Structures in Latin America, Europe and Asia* (Louvain 1989) and *Money, Coins and Commerce: Essays in the Monetary History of Asia and Europe* (Louvain 1991). E. J. Hamilton's *American Treasure and the Price Revolution in Spain (1501–1650)* (Cambridge, Massachusetts, 1934) addresses the matter from the Spanish perspective, while F. C. Spooner examines the position in France in *The International Economy and Monetary Movements in France, 1493–1725* (Harvard 1972). A different aspect of money of the period is considered by T. J. Sargent and F. R. Velde in *The Big Problem of Small Change* (Princeton 2002), building on earlier work by Cipolla (see chapter 3).

The only general survey of coins for the early modern period specifically is E. E. and V. Clain-Stefanelli, *Monnaies européennes et monnaies coloniales américaines entre 1450 et 1789* (Fribourg 1978). There exist many catalogues and lists of coins, some based on geography (national and regional coinage), some on chronological periods and some on denominations and types of coins (e.g. J. S. Davenport's catalogues of silver thalers and thaler-sized coins), though this sort of work rarely provides much context or explanation of monetary history.

For particular countries, several works cover both medieval and early modern periods, notably N. Mayhew's *Sterling: The History of a Currency* (London 2000) and C. E. Challis's *New History of the Royal Mint* (London 1992). For Britain, the Centenary Volume of the *British Numismatic Journal* provides bibliographic surveys of relevant work, with chapters on the Tudors, Stuarts and token coinage. C. E. Challis's specialist study *The Tudor Coinage* (Manchester 1978) is a unique survey of a country's monetary policies and practices for anywhere in Europe in the early modern period. E. Besly has produced an excellent and accessible modern survey of the coinage of the period of the Civil War, *Coins and Medals of the English Civil War* (London 1990).

There are many books and articles on paper money and the history of banking. E. Green's *Banking: An Illustrated History* (Oxford 1989) tells the story of banking from medieval Italy to the present day, and the articles in V. Hewitt (ed.), *The Banker's Art: Studies in Paper Money* (London 1995) cover a similarly large range of times and places. Accounts of the development of paper currency and banking systems in Europe and America can be found in P. L. Cottrell and B. G. Anderson, *Money and Banking in England: The Development of the Banking System, 1694–1914* (London 1974), J. J. McCusker, *Money and Exchange in Europe and America, 1660–1773: A Handbook* (North Carolina 1978), or H. van der Wee, 'Monetary, credit and banking systems', in E. E. Rich and C. Wilson, *Cambridge Economic History of Europe*, vol. 5 (Cambridge 1977). Scottish banking history is covered in S. G. Checkland, *Scottish Banking: A History*, 1: *1693–1973* (Glasgow 1975), while the Bank of England has a detailed history written by J. Clapham: *The Bank of England: A History*, 1: *1694–1797* (Cambridge 1944). The paper money of America is surveyed and described by E. P. Newman in his book *The Early Paper Money of America* (3rd edn, Iola 1990).

Chapter 8
AFRICA AND OCEANIA

The many non-coin currencies used in different parts of Africa have been a source of interest for anthropologists and numismatists alike. Classic works on the subject, although they are perhaps now a little out of date, are A. H. Quiggin, *A Survey of Primitive Money* (London 1949), and P. Einzig, *Primitive Money* (London 1948). More recently, C. Optiz has published his *Ethnographic Study of Traditional Money* (Ocala 2001), which is both detailed and richly illustrated. The different ways that these kinds of money are used has been explored in G. Dalton (ed.), *Tribal and Peasant Economies: Readings in Economic Anthropology* (Austin, Texas, 1967) and J. Melitz, *Primitive and Modern Money: An Interdisciplinary Approach* (Reading, Massachusetts, 1974). More recent work includes O. Humphries and S. Hugh-Jones (eds), *Barter, Exchange and Value: An Anthropological Approach* (Cambridge 1992) and J. Parry and M. Bloch (eds), *Money and the Morality of Exchange* (Cambridge 1989). There is much interesting recent work in the collection of essays edited by J. I. Guyer, titled *Money Matters: Instability, Values and Social Payments in the Modern History of West African Communities* (London 1995).

Some kinds of money have been the subject of more detailed studies, including the cloth currencies of the Lele people, studied in detail in M. Douglas, 'Raffia cloth distribution in the Lele economy', *Africa* xxv (1950), pp. 109–22 (reprinted in Dalton, *op. cit.*, pp. 103–22). The copper currencies of West and Central Africa are discussed in E. W. Herbert's excellent *Red Gold of Africa: Copper in Precolonial History and Culture* (Wisconsin 1984), which draws on specialist studies including M. S. Bisson, 'Copper currency in central Africa: the archaeological evidence', *World Archaeology* 6:3 (London, February 1975).

See also:
Ben-Amos, P. G., *The Art of Benin* (2nd edn, London 1995)

Mack, J., *Madagascar: Island of the Ancestors* (London 1986)
O'Hanlon, M., *Paradise: Portraying the New Guinea Highlands* (London 1993)
Rivallain, J., *Echanges et pratiques monétaires en Afrique du XVe au XIXe siècle à travers les récits de voyageurs* (Paris 1994)

Chapter 9
THE MODERN PERIOD

The modern period has seen significant changes to money and the ways it is used, including the rise of economic theory and the ending of gold and silver standards against which paper money and base metal coins were valued. The many different coins and paper money from this period are found in the catalogues published by Krause Publications annually, including the *Standard Catalog of World Coins* and the *Standard Catalogue of World Paper Money*. In addition to catalogues like these, listing every note or coin issued, there are a number of general works relating to money in the modern world. Two recent examples are P. D. Van Wie, *Image, History and Politics: The Coinage of Modern Europe* (Lanham, Maryland, 1999) and D. Standish, *The Art of Money: The History and Design of Paper Currency from around the World* (San Francisco 2000).

Covering monetary history throughout time and across the world, but particularly strong in the modern sections, G. Davies, *A History of Money from Ancient Times to the Present Day* (Cardiff 2002) is an excellent introductory work which helps to put the more detailed studies into context. More than seventy years earlier, written at a turbulent time in world monetary history, N. Angell, *The Story of Money* (London 1930) is neither a straightforward account of monetary history, nor of economic theory, but considers the relationship between money and people. Other general books treating the history of money and banking in the modern world include J. K. Galbraith, *Money: Whence it Came, Where it Went* (Boston 1975), and R. S. Sayers (ed.), *Banking in Western Europe* (Oxford 1962).

For information about English local banks and banking in the eighteenth and nineteenth centuries, see L. S. Pressnell, *Country Banking in the Industrial Revolution* (Oxford 1956). On the American Revolution, see W. G. Anderson, *The Price of Liberty: The Public Debt of the American Revolution* (Charlottesville 1983), and for the money of the French Revolution, see A. Dowle and A. de Clermont, *Monnaies modernes, 1789 à nos jours* (Fribourg 1972) or J. Lafaurie, *Les assignats et les papiers monnaies émis par l'état au XVIIIe siècle* (Paris 1981).

General works on the history of economics include E. Roll, *A History of Economic Thought* (4th edn, London 1973) and two of J. K. Galbraith's publications, *A History of Economics* (London 1987) and *The World Economy since the Wars* (London 1995). The online encyclopaedia of Economic and Business History at www.eh.net contains a number of interesting articles written by leading specialists in the field, and is an invaluable resource. The primary sources discussed in chapter 9 are: A. Smith, *An Inquiry into the Nature and Causes of the Wealth of Nations* (5th edn, 1789); D. Ricardo, *On the Principles of Political Economy and Taxation* (3rd edn, London 1817); K. Marx, *Das Kapital: Kritik der politischer Ekonomic*, ed. F. Engels (1867); and J. M. Keynes, *The General Theory of Employment, Interest and Money* (London 1936).

World Money Museums

Most archaeological museums have coins in their collections, many art museums have collections of coins and medals, and a significant number of central banks have museums or visitor centres attached to them. Therefore, the listing of money museums that follows is necessarily selective, and could easily have been two or three times its current length and still not been complete. More information about money museums is available from ICOMON, the ICOM international committee which looks after their interests and maintains lists of money museums of the world, at http://icom.museum/international/icomon.html

Europe

Here there is perhaps the greatest concentration of money museums and museums with displays of coins, medals or paper money. *Austria* has the money museum at the National Bank and the coin cabinet of the Kunsthistorisches Museum, both in Vienna, as well as collections and displays in Graz and the Tirol. In *Belgium* are the collections of the Bibliothèque Royale in Brussels and the money museum of the National Bank of Belgium. Archaeological museums in *Bulgaria* and *Croatia* have collections of coins, and the rich monetary history of *Cyprus* is reflected in the displays at the Bank of Cyprus. The *Czech Republic*'s rich heritage can be seen at the mint museum in Kutna Hora, as well as in the Czech National Bank museum in Prague. The National Museum of *Denmark* in Copenhagen has large and important collections; in *Estonia* there are displays at the Bank of Estonia and the Estonian History Museum in Tallinn; and in *Finland* there are displays and collections at the Bank of Finland Museum and the National Museum of Finland. *France* has several excellent collections and displays, including the Musée de la Monnaie and the Bibliothèque Nationale in Paris, and local museums and archives. *Germany* is similarly well provided for, with money museums and important collections in Cologne, Dresden, Frankfurt, Halle and Hannover, among other places. In *Greece*, the National

Numismatic Museum in Athens has significant collections from antiquity to the present day. The National Bank of *Hungary* opened a redesigned visitor centre in 2004, and *Iceland*'s Numismatic Museum was established jointly by the Central Bank and the National Museum of Iceland. At the National Museum of *Ireland*, Collins Barracks, there are displays tracing 1,000 years of Irish monetary history. Many museums in *Italy* have coin collections, thanks to the country's rich history and archaeological heritage, most notably in Rome and Naples, as well as at important sites including Syracuse. The Bank of *Latvia* has a visitor centre, as does the Bank of *Lithuania*, and in *Luxembourg* there is the Bank Museum, opened in 1995. On the island of *Malta*, the 'monetarium' at the National Museum of Fine Arts in Valletta can be viewed by appointment. In the *Netherlands*, the merging of three museums and collections has led to the foundation of a new money museum in Utrecht, which opens in 2007. In *Norway*, numismatic collections are on display in Oslo at the Historical Museum, and in *Portugal* there are a number of collections, including those at the Calouste Gulbenkian Foundation in Lisbon and in the museum of the Bank of Portugal, as well as a specialist paper money museum in Porto. In *Romania* there are collections and displays at the National Museum of Antiquities and at the National Bank of Romania, in Bucharest. *Russia* has some very substantial collections, notably at the State Historical Museum in Moscow and the Hermitage Museum in St Petersburg. In *Serbia*, museums in Belgrade and Sabac are among those with coin collections and displays; in *Slovakia*, the Museum of Coins and Medals in Kremnica is among the oldest museums in the country; and coins are among the many objects in the collections of the National Museum of *Slovenia* in Ljubljana. In *Spain*, the Spanish mint museum in Madrid, the Casa de la Moneda, has several rooms of displays on the history of money, and there are also many interesting objects in the money collections on display in Barcelona in the Palau de la Virrena. *Sweden* boasts the

Royal Coin Cabinet in Stockholm, which has a large collection and display area, and is linked to the Tumba paper mill museum just outside Stockholm. *Switzerland*, thanks to its cantonal structure, is blessed with several interesting coin collections and money museums, in Basel, Lausanne, Neuchâtel and Zürich, among others, and archaeological museums in the *Ukraine* and the former *Yugoslav Republic of Macedonia* feature coins among their collections. Finally, in the *United Kingdom* there are several major collections and displays relating to money, including the British Museum, the Bank of England Museum, the Royal Mint Museum, and university collections including the Ashmolean Museum (Oxford), the Fitzwilliam Museum (Cambridge), Manchester Museum, and the Hunterian Museum (Glasgow).

America

In the past, money museums in America were dominated by those in North America, and in particular in the USA. In the past few decades, however, increasing numbers of Central and South American central banks have developed museums and cultural centres. Among these are the national bank museum in Buenos Aires, *Argentina*, which also boasts a Museum of Foreign Debt dealing with the country's sometimes troubled relationship with international trade and finance. *Arbua*, *Belize* and *Bermuda* all have museums attached to their central banks, featuring the monetary history of those countries. In *Bolivia*, the Potosi mint, which produced many thousands of coins, is now a money museum. The Casa da Moeda in Brasilia is home to a money museum set up by the Central Bank of *Brazil*, and there are significant collections and displays at the Museum of National History in Rio de Janeiro. The Currency Museum of the Bank of *Canada* has significant collections relating in particular to Canadian currency, including archives and objects transferred from other organisations. In *Chile*, there is a museum in the old mint building in Santiago, the Casa de la Moneda, and important collections in the National History Museum, also in Santiago. In *Colombia*, the Central Bank of Colombia runs the Gold Museum in Bogota, and the National Museum of Colombia also has collections and displays relating to money. In *Costa Rica*, there are exhibitions of money in the underground displays at the Museum of the Central Bank in San José, and the Numismatic Museum in *Cuba* is housed in the former headquarters of the Banco Mendoza in Havana. In the *Dominican Republic*, the Numismatic and Philatelic Museum houses significant collections of coins and stamps from the Caribbean, and in *Ecuador* the National Museum of the Central Bank of Ecuador houses important art and archaeological collections. The national banks of *Jamaica*, *Mexico* and *Panama* all have money museums attached to them, and coins and paper money are among the objects on display at the museum of the Central Bank of *Peru*. In *Suriname*, the Central Bank of Suriname has a Numismatic Museum, and in *Trinidad and Tobago* a new money museum opened at the Central Bank in 2004, developed as part of the fortieth anniversary celebrations of the bank. In the *United States* there are a large number of money collections and displays, including those at branches of the Federal Reserve Bank and the Bureau of Engraving and Printing. The Smithsonian Institution in Washington has money collections containing more than one million objects, and the collections and displays of the American Numismatic Association in Colorado Springs and the American Numismatic Society in New York include important objects relating to the history of money. Smaller museums also have interesting displays relating to aspects of monetary history, including the American Museum of Financial History in New York, which focuses on economics and finance. Finally, the Central Bank of *Uruguay* has a money museum, as does the Central Bank of *Venezuela*, at its offices in Caracas.

Africa

Africa currently has the fewest money museums, but there are nonetheless significant collections of money in museums across the continent and temporary displays sometimes bring these out on show. Over the coming decades, increased investment in museums and cultural activities will hopefully lead to more of these important and interesting collections being on display. In *Egypt*, the Egyptian Museum in Cairo includes coins and other money objects among its many treasures. To the south, *Ethiopia*'s rich history is showcased at the archaeological site of Axum, which has a museum to display the small artefacts, including coins, and the University of Addis Ababa has a collection of coins, banknotes and postage stamps. In West Africa there is a currency museum at the Central Bank of the *Gambia*, and the National Museum of *Ghana* in Accra has displays about the history of money. Representing its important role in the Indian Ocean trade, *Kenya* has interesting and important money collections held at the National Museums of Kenya in Nairobi. In *Morocco*, the Bank al-Maghrib has a collection of currency which was transferred from Casablanca to a new Numismatic Museum in Rabat in the 1990s. In *Mozambique*, there is a money museum in a landmark building in Maputo known as the 'yellow house', which displays the history of currency in Mozambique. There have in the past been temporary exhibitions arranged by museums in *Nigeria*, and there are significant collections in museums there. In *Senegal*, there is a money museum in Dakar, based at the Central Bank of the West African States, which covers the monetary history of West Africa. In *South Africa*, there are a number of bank museums, as well as the Coin World museum at the South African mint, between Johannesburg and Pretoria. Finally, moving from the far south to the far north of Africa, the Central Bank of *Tunisia*'s Currency Museum displays objects from antiquity to the present day.

Asia and Oceania

From Turkey in the West to Japan in the East, Asia is the largest and most populous continent. Home to several of the world's great ancient civilisations – including those of Mesopotamia, the Indus Valley and ancient China – Asia has a rich trading and monetary history, reflected in museums across the continent. Australia and Oceania, usually considered to be a separate continent, are included here with Asia. In *Afghanistan*, the National Museum has an important collection of coins spanning thousands of years of the country's history, many of which survived the wars of the past few decades only because they were hidden away by museum staff. In *Australia*, the numismatic and philatelic collections of Museum Victoria include early Australian coins as well as material from the Sydney and Melbourne mints, and the Western Australia Maritime Museum has collections of shipwreck coins. There are specialist money museums in Kadina, South Australia, at the Reserve Bank of Australia in Sydney, and at the visitor centre of the Royal Australian Mint in Canberra. The Museum of the History of *Azerbaijan* has in its collection many thousands of coins, and the *Bahrain* National Museum in Manama has coins among its art, archaeological and historical collections and exhibits. The *Bangladesh* National Museum was founded when the Shillong coin cabinet was transferred to Dhaka, and the coin collections remain an important resource. *China*'s rich monetary history is reflected in its museums, particularly the Gallery of Ancient Chinese Coins in the Shanghai Museum and the China Numismatic Museum in Beijing. *India* is similarly well provided with money museums and collections and displays of coins and paper money, including at the National Museum in Delhi, the Indian Museum in Kolkata and the Government Museum in Chennai. The Bank of *Indonesia* has a museum, and in *Iran* there is an important coin collection at the National Museum of Iran, as well as a specialist Money Museum in Tehran. The collections of the *Iraq* National Museum are significant, and although unfortunately a

small number of gold coins were looted
during 2003, the main coin collection
remained intact. In *Israel*, several museums
have displays and collections relating to
money, including the Israel Museum and
Bank of Israel Museum in Jerusalem, the
Eretz Israel Museum in Tel Aviv and the
National Maritime Museum in Haifa. *Japan*
has money museums at some of its banks,
including the Bank of Japan and the UFJ
Bank, as well as a display on paper money
at the Printing Bureau Museum in Tokyo.
The Central Bank of *Jordan* museum covers
money in Jordan over the past two
thousand years, and the National Bank of
Malaysia has a money museum and art
centre at its base in Kuala Lumpur. In *New
Zealand*, both Te Papa (the National
Museum of New Zealand) and the Bank of
New Zealand in Wellington have
collections of money objects. The *Pakistan*
National Museum in Karachi has a
significant collection of coins, and the State
Bank of *Pakistan* is in the process of
developing its collections and displays. In
the *Philippines*, the Central Bank in Manila
has a money museum, and in the *Republic of
Korea* several banks have museums of
money and banking, including the Woori
Bank, Bank of Korea and Chohung Bank.
There is a specialist money museum in
Riyadh, *Saudi Arabia*, at the Saudi Arabian
Monetary Agency, and the Saudi National
Museum also has collections of coins. In
Singapore there are displays about money at
the Mint Coin Gallery at the Singapore
mint. *Sri Lanka* has several money museums
and money displays, with important
collections at the National Museum in
Colombo and at the Central Bank of Sri
Lanka in Kotte. *Syria*'s long monetary
history is reflected in the collections and
displays of the National Museum in
Damascus. The Bank of *Thailand* has
collections and displays about Thailand's
monetary history in the Bangkhunprom
Palace in Bangkok, a historic building and
former royal palace. In Istanbul, *Turkey*,
there is a city museum and cultural centre
in the old Imperial Mint buildings, and the
Turkish State Mint has displays of coins and
other objects relating to the mint. Since

Turkey was among the first places in the
world to mint coins, there are significant
coin collections in its archaeological
museums, most notably the Hall of Coins at
the Antalya Archaeological Museum.
Finally, there are money collections and
displays in the *United Arab Emirates* at the
Sharjah Numsimatic Museum, and in
Uzbekistan at the State Museum of the
History of Uzbekistan and the National
Bank of Uzbekistan.

ILLUSTRATION ACKNOWLEDGEMENTS

The authors and publishers are grateful to
the following for permission to reproduce
illustrations of which they own copyright:

American Express: 357c; American Institute
of Indian Studies, Ramnagar, India: 176;
American Numismatic Society, New York:
131, 150; Aphrodisias Archive, Institute of
Fine Arts, New York: 80g; Bank of England:
274, 321a; Barclays Group Archives: 357d;
Steve Bell: 353; Bibliothèque Nationale,
Paris: 160 (MS 5847, f. 105); Bildarchiv
Preussischer Kulturbesitz, Berlin: 81;
Bodleian Library, Oxford: 82 (MS Canon
Misc. 378, f. 142v); Hector Breeze: 5;
Bristol Museums and Art Gallery: 320;
British Library: 105 (MS 70560 Add. 28162,
f. 9v), 118, 171 (India Office Library),
243 (Add. MS 19927, ff. 12v-13);
Burgerbibliothek, Bern: 254a;
Corbis Images UK, Ltd: 349
(© Bettman/CORBIS), 350 (© JP
Laffont/Sygma/Corbis); Joe Cribb: 201c;
Diners Club: 357b, 361; Elizabeth
Errington: 97i; HSBC Holdings plc: 215,
357e; Kungl Myntkabinettet, Statens
Museum för Mynt-, Medalj- och
Penninghistoria, Stockholm: 97b; Mansell
Collection: 71; Mary Evans Picture Library:
348; National Portrait Gallery, London: 270;
The New York Public Library, Rare Books
Division, Astor, Lenox and Tilden
Foundations: 279d; M. O'Grady: 276, 341;
Michael O'Hanlon: 296; Photos12.com –
Collection Cinéma/Mervyn Le Roy: 2;
Venetia Porter: 144; Réunion des Musées
Nationaux, Paris: 3, 8; Rosgarten Museum,
Konstanz: 254b; Simmons and Simmons,
London: 172; Staatliche Museen, Kassel:
260; Trinity College, Cambridge: 94f
(Trinity MS R.17.1 Canterbury Psalter,
f. 230); Victoria and Albert Museum,
London: 94b; Western Union Holdings, Inc.
(The Western Union name, logo and
related trademarks and service marks,
owned by Western Union Holdings, Inc.,
are registered and/or used in the U.S. and
many foreign countries): 357a

Index